THE POWER OF
COMMUNITY-ENGAGED
TEACHER PREPARATION

THE POWER OF
COMMUNITY-ENGAGED
TEACHER PREPARATION

Voices and Visions of Hope and Healing

EDITED BY

Patricia Clark
Eva Zygmunt
Susan Tancock
Kristin Cipollone

Foreword by Tyrone C. Howard

TEACHERS COLLEGE PRESS

TEACHERS COLLEGE | COLUMBIA UNIVERSITY

NEW YORK AND LONDON

Published by Teachers College Press,® 1234 Amsterdam Avenue, New York, NY 10027

Copyright © 2021 by Teachers College, Columbia University

Front cover photo by FatCamera / iStock by Getty Images.

Library of Congress Cataloging-in-Publication Data is available at loc.gov

ISBN 978-0-8077-6522-7 (paper)
ISBN 978-0-8077-6523-4 (hardcover)
ISBN 978-0-8077-7950-7 (ebook)

Printed on acid-free paper
Manufactured in the United States of America

For those with the courage to reconsider teacher education;
for the future teachers they will prepare;
and for the children, families, and communities
whose voices and visions they will honor;
because it is time.

Knowledge emerges only through invention and re-invention, through the restless, impatient, continuing, hopeful inquiry human beings pursue in the world, with the world, and with each other.

—Paulo Freire, *Pedagogy of the Oppressed*

Contents

The Power of Community-Engaged Teacher Preparation

Voices and Visions of Hope and Healing

The upheavals of 2020 created a reality that many educators could never have envisioned. The impact of COVID-19—the millions infected, the hundreds of thousands of lives lost, the downturn of an economy, and the increasing social–emotional fallout—has left few untouched. Moreover, the racial unrest around the deaths of George Floyd, Breonna Taylor, and Ahmaud Arbery have reminded us all that racial justice remains elusive for too many Black people and other people of color in the United States. The year 2020 has transformed how we engage with friends and family, significantly altered the manner in which our students learn, and forced many of us to create a new normal in much of what we do. To that end, institutions that prepare and support teachers must create and establish a new normal for how we do our work. Now is the time; anything less only perpetuates inequities and injustice for our most vulnerable students. Many of our students have experienced unprecedented levels of loss, anguish, anger, fear, and uncertainty. Teachers cannot go back to business as usual. Today's new normal requires that teacher preparation programs provide educators with the knowledge, skills, dispositions, and mindsets to work in today's context. To be clear, many of our students need something different, they need something transformative; many have seen their lives uprooted, their loved ones lost, and their most basic needs not being met. In short, our students need hope and healing (Ginwright, 2016). This timely and beautifully edited volume, *The Power of Community-Engaged Teacher Preparation: Voices and Visions of Hope and Healing*, brings together a collection of powerful authors who offer theoretical considerations, evidence-based approaches, and practical considerations for not just teacher education as usual but *community-engaged teacher education.*

The current moment of academic, social, and emotional distress requires that we respond to students in a different way, a more thoughtful, caring, and community-informed way. At this time, traditional teacher preparation requires nontraditional approaches. In times of anguish, heartbreak, grief, and loss, which many students are experiencing, students need healing and loving communities. Such ecosystems need to be replete with a cadre of individuals who understand, recognize, and honor the multiple layers of identities and the varied structures and systems that influence students' day-to-day realities. To be clear, many of those individuals are located in the very communities in which our students live. The individuals who can inform teacher preparation are in our students' households and at their local churches, mosques, and synagogues. These loving and caring individuals often work at the local grocery markets, neighborhood parks, hospitals, senior centers, or recreation centers. These individuals are the caregivers who have known students since birth and know them better than anyone. They know, understand, and create the cultural fabric that shapes the ecosystem that students interact with on a daily basis. The sad yet untold truth is that not enough of these individuals are in the schools and classrooms that our students attend. Thus, to bridge the knowledge, caring, and empathy gap that exists in many schools, we must prepare teachers in a manner that sees community as vital to the work and that situates teacher learning within a cultural context that is tied to communities where students live, learn, thrive, and seek to be their best selves. Education scholar Patrick Camangian (2020) maintains that the "something different" that students need must be a more holistic, healing, and humanizing approach to teaching and learning that recognizes these social identities, which have a profound influence on learning. He suggests that

> humanization provides the real social and emotional learning that historically marginalized communities deserve. By lacking an explicit analysis of the intersecting systems of racism, sexism, homophobia, and classism, SEL is not encompassing enough of a framework to address the dehumanization that marginalized communities experience. (p. 126)

What our students need in this moment is what Dr. Martin Luther King Jr. referred to when he talked about a need for "a beloved community"—one that would require "qualitative change in our souls as well as a quantitative change in our lives" (King, 1966, p. 30). Community-engaged teacher education can and must create the engaged and beloved community through a preparation process that is willing to rethink where our teacher candidates learn, how they learn, and who they learn with on their quest to become transformative educators. To be clear, teacher education has to rethink the manner in which opportunity plays out for poor children, BIPOC children, children in foster care, youth experiencing homelessness, LGBTQ+ children, and children with various disabilities. To that end, an intentional focus must be centered on the very opportunities that are afforded in some communities compared to others. For example, a community-centered approach to education would situate itself within an antiracist framework, which challenges racist practices in schools and does so in an unapologetic manner. Education scholar Bettina Love says that "White rage in our schools murders dark students' spirits . . . Spirit-murder is not only about race and racism; dark people's other identity categories, such as gender, citizenship, religion, language, class, ethnicity, nationality, and queerness, are additional, distinct, factors driving discrimination, bigotry and violence" (pp. 38–39).

This work of community-centered education anchors community at its core. It recognizes that schools sit in the hubs of our communities, and that our ecosystems are vital to the development of educators who are willing to do the hard work and the heart work that are vital to educating students. For too long, teacher education has been very university centered, without any real-world connection to the communities in which schools are located (Shirley et al., 2006). Critiques of this model have been warranted and must inform a more complex and innovative approach to how we prepare the next generation of educators. In order to respond to and prepare educators for our new normal, teacher education programs must make a bold and unrepentant commitment to transform their focus and strategies to work more intimately with their schools, communities, families, and community-based organizations to locate teacher preparation programs directly in the schools and communities in which this work will be done (Noel, 2016; Zeichner, 2010). Accessing the historical knowledge, current-day expertise, and pressing needs of students requires a type of teacher education that operates from an asset base of the communities where students live, learn, and play; an understanding of the often overlooked or misunderstood intellect of caregivers who are dedicated and devoted to the best of their youth; and a connectedness to the organizations that have mastered ways to engage students, all of these "utilizing the expertise that exists in the broader community to educate prospective teachers about how to be successful teachers in their communities" (Noel, 2016, p. 95). By situating programs in communities, "teacher candidates are able to discover the strengths and challenges of urban communities rather than be solely informed by preexisting assumptions, societal stereotypes and judgment" (Waddell, 2013, p. 3). Our time is now to know, care, and act in a different way. Communities have frequently been the loving hubs of our society, providing and protecting children in ways that schools often do not. In this work, the authors not only tell us what can be done, they demonstrate—based on their own efforts—how it is done, the challenges involved, and the amazing outcomes that can result when we stay the course in this work.

—Tyrone C. Howard, University of California, Los Angeles

REFERENCES

Camangian, P. (2020). *"It's not so much . . . for a grade": Humanization as real social and emotional learning. All students must thrive.* International Center for Leadership in Education.

Ginwright, S. (2016). *Hope and healing in urban education: How urban activists and teachers are reclaiming matters of the heart.* Routledge.

Glass, R. D., & Wong, P. L. (2013). Learning to produce knowledge: Reconstructing teacher preparation for urban schools. In J. Noel (Ed.), *Moving teacher education into urban schools and communities: Prioritizing community strengths* (pp. 20–35). Routledge.

King, M. L., Jr. (1966). Nonviolence: The only road to freedom. *Ebony, Oct. 1966,* 27–34.

Love, B. L. (2019). *We want to do more than survive: Abolitionist teaching and the pursuit of educational freedom.* Beacon Press.

Noel, J. (2016) Community-based urban teacher education: Theoretical frameworks and practical considerations for developing promising practices. *The Teacher Educator, 51*(4), 335–350. https://doi.org/10.1080/08878730.2016.1210429

Shirley, D., Hersi, A., MacDonald, E., Sanchez, M. T., Scandone, C., Skidmore, C., & Tutwiler, P. (2006). Bringing the community back in: Change, accommodation, and contestation in a school and university partnership. *Equity & Excellence in Education, 39*(1), 27–36.

Waddell, J. (2013). Communities as critical partners in teacher education: The impact of community immersion on teacher candidates' understanding of self and teaching in urban schools. *Current Issues in Education, 16*(2), 1–16.

Zeichner, K. (2010). Rethinking the connections between campus courses and field experiences in college- and university-based teacher education. *Journal of Teacher Education, 61*(1–2), 89–99.

Zygmunt, E., & Clark, P. (2016). *Transforming teacher education for social justice.* Teachers College Press.

Preface

Community-engaged teacher preparation, by definition, is driven by context, and the context of our world has changed dramatically since we embarked on the journey of gathering the voices that would be privileged in this book. What has remained steadfast, however, is the need for teachers who are prepared to be context-driven, that is, to not only understand the daily events that inform children and families' lived experience, but also to contextualize those experiences within broader historical contexts. It is this understanding that has inspired the ambitious aspiration of reimagining what we currently perceive as "teaching" into the possibility of "reaching" and thereby transforming the spaces and places where our youngest citizens spend their formative years into harbors of healing and hope.

The poet Audre Lorde spoke the words, "To refuse to participate in the shaping of our future is to give it up. Do not be led into passivity by false security or by despair. Each of us must find our work and do it" (1982/2012). Rather than surrender to the present circumstance in teacher education, this book tells the stories of the work that communities, schools, and universities are doing together, boldly and creatively redefining the parameters of possibility. One could argue, amidst the discontent and division that plague our nation and the spaces beyond our border, that this work has never been more urgent.

The genesis of this book began in 2008 when its editors began conversations with leaders and elders in the Whitely community—a historically African American neighborhood in Muncie, Indiana. Interestingly, Muncie was selected by sociologists Robert and Helen Lynd in the 1920s as a city representative of "contemporary American life" for their landmark study on American values, practices, and politics (Lynd & Lynd, 1929). However, Muncie's African American population, which comprised 6% of the population, was intentionally omitted from the study, so as not to "confound" the findings by race. This study and its glaring omission forecasted the African American experience in Muncie for the next 100 years, with practices of enduring exclusion continuing to influence the current landscape. It is this marginalization, particularly relevant to input regarding local schools, that informed our initial conversation with neighborhood residents.

Elders approached us to share an enduring frustration that although the children of the neighborhood were in school all day, every day (with a documented 98% attendance rate), a mere 30% of students were scoring in the proficient range in state literacy and math assessments. They perceived educators who did not live in the community as having significant deficit perspectives of students and families while at the same time lacking the contextual knowledge necessary to understand community strengths, values, and resources. They expressed their interest in a novel partnership through which to embed future teachers' preparation in the Whitely community, match candidates with mentor families in the neighborhood, and thus develop context-specific knowledge of children's lived experience. In this way, candidates could take the content they were responsible for teaching and match it to children's experience to make it more relevant, engaging, and culturally responsive and sustaining. By situating their learning in the community, residents argued, future teachers could also learn the significant history of the community, along with its language and teaching traditions. Ultimately, neighbors wished to be instrumental in the development of teachers who would not only value but honor and privilege the wisdom and expertise of the community in both the content and pedagogy that informs children's experience in school. With a willing spirit and a desire to address the damage that had taken place in previous university–community partnerships, which often ended in failure and frustration on the part of the community, we cautiously committed to a new concept of collaboration.

Fast-forward 13 years, and we continue in our commitment to this work, considering our community colleagues as co-teacher educators who are instrumental in candidates' learning. Through their careful review, input, and critique of the lessons candidates will teach, the books that children should be reading, their hospitality in inviting candidates into their homes and other prominent community spaces, and their careful shepherding of critical service-learning projects that address community-identified needs for mobilization and revitalization, neighborhood residents have created the context for authentic community engagement, which continues to be transformative for us all.

As our local efforts have emerged, we have been fortunate to welcome others to Muncie to learn and to be inspired to transform their programs of educator preparation to be more authentically engaged in the communities in which their universities are situated. In 2015 we held an inaugural Summer Institute on Community-Engaged Teacher Preparation at Ball State University, where a small gathering of teacher educators and their school and community partners attended with the idea that they would emerge after three days with a plan for their own communities and teacher preparation programs. Now in its 6th year, the Summer Institute provided the impetus for the organization of the Alliance for Community-Engaged Teacher Preparation—a group of teacher educators and their school and community partners committed to furthering this paradigm.

The chapters in this book privilege the voices of some of our earliest Summer Institute participants, whose programs have been emerging for several years, and those of our candidates and community partners here in Muncie, as well as some of the Alliance's newest members, whose programs are in their infancy but whose commitment to the long-term is absolute. The chapters, authored by school, university, and community partners, speak to the innovation, creativity, commitment, and persistence required to reinvent teacher preparation. They also underscore the complexity of this work, the humility necessary to reflect and reconsider, and the true spirit of authentic university–school–community solidarity required to seek and secure equity for children in schools.

As we move from this preface into the chapters that follow, we express our gratitude and acknowledge our privilege to be engaged in this all-important work alongside our school and community colleagues. Additionally, we vow, with vigilance to our collective vision, to renew our commitment to furthering community-engaged teacher preparation as a promising paradigm. Ultimately, it is our hope that the stories within these pages compel the larger field of educator preparation with the courage to join us.

REFERENCES

Lorde, A. (2012). *Learning from the 60s*. Blackpast. https://www.blackpast.org/african-american-history/1982-audre-lorde-learning-60s (Original work published 1982)

Lynd, R., & Lynd, H. (1929). *Middletown: A study in contemporary American culture*. Hardcourt, Brace, & Company.

Acknowledgments

In 2016, our first book, *Transforming Teacher Education for Social Justice*, detailed the history of our inaugural 6 years of community-engaged teacher preparation at Ball State University. At that time we celebrated our entire community of practice, including our school partners and community colleagues with whom we worked tirelessly to dream of a new way of preparing teachers and to develop a community-contextualized model to execute that vision.

As we offer this new edited volume, which details places and spaces where community-engaged teacher preparation is taking place, we would like to thank our colleagues across the country and world who are embracing a new way of preparing teachers, and with whom we have had the good fortune to ally. We are indebted for the inspiration you are to us as you work with school and community partners in creative ways to more authentically move your programs of educator preparation into the communities in which your universities are situated. We have met many of you through the Ball State Summer Institute on Community-Engaged Teacher Preparation, and it has been joyful to watch your efforts emerge. Thank you for coming to Muncie, and for inviting us into your communities of practices so that we can learn.

How the larger field of education, in general, and educator preparation, in particular, acknowledges the paradigm of community-engaged teacher preparation is all-important in how it is received by colleges of education across the country and world who are charged with developing the programs to prepare teachers that *all* children need. Accordingly, we would like to thank the American Association of Colleges for Teacher Education (AACTE), the American Educational Research Association (AERA), the American Association of State Colleges and Universities (AASCU), the Association of Public Land Grant Universities (APLU), the Engagement Scholarship Consortium, Campus Compact, and the Indiana Commission on Higher Education for their recognition of community-engaged teacher preparation as a compelling and justifiable direction for the field.

We additionally acknowledge the commitment our institution has made to this work over the years, which has been significant. From its initial investment in supporting a new paradigm of teacher preparation to providing start-up support for our Summer Institute on Community-Engaged Teacher Preparation (now in its 6th year) and our Alliance for Community-Engaged Teacher Preparation, leadership at Ball State University has been instrumental in championing community-engaged teacher preparation, and thus inspiring other colleges of education to follow suit. For the support we have been given from department chairs and deans and university presidents over the last 12 years, we offer our significant gratitude.

We thank Muncie Community Schools for their hospitality in welcoming our candidates, and we appreciate their emerging commitment to culturally responsive teaching and learning. We are especially indebted to the MuncieP3 after-school complementary learning program for providing a caring, creative, constructive, and, most importantly, joyful environment where local community and culture are honored and children and families are free to dream.

We also offer appreciation to Brian Ellerbeck at Teachers College Press for his patience and persistence in encouraging us to refine the conceptual underpinnings of this edited volume. We were privileged to work with Brian on our first book and continue to be grateful for the questions he poses and the challenges he presents in order to best frame this work. It is much stronger due to his guidance.

We would be remiss in neglecting to acknowledge the 11 cohorts of preservice teacher candidates who have walked with us as we forged a new path. How we have appreciated their trust in the process, their patience, and their persistence in opening their minds and hearts to truths that transcend and transform.

Finally, we continue to celebrate members of the Whitely neighborhood of Muncie, Indiana, and how they have inspired us to understand how universities with programs of educator preparation can work in solidarity with communities to privilege context-specific funds of knowledge and cultural wealth in the development of teachers committed to constructs of equity and social justice. Members of the Whitely neighborhood have been additionally generous in sharing their expertise in community-engaged teacher preparation with national and international audiences who have come to Muncie to learn. To the members of the Whitely neighborhood, we offer our honor, respect, and unwavering gratitude. You have shown us the way.

THE POWER OF
COMMUNITY-ENGAGED
TEACHER PREPARATION

Educator Preparation and the Rhetoric of "With Liberty and Justice for All"

Eva Zygmunt and Patricia Clark

In 32 of our 50 United States, it is mandated by law that the Pledge of Allegiance to the flag be recited as part of students' daily experience in public school. According to public education enrollment projections, this year alone some 36 million students will hear, listen to, or be required to recite this allegiance every day for the 180–190 discrete units of the school calendar (National Center for Education Statistics [NCES], 2018). Given an average of 11 years of mandated schooling (NCES, 2017), an American child with even mediocre attendance will be exposed to the language in the pledge nearly 1,700 times before reaching adulthood. This ritual is reified as an act of patriotism to a nation whose birth was predicated upon the proposition that "all men are created equal," and is conducted as a morning missive in spaces designed, in theory, to be "the great equalizers" (Mann, 1849).

CURRENT INEQUITY IN AMERICAN SCHOOLS

One need not look far to find evidence that "liberty and justice" are not principles at work for *all* American students. Evidence continues to show that children of color and those from families with lower socioeconomic status are failing at a rate significantly higher than their White and more advantaged peers (Bohrnstedt et al., 2015; Hemphill & Vanneman, 2010; Reardon, 2011; Vanneman et al., 2009). With educational segregation still rampant at the 67th anniversary of the *Brown v. Board of Education* decision, schools serving majority populations of lower-income and minority children have some of the worst facilities and the least-prepared teachers (Orfield & Frankenberg, 2014). And while United States class-rooms are becoming increasingly diverse (NCES, 2020), we continue to prepare a majority of White, female, middle-class, monolingual educators to tackle the complex issues of equity in education. With good reason, institutions of teacher education are under increased scrutiny for their relevance to the dynamics and demographics of the 21st century (Darling-Hammond, 2013).

Many schools, urban, rural, and suburban, remain racially and economically segregated, with those responsible for teaching students neither living in the communities they teach nor possessing knowledge of students' lived experience outside of school. This lack of contextual cognizance has the potential to reinforce teachers' deficit perspectives of communities, compromising their expectations for students' success. Data on suspensions, placement in special education, and teacher expectations bear witness to the effects of deficit perspectives (Skiba et al., 2011). Further, the use of "no excuses" exclusionary disciplinary practices (Gregory et al., 2011) disproportionately impacts students of color, and has been linked in the literature to a school-to-prison pipeline (Alexander, 2012; Heitzeg, 2016; Mallett, 2015). It is also well established that a persistent opportunity gap (Carter & Welner, 2013) or education debt (Ladson-Billings, 2006) exists between racially, socio-economically, and linguistically nondominant and dominant students. Research has demonstrated that teachers' expectations of student ability are frequently tied to the class and race positions students occupy (Anyon, 2014; Gershenson et al., 2016; Rist, 1970), and that expectations often become self-fulfilling prophecies with regard to achievement (McKown & Weinstein, 2008). Many students who experience racial stereotyping and discrimination are the unfortunate recipients of curriculum that falls desperately short of being culturally relevant, responsive, or sustaining (Hope et al., 2015). These experiences can influence students' perceptions about their value to society and their aspirations of who they can become (Hughes et al., 2011). Teacher expectations, which privilege certain students to the detriment of others, can also negatively impact students from the dominant culture, as they position them as superior, a posture that further insulates them from acknowledging their privilege and understanding persistent inequity (Derman-Sparks & Ramsey, 2011).

While the impact of culturally responsive and sustaining pedagogies on student success has been documented in empirical research (Esposito & Swain, 2009; Howard, 2003; Milner, 2011; Tate, 1995), evidence suggests that what it means to be truly culturally responsive is often misunderstood (Enyedy & Mukhopadhyay, 2007; Young, 2010) and that the theory has been interpreted as a set of fixed behaviors (Ladson-Billings,

1995a, 1995b). Applied within the context of teacher education, this misorientation is antithetical to the original construct of culturally responsive practice and furthers the reproduction of inequity.

EDUCATOR PREPARATION AS COMPLICIT
IN THE PROPAGATION OF INEQUITY

bell hooks (1991) discusses culturally sustaining school environments as "homeplaces," spaces where souls are nurtured, comforted, and fed, where racial healing happens and dignity is restored. Inspired by hooks, Bettina Love (2019) describes a regrettably more common "educational survival complex" (p. 27) in which many students of color are left learning to merely survive, not thrive, and in which they experience what she names "spirit-murdering" (p. 34). According to Love:

> The educational survival complex has become so rationalized and normalized that we are forced to believe, against our common sense, that inadequate school funding is normal, that there is nothing that can be done about school shootings, that racist teachers in the classrooms are better than no teachers in the classrooms. We have come to believe that police officers in our schools physically assaulting students is standard practice. (pp. 101–102)

In this book, we make the argument that the field of educator preparation is complicit in creating and sustaining the educational survival complex. With a retreat from the ethics of equity and social justice over the last several decades, the field, including the accrediting bodies responsible for ensuring program quality, is currently informed by market-driven standardization that belies precepts of context-informed practice (Sleeter, 2008). Our current context finds us limiting the admission of a diverse sector of candidates based on stringent criteria unsupported by research (Freedle, 2010; Santelices & Wilson, 2010); relegating requisite candidate dispositions to a set of benign professional behaviors instead of authentic assessments of candidates' ethical and moral obligations (Wilkerson, 2006; Wise, 2006); homogenizing what constitutes program quality (Greenberg et al., 2014); and wrongly regimenting what constitutes an "effective teacher" (An, 2016; Greenblatt, 2018; National Association of Multicultural Education, 2014; Picower & Marshall, 2016; Souto-Manning, 2019; Tuck & Gorlewski, 2016). According to Cochran-Smith and colleagues (2018), these mandates devalue teacher educators' local knowledge and undercut their professional expertise in developing and engaging in programs and practices informed by and responsive to community-identified need.

To remedy structures that are distinctly deficient, decidedly discriminatory, and perpetually propagative of social inequity, a new approach is imperative. As Love (2019) emphasizes, "We need spaces that not only protect those who are most vulnerable, but also heal them" (p. 98). Toward this end, we propose community-engaged teacher preparation, accomplished in solidarity with members of historically marginalized populations, as a promising model (Zygmunt & Cipollone, 2019; Zygmunt & Clark, 2016; Zygmunt et al., 2018). This model, achieved through privileging community funds of knowledge (Moll et al., 1992) and cultural wealth (Yosso, 2005), creates classrooms "aimed at facilitating interactions where people matter to each other, fight together in the pursuit of creating 'homeplaces' that represent their hopes and dreams, and resist oppression all while building a new future" (Love, p. 68). According to Filipiak (2019), "teaching for justice requires that we love the children we teach. And to love young people, we have to fundamentally believe that they matter. Mattering isn't a feeling; it's an action. It's respecting the richness of young people's identities and acting in the best interest of their humanity."

The aim of this book is to give clear guidance on what is meant by culturally relevant and sustaining pedagogies and provide examples of how this work is being operationalized in community-engaged teacher education. We will both share and honor the mechanisms through which teacher educators in large urban cores, Midwestern cities, small towns, and rural villages are working in solidarity with members of marginalized communities in the preparation of teachers for equity and social justice. The premise that the health and success of our institutions of higher education, our schools, and our neighborhoods and communities are collectively intertwined guides this work and our vision of what can be when we "freedom dream" (Love, 2019) of a new tomorrow.

In 1999, Cochran-Smith declared the three principal emphases of teacher education to be social responsibility, social change, and social justice. Similarly, in 2000, Sonia Nieto argued for equity to be placed at the forefront of teacher education. Over 2 decades have passed since these declarations, and some would argue that the field is further distanced from these precepts now than we were at what seemed to be a potential tipping point in the direction of commitment to equity. There is much work ahead in equitizing the field of educator preparation toward the end of ensuring that those with the privilege of teaching, indeed those "worthy" of such a privilege (Howard, 2009), are brought up as future teachers in systems that honor the constructs of equity and social justice as core to their reason for being. As a mechanism for such, Sleeter (2008) emphasized the importance of collaboration with underserved communities in order to push back against a neoliberal agenda thwarting efforts toward preparing educators equipped to consciously and critically adopt the principles and practices of equity and social justice. In this book, we offer the construct of community-engaged teacher preparation as proliferative of this plea.

COMMUNITY-ENGAGED TEACHER PREPARATION DEFINED

Community-engaged teacher preparation entails situating teacher education in the cultural contexts in which children grow and learn: physically embedding teacher preparation within communities and affording opportunities for context-specific, situated learning (Lave & Wenger, 1991). Differentiated from *community-based* initiatives, which simply occupy a space away from campus, a *community-engaged* approach works toward the authentic integration of programs of educator preparation in historically marginalized communities, working in solidarity with their members. The elevating and honoring of funds of knowledge (Moll et al., 1992) and community cultural wealth (Yosso, 2005) is a decisive element of candidates' experience, education, and preparation to be critically conscious, socially just, and equity-focused community teachers (Murrell, 2001). With a growing research base to support the benefits of this approach (Lee et al., 2013; Lees, 2016; Zeichner, 2006, 2010; Zygmunt & Cipollone, 2019; Zygmunt & Clark, 2016; Zygmunt et al., 2018), community-engaged teacher preparation is emerging as an innovative paradigm in the preparation of teachers with the will and skill to advance educational equity.

Community-engaged teacher preparation is predicated on the concerted cultivation of collaborative relationships among universities, communities, and schools. Grounded in the equalization of power structures that traditionally privilege the expertise of the university and the knowledge of the school over the wisdom of the community, this approach positions community members as experts and colleagues in the preparation of future teachers. The approach honors significant relationship-building between candidates and community members; ensures opportunities for candidates' critical service learning alongside neighborhood residents based on community-identified need; engages candidates in intentional experiences through which to develop a critical consciousness; and provides opportunities through which to operationalize their learning in the development and implementation of experiences for children that are culturally relevant, responsive, and sustaining.

Community-engaged teacher preparation is intentionally grounded in the development of community teachers (Murrell, 2001) who understand systems of power and privilege and are compelled to work collaboratively toward a socially just society in order to rectify conditions that disadvantage populations of children. Opportunities to intentionally and critically reflect upon one's cultural lens, personal bias, assumptions, values, and beliefs in concert with an examination of societal oppression and the mechanisms that maintain and perpetuate injustice are essential elements in the equation of community-engaged teacher preparation.

We have structured this book into three overlapping sections reflective of the characteristics of community-engaged teacher preparation—overlapping because it is not possible to tease apart the essential components without compromising the whole. These components emphasize that community-engaged teacher preparation depends on collaborative relationships among universities, communities, and schools, which are grounded in the equalization of power structures, and which position community members as colleagues in the preparation of future teachers who are compelled to work toward a socially just society.

The first section focuses on the imperative of valuing and elevating the assets of the community in the preparation of teachers. Its first chapter begins with the impassioned plea of a community member reflecting on past and current relationships with the university and schools, and leading us through a new way to envision the preparation of teachers for minoritized communities. The next chapter in this section discusses a community mentoring initiative, which was part of a teacher preparation program, and the impact it had on candidates. The first section concludes with a chapter that examines ways in which community mentors can guide and enhance the efforts of university faculty to prepare teachers for the communities in which they work. The authors of this chapter take a critical look at what has worked well and what might be changed to better prepare the teachers we need.

Sustained, collaborative relationships among universities, schools, and communities, which create a community of practice and a shared vision for the education of children and youth, are at the heart of community-engaged teacher preparation. In the second section, we see this being enacted in three very different settings—one in an urban community on the east coast of the United States, one in Australia, and one in a rural Texas community. In all of this section's chapters, we hear from community members, school personnel, and university faculty who reflect on the development of their collaborative partnership and what it has meant for teacher candidates.

The two chapters in the third section focus on the ways in which community-engaged teacher preparation programs foster the development of "community teachers" committed to social justice and equity. The first chapter in this section provides readers with a critical look at how both faculty and program graduates view the successes and challenges of a fairly new urban social justice teacher preparation program. In the section's second chapter, current and former teacher candidates reflect on how their views of the world have changed because of their participation in a community-engaged teacher preparation program, as well as what this has meant for them personally and professionally as they begin their teaching careers.

Each section of the book is introduced with an overview of one of the overlapping components of community-engaged teacher preparation; the chapters within each section then highlight how that component is essential to the work of preparing "community teachers" (Murrell, 2001). Following the chapters, each section concludes with a reflection on how the work being done is part of a greater effort to reimagine the preparation of teachers.

In this book, we argue that the vision of social justice in teacher education has been "disrupted, but not displaced" (Brodie, 2007) and that a resurgence in commitment and conviction is on the horizon, fueled by a rectifying resolve to develop a new cadre of teachers with the will and skill to enact pedagogies informed by a moral and ethical obligation to end social inequity. With esteem and admiration, we share exemplars of the spaces in which this work is taking place, with an intention to inspire others to dream of the possibilities before them. In 1909, Goethe wrote, "boldness has beauty and power and magic in it." With this book, we invite such boldness among our colleagues in the field of educator preparation and, in the words of Goethe, encourage them to "begin it now."

REFERENCES

Alexander, M. (2012). *The new Jim Crow: Mass incarceration in the age of color-blindness*. The New Press.

An, S. (2016). Teaching elementary school social studies methods under edTPA. *The Social Studies*, 107(1), 19–27.

Anyon, J. (2014). *Radical possibilities: Public policy, urban education, and a new social movement* (2nd ed.). Routledge.

Bohrnstedt, G., Kitmitto, S., Ogut, B., Sherman, D., & Chan, D. (2015). *School composition and the Black–White achievement gap*. National Center for Education Statistics.

Brodie, J. (2007). Reforming social justice in neoliberal times. *Studies in Social Justice*, 1(2), 93–105.

Carter, P., & Welner, K. G. (2013). *Closing the opportunity gap: What America must do to give every child an even chance*. Oxford University Press.

Cochran-Smith, M. (1999). Learning to teach for social justice. In G. Griffin (Ed.), *Ninety-eighth yearbook of the National Society for the Study of Education* (pp. 114–144). University of Chicago Press.

Cochran-Smith, M., Carney, M., Keefe, E., Burton, S. Chang, W., Fernandez, M. Miller, A., Sanchez, J., & Baker, M. (2018). *Reclaiming accountability in teacher education*. Teachers College Press.

Darling-Hammond, L. (2013). *Powerful teacher education: Lessons learned from exemplary programs*. Jossey-Bass.

Derman-Sparks, L., & Ramsey, P. G. (2011). *What if all the kids are White? Anti-bias multicultural education with young children and families*. Teachers College Press.

Enyedy, N., & Mukhopadhyay, S. (2007). They don't show nothing I didn't know: Emergent tensions between culturally relevant pedagogy and mathematics pedagogy. *Journal of Learning Sciences*, 16(2), 139–174.

Esposito, J., & Swain, A. N. (2009). Pathways to social justice: Urban teachers' uses of culturally relevant pedagogy as a conduit for teaching for social justice. *Perspectives on Urban Education*, 6(1), 38–48.

Filipiak, D. (2019). *An equitable English education begins with dignity*. National Council of Teachers of English. https://ncte.org/blog/2019/04/an-equitable-english-education-begins-with-dignity

Freedle, R. (2010). On replicating ethnic test bias effects: The Santelices and Wilson study. *Harvard Educational Review*, 80(1), 394–404.

Gershenson, S., Holt, S., & Papageorge, N. (2016). Who believes in me? The effect of student-teacher demographic match on teacher expectations. *Economics of Education Review*, 52, 209–224.

Goethe, J. (1909). *Faust*. Collier.

Greenberg, J., Walsh, K., & McKee, A. (2014). *Teacher prep review 2014: A review of the nation's teacher preparation programs*. National Council on Teacher Quality.

Greenblatt, D. (2018). Neoliberalism and teacher certification. *Policy Futures in Education*, 16(6), 804–827.

Gregory, A., Cornell, D., & Fan, X. (2011). The relationship of school structure and support to suspension rates for Black and White high school students. *American Educational Research Journal*, 48, 904–934.

Heitzeg, N. (2016). *The school-to-prison pipeline: Education, discipline, and racialized double standards*. Praeger.

Hemphill, F. C., & Vanneman, A. (2010). *Achievement gaps: How Hispanic and White students in public schools perform in mathematics and reading on the National Assessment of Educational Progress* (NCES 2011-459). National Center for Education Statistics, Institute of Education Sciences, U.S. Department of Education.

hooks, b. (1991). *Yearning: Race, gender, and cultural politics*. Turnaround.

Hope, E., Skoog, S., & Jagers, R. (2015). "It'll never be the White kids, it'll always be us": Black high school students' evolving critical analysis of racial discrimination and inequity in schools. *Journal of Adolescent Research*, 30(1), 83–112. https://doi.org/10.1177/0743558414550688

Howard, G. (2009). Dispositions for good teaching. In M. Fehr & D. Fehr (Eds.), *Teach boldly: Letters to teachers about contemporary issues in education* (pp. 189–198). Peter Lang.

Howard, T. C. (2003). Culturally relevant pedagogy: Ingredients for critical teacher reflection. *Theory into Practice*, *42*(3), 195–202.

Hughes, D., McGill, R., Ford, K., & Tubbs, C. (2011). Black youths' academic success: The contribution of racial socialization from parents, peers, and schools. In N. E. Hill, T. L. Mann, & H. E. Fitzgerald (Eds.), *African American children and mental health: Vol. 1. Development and context* (pp. 95–124). ABC-CLIO.

Ladson-Billings, G. (1995a). Toward a theory of culturally relevant pedagogy. *American Educational Research Journal*, *32*(3), 465–491.

Ladson-Billings, G. (1995b). But that's just good teaching! The case for culturally relevant pedagogy. *Theory into Practice*, *34*(3), 159–165.

Ladson-Billings, G. (2006). From the achievement gap to the education debt: Understanding achievement in U.S. schools. *Educational Researcher*, *35*(7), 3–12.

Lave, J., & Wenger, E. (1991). *Situated learning: Legitimate peripheral participation*. Cambridge University Press.

Lee, R., Showalter, B., & Eckrich, L. (2013). Beyond the ivory tower: The role of contextually based course redesign in a community-embedded urban teacher preparation model. In J. Noel (Ed.), *Moving teacher education into urban schools and communities* (pp. 56–72). Routledge.

Lees, A. (2016). Roles of urban indigenous community members in collaborative field-based teacher preparation. *Journal of Teacher Education*, *67*(5), 363–378.

Love, B. L. (2019). *We want to do more than survive: Abolitionist teaching and the pursuit of educational freedom*. Beacon.

Mallett, C. (2015). *The school to prison pipeline: A comprehensive assessment*. Springer.

Mann, H. (1849). *Twelfth annual report for 1848 of the secretary of the Board of Education of Massachusetts*.

McKown, C., & Weinstein, R. S. (2008). Teacher expectations, classroom context, and the achievement gap. *Journal of School Psychology*, *46*(3), 235–261.

Milner, H. R. (2011). Culturally relevant pedagogy in a diverse urban classroom. *The Urban Review*, *43*(1), 66–89.

Moll, L. C., Amanti, C., Neff, D., & González, N. (1992). Funds of knowledge for teaching: Using a qualitative approach to connect homes and classrooms. *Theory into Practice*, *31*(2), 132–141.

Murrell, P. C., Jr. (2001). *The community teacher: A new framework for effective urban teaching*. Teachers College Press.

National Association of Multicultural Education (NAME). (2014). *NAME position statement on the edTPA*. https://nameorg.org/docs/Statement-rr-edTPA-1-21-14.pdf

National Center for Education Statistics (NCES). (2017). *Compulsory school attendance laws, minimum and maximum age limits for required free education, by state: 2017.* https://nces.ed.gov/programs/statereform/tab5_1.asp

National Center for Education Statistics (NCES). (2018). *Number of instructional days and hours in the school year, by state: 2018.* https://nces.ed.gov/programs/statereform/tab5_14.asp

National Center for Education Statistics (NCES). (2020). *The condition of education 2020.* https://nces.ed.gov/programs/coe/pdf/coe_cge.pdf

Nieto, S. (2000). Placing equity at the front and centre. *Journal of Teacher Education, 51*(3), 180–187.

Orfield, G., & Frankenberg, E. (2014). *Brown at 60: Great progress, a long retreat and an uncertain future.* The Civil Rights Project. http://civilrightsproject.ucla.edu/research/k-12-education/integration-and-diversity/brown-at-60-great-progress-a-long-retreat-and-an-uncertain-future

Picower, B., & Marshall, A. M. (2016). "Run like hell" to "look before you leap": Teacher educators' responses to preparing teachers for diversity and social justice in the wake of edTPA. In J. Carter & H. Lochte (Eds.), *Teacher performance assessment and accountability reforms* (pp. 189–212). Palgrave Macmillan.

Reardon, S. F. (2011). The widening academic achievement gap between the rich and the poor: New evidence and possible explanations. In R. Murnane & G. Duncan (Eds.), *Whither opportunity? Rising inequality and the uncertain life chances of low-income children* (pp. 91–116). Russell Sage Foundation Press.

Rist, R. (1970). Student social class and teacher expectations: The self-fulfilling prophecy in ghetto education. *Harvard Educational Review, 40*(3), 411–451.

Santelices, M., & Wilson, M. (2010). Unfair treatment? The case of Freedle, the SAT, and the standardization approach to differential item functioning. *Harvard Educational Review, 80*(1), 106–133.

Skiba, R., Horner, R., Chung, C.-G., Rausch, M., May, S., & Tobin, T. (2011). Race is not neutral: A national investigation of African American and Latino disproportionality in school discipline. *School Psychology Review, 40*(1), 85–107.

Sleeter, C. (2008). Equity, democracy, and neoliberal assaults on teacher education. *Teaching and Teacher Education, 24*(8), 1947–1957.

Souto-Manning, M. (2019). "Good teaching" and "good teachers" for whom?: Critically troubling standardized and corporatized notions of quality in teacher education. *Teachers College Record, 121*(10), 1–44.

Tate, W. F. (1995). Returning to the root: A culturally relevant approach to mathematics pedagogy. *Theory into Practice, 34*(3), 166–173.

Tuck, E., & Gorlewski, J. (2016). Racist ordering, settler colonialism, and edTPA: A participatory policy analysis. *Educational Policy, 30*(1), 197–217.

Vanneman, A., Hamilton, L., Baldwin Anderson, J., & Rahman, T. (2009). *Achievement gaps: How Black and White students in public schools perform in mathematics and reading on the National Assessment of Educational*

Progress (NCES 2009-455). National Center for Education Statistics, Institute of Education Sciences, U.S. Department of Education.

Wilkerson, J. R. (2006, April 20). Measuring teacher dispositions: Standards-based or morality-based? *Teachers College Record*. http://www.tcrecord.org/books/Content.asp?ContentID=12493

Wise, A. (2006, January 16). Response to George Will's column "The truth about teaching." *Newsweek*.

Yosso, T. (2005). Whose culture has capital? A critical race theory discussion of community cultural wealth. *Race, Ethnicity, and Education, 8*(1), 69–91.

Young, E. (2010). Challenges to conceptualization and actualizing culturally relevant pedagogy: How viable is the theory in classroom practice? *Journal of Teacher Education, 61*(3), 248–260.

Zeichner, K. (2010). Rethinking the connections between campus courses and field experiences in college- and university-based teacher education. *Journal of Teacher Education, 61*(1–2), 89–99.

Zeichner, K. (2006). Reflections of a university-based teacher educator on the future of college- and university-based teacher education. *Journal of Teacher Education, 57*(3), 336–340.

Zygmunt, E., & Cipollone, K. (2019). Community-engaged teacher preparation and the development of dispositions toward equity and social justice. In R. Papa (Ed.), *Springer handbook on promoting social justice in education*. Springer.

Zygmunt, E., Cipollone, K., Tancock, S., & Clark, P. (2018). Community-engaged teacher preparation. In J. Lampert (Ed.), *Oxford encyclopedia of global perspectives on teacher education*. Oxford University Press. https://doi.org/10.1093/acrefore/9780190264093.013.476

Zygmunt, E., & Clark, P. (2016). *Transforming teacher education for social justice*. Teachers College Press.

COMMUNITY MEMBERS AS COLLEAGUES

PRIVILEGING FUNDS OF KNOWLEDGE AND COMMUNITY CULTURAL WEALTH

Collegial relationships between schools and programs of educator preparation are not uncommon and are, by most standards, essential in order to ensure a productive clinical practice experience for preservice teacher candidates. Professional Development Schools (Darling-Hammond, 1997; Holmes, 1995, 1986) foster this collegiality through concerted collaboration between schools and university faculty whereby goals for partnership are articulated, research is conducted, and professional development needs are established and accommodated. Teacher residency models further advance the professional connection between schools and universities by melding theory and practice in year-long experiences situated entirely in schools under the guidance of university faculty and mentor teachers. While such partnerships between schools and universities have become increasingly well established in the evolution of teacher preparation, a regard for the role of the community in these efforts has been essentially absent. Community-engaged teacher preparation seeks to remedy this omission by positioning members of the community as colleagues in the preparation of future teachers, inviting inherent funds of knowledge and community cultural wealth into the fabric of educator preparation.

Configurations of collegiality in community-engaged teacher preparation programs vary, but are, most importantly, grounded in reciprocal, caring relationships configured around a united vision

for children's success. Pairing candidates with mentor families in the
neighborhoods in which they practice-teach can provide valuable
insight into children's lived experience and afford opportunities
for candidates' authentic participation in the community, which
might otherwise be unavailable. Staff members in community-based
organizations can provide important contexts for neighborhood
resources in support of children and families. Community elders and
neighborhood leaders are sources of cultural and historical wealth.
Neighborhood clergy often provide important connections within the
community and may well provide examples of pedagogical approaches
that are more culturally congruent with children's lived experience.

Through the relationships we develop, the united vision we
construct, and the power we share, members of universities, schools,
and communities come to know one another authentically, developing
trust in and respect for the wealth of knowledge, the resources, and
the experiences that define our collective work. While the knowledge
and capital of universities and schools have been traditionally
recognized and elevated, historically marginalized communities have
typically been perceived in terms of their deficits, instead of the
resilience, resistance, and resolve that have informed their struggle
for survival, despite overwhelming obstacles. Community funds of
knowledge are the skills and knowledge, developed over time, that
enable individuals and families to function within a given culture
(Moll et al., 1992). Understanding of and appreciation for such funds
of knowledge position educators with the capacity to connect the
content they are responsible for teaching to children's lived experience,
rendering learning more authentic, relevant, and engaging. Funds of
knowledge are discovered and uncovered only through time spent and
relationships developed in particular spaces, and such cognizance does
not happen accidentally. With intention for respectful exploration
and community connection, funds of knowledge emerge as tangible
linkages that give meaning to teachers' teaching and students'
learning. Without an understanding of and appreciation for these
funds of knowledge, educators miss a valuable opportunity to truly
know students within the context of their communities.

Components of community cultural wealth (Yosso, 2005)
represent the tenacity and determination through which obstacles
such as systemic racism and classism have been effectively navigated.

As opposed to the financial assets that traditionally characterize wealth, these tenets define the capital through which individuals have endeavored to persevere in spite of oppression. The means through which communities preserve faith and keep dreams alive, the ways in which individuals navigate spaces of patent persecution, the strategies through which linguistic traditions are maintained, and the mechanisms through which communities strive for equal rights and collective freedom represent traditions of wealth. As educators come to know and understand communities for the inherent wealth they possess, they can build intentional linkages between the content and pedagogy that inform students' experience in schools. A steadfast mindset that *all* communities possess funds of knowledge and cultural wealth, and that it is the responsibility of educators to cultivate the relationships through which such wealth is shared and honored as an essential ingredient of children's education, forms the basis of community-engaged teacher preparation.*

The chapters in this section highlight the ways in which three distinct community-engaged teacher preparation programs have intentionally sought to privilege and give voice to the funds of knowledge and community cultural wealth in the particular neighborhoods in which they are situated. Each of these programs view their community partners as colleagues, without whom the work of preparing teachers who are committed to culturally relevant and sustaining practice could not succeed.

REFERENCES

Darling-Hammond, L. (1997). *The right to learn: A blueprint for creating schools that work.* Jossey-Bass.

Holmes Group. (1986). *Tomorrow's teachers: A report of the Holmes Group.* Holmes Group.

Holmes Group. (1995). *Tomorrow's schools: Principles for the design of professional development schools.* College of Education, Michigan State University.

---

*This material is excerpted from "Community-Engaged Teacher Preparation," by E. Zygmunt, K. Cipollone, S. Tancock, and P. Clark, 2018, in *The Oxford Encyclopedia of Global Perspectives on Teacher Education*, edited by Jo Lampert. Reproduced by permission of Oxford University Press. http://global.oup.com/academic. For permission to reuse this material, please visit http://global.oup.com/academic/rights.

Moll, L. C., Amanti, C., Neff, D., & González, N. (1992). Funds of knowledge for teaching: Using a qualitative approach to connect homes and classrooms. *Theory into Practice, 31*(2), 132–141.

Yosso, T. J. (2005). Whose culture has capital? A critical race theory discussion of community cultural wealth. *Race, Ethnicity, and Education, 8*(1), 69–91.

Zygmunt, E., Cipollone, K., Tancock, S., & Clark, P. (2018). Community-engaged teacher preparation. In J. Lampert (Ed.), *Oxford encyclopedia of global perspectives on teacher education.* Oxford University Press. https://doi.org/10.1093/acrefore/9780190264093.013.476

I Am My Community

Privileging Funds of Knowledge and Community Cultural Wealth

Wilisha Scaife and Eva Zygmunt

I AM MY COMMUNITY! I am the HOPE of our elders and I bear the DREAMS of our children. I AM MY COMMUNITY! I know the stories, I feel the pains, I know the struggles, and I can celebrate the gains. I AM MY COMMUNITY!!!

I have many answers but there is no inquiry . . . I know the truth, but you become judge and the jury. Because you look and don't SEE, you don't recognize me, but I AM MY COMMUNITY!

I AM MY COMMUNITY!!! I know the mother down the street who loves but lost her babies, I AM that mother. I know the grandparent who raised their grandchildren and watch so many others. They are my grandparents. I know the young man on the corner, hiding his shame behind his back, when I walk by, "Hi Mrs. Scaife . . . !" He means no harm, . . . says he's just "trying to survive . . ." He is my son, my nephew, my cousin. (You may have had him in your class, he might have been that student you just didn't have time for—his mother didn't show, and you didn't try to know . . .)

But you don't see US, because you don't look. Instead you see yourself as the "expert" because you had "the book," you know, the classes YOU took, so . . . you don't need me. I come to mind when you need to BLAME, want to JUDGE, and then you hold a grudge and talk about me with your coworkers and that negative little nudge.

BUT YOU NEVER KNEW ME, you don't know MY COMMUNITY, and as a result, you don't know OUR KIDS! You can't SERVE our kids. You barely teach our kids because you don't REACH our kids. See, our kids are the sum of MY COMMUNITY and MY COMMUNITY is me, so you must SEE ME and KNOW ME to see them, to reach them, to teach them, and if you don't, they fail . . . But guess what, YOU FAIL and, unfortunately, WE ALL FAIL!

So what's the resolve? Well, since I AM MY COMMUNITY, come to me!
Reach out to me! See me! Know me! You may know reading, science and
math but I know our kids, our community, our struggle, OUR PATH! You
see, you are an expert but, in that category, YOU ARE NOT ALONE! I AM
THE EXPERT on my family and my home!
I hear you. You say, "We spend more time with these kids than their
parents do." Don't believe the lie, I've done the calculations, that simply is
not true. Chronologically it's impossible, and emotionally, it can't stand,
see, 'cause even when it's not the parent, it's my family and community
who, FOR YEARS, holds that child's hand.
So humble yourself and with new motivation, find the wisdom that is
good; get out of your bubble, out of YOUR comfort zone, and take a walk
around MY neighborhood. You've come to TEACH our kids, you've got to
REACH our kids, and you can't do that alone; it's not the principal or your
school colleagues, it's community and home. Talk to elders, small business
owners, parents and family. Come my way—come over here because . . .
I AM MY COMMUNITY!

—Wilisha Scaife, "I Am My Community"
(original spoken word poem, 2017)

There is something in my core that believes that certain people come together in certain spaces for certain reasons at certain times. Some call it fate;
others, destiny. Some attribute it to a larger predetermined orchestration
of objectives, while others look to the alignment of the planets and the
intention of the universe. Of course, there are those who believe the true
seekers shall find, and that those with fervent faith invite such things upon
themselves. All I know is that it happens. This is a story of such happening.

As we toil in the telling of this story, Wilisha, an esteemed member of
the Whitely neighborhood of Muncie, Indiana (whose voice is included in
the story throughout), and Eva, a faculty member at Ball State University
(who grounds Wilisha's narrative in the literature and provides a reflection
on Wilisha's words), have tinkered with how to juxtapose our expression
in a way that speaks to both our individual and collective experience with
a novel paradigm in the training of future teachers. Our intention is to
weave our voices into a compelling narrative—to communicate the nu-
ances of our concerted university/community collaboration over the last
decade and to share how these have informed our continued commitment
to children and families. Our ultimate intention is to honor our conviction
that much of the answer to the academic success of children lies in the
wisdom, expertise, and cultural wealth of the communities in which they
are privileged to live and learn—if only we would listen.

As a frame for the story that will unfold, Wilisha articulates an all-too-
familiar pattern of university engagement that furthers the oppression of

marginalized and minoritized communities. She then underscores an unex-
pected and unprecedented turn in the typical tide that created the opportunity to pause and the potential to reconsider.

IT'S THE SAME STORY, UNTIL IT'S NOT

Our experience was like so many other high-poverty, predominantly Black,
and marginalized communities: the university would come in with grand
ideas and assumptions about our poverty, throw an assessment at us that
was sure to validate their deficit perspective, initiate a program that would
veil their true intentions, and then take their "findings" and "successes"
back to the university to celebrate the work they did in yet another "poor
community." Not this time! This time our gatekeepers were in place and
ready to question the investigators and send them packing, back to campus.

As a community, we had learned that we are an important asset to
the city and that we need to be valued. We were no longer interested in
people coming in to dictate our vision and determine our needs; we were
self-assessing and drawing knowledge and resources from within first. Our
gatekeepers met with campus folks to ask the questions: What do you really
want from us? How will our families and children benefit? And, how will
you tell our story? The gatekeepers were principals, community activists,
and church leaders. And they were directly connected to our community
leaders and champions (parents, elders, small business owners, etc.). Our
gatekeepers explained to the campus visitors that you must gain the trust of
families and community members, and this is not a rush job; it takes building
relationships and gaining permission (slowly, over time) and then access
into the deeper parts of family and community.

Our gatekeepers explained that Whitely is a community that values
faith, family, and the education of our children, and you must see our value
in those things. You must be willing to go to the community places and
spaces that represent such values. You may not believe in God or reverence
organized religion, but you must be willing to go to the church house before
you can ever be invited to the family house; you must eat at the table of a
community council meeting before you could ever expect an invitation to the
table of a community member. We need to see you genuinely engaged and
authentically active in our little community.

This group of campus professors and leaders agreed. They did not push
or prod; instead, they stepped back, asked questions, listened to, loved,
and learned from the champions and gatekeepers. These campus folks
recognized that they had a lot to learn about community, *from* community,
and they asked if they could come alongside. With some suspicion, we
welcomed the campus leaders in. When they told us that they wanted

to bring students into our community to learn from us, our suspicions stirred again. Surely these students have been told lies about us, about our community. Surely these students' parents warned them about the dreaded Whitely neighborhood. Surely they would be coming just to see if what they were told was true, and upon seeing one thing that even resembled the warnings they were given, they would run out of our community declaring to all that Whitely was as wicked as they had been told. And if this cohort of students would be doing what others had done before, that's exactly what would have happened. Oh yes, we've had students come through our little neighborhood before. They have rolled in on their college guided tour bus, to gaze at those they had been told were "riffraff," or worse, "animals." Yes, like walking on the safe path in a large zoo, with the animals caged in, the tour bus provided them just enough visibility to be in awe, enough of a boundary to stare intently, yet enough protection and speed to later laugh and say, "Whoa, we made it out of there . . ." There had to be a feeling of dangerous intrigue, as many of these students rolled through my community but never got off the bus.

Research supports legitimate suspicion and well-founded fear of the patterns of community engagement in which universities and their students all too frequently engage (Schorr, 1997). "Studied" from outsiders' perspectives of deficit and weakness instead of assets and community wealth (Yosso, 2005), university exploitation of marginalized and minoritized populations, often for the personal gain resulting from published "findings," is an act of violence—one that has been historically sanctioned, and one that, in the story we recount, required careful reparation. Freire (1972) wrote, "one cannot expect positive results from an educational program which fails to respect the particular view of the world held by the people. Such a program constitutes cultural invasion, good intentions notwithstanding" (p. 93). Owning the standing and status of the mistakes of the past professoriate, while beyond daunting, strengthened our resolve to redefine a new paradigm of collaboration and partnership, grounded in the strength and conviction of the community in communicating its own agenda for growth and development. We were steadfast in our hope to transform what might be tenable—to reconceive the parameters of possibility—to flip the script on the traditional paradigm of university/community relations, redefining the community as the architect of imagination.

Freire (1997) wrote, "The idea that hope alone will transform the world, and action undertaken in that kind of naivete, is an excellent route to hopelessness, pessimism, and fatalism" (p. 8). It was abundantly clear that we needed to do much more than simply hope. Jeff Duncan-Andrade (2009) discusses a "hokey hope" that ignores both the inequities faced by minoritized and marginalized communities, as well as the paths through which they have historically navigated oppression and mobilized for change. Fundamental to our beginnings was an imperative to listen and learn, and by doing so to establish the trusting relationships essential to concerted collaboration; to absolutely never assume an understanding of an experience we had not lived, and instead to let this narrative unfold through the voices of members of the community. Duncan-Andrade juxtaposes "hokey hope" with "critical hope" that not only requires contextual cognizance but also "demands a critical and active struggle" against injustice (p. 185). It was to this struggle that we intended to commit.

In *Teaching Community: A Pedagogy of Hope*, bell hooks (2003) offers: "To build community requires vigilant awareness of the work we must continually do to undermine all the socialization that leads us to behave in ways that perpetuate domination" (p. 36). Nowhere does this hold more true than within the walls of the academy, where status and station inform positionality and privilege, belying even the best of intentions for authentic community engagement. Martin Buber (2013) offers: "We can be redeemed only to the extent to which we see ourselves" (p. 123). Owning the mistakes of the past, and how our affiliation with the university rendered us complicit by association, forced a posture of humility in order to work toward the reconciliation required to move forward.

THEY ACTUALLY GOT OFF THE BUS

We were ready to be angry with the university, to shake our heads and say, "We knew it was too good to be true." It was one of those "we will believe it when we see it" moments when the professors told us that these new students would not be on a tour bus but would literally (and figuratively), "get off the bus." Seriously, these students would come in, spend the entire semester in our community, get to know our families, participate in our events, visit our churches, eat at our tables . . . ? "Only if you allow us to do so," was the humble response of the campus professors. "What do you want in return?" was the wise question one of our gatekeepers asked of the professors. "We want to develop community-engaged teachers. We believe that teaching is more than understanding content—more than having strategies to deliver that content. We believe that in order to be a truly exceptional teacher, you need to understand the context of children's lives—who they are and the richness from where they come—so that you can take the content you are responsible for teaching and match it to children's lived experience to make it more relevant, engaging, and culturally responsive and sustaining." Could this be true? No probing, no assessing the stability of our homes and families? No determining whether we were good enough? No critique of our parenting styles or why we believe what we believe? They were sincerely committed to spending time getting to know us, what we know and what we wanted them to know about our children, families, and community. This was hard to believe and so out of character for a university. The university is "The Man." The university is the powerhouse of educators and experts; what could they possibly learn from a poor Black community, and more importantly, WHY would they want to learn from us?

After many gatherings and relationship-building opportunities between the university staff and community leaders and champions, it was time for the students to join the party. Each student was assigned a community mentor (an idea that sprang from the community), which was extremely significant. One of the first things that the mentors and students did together (as a large group) was take a community tour. No, no, no . . . not a bus tour! It was a walking tour down the streets, over the hills, and even through some of the buildings of our community; a poor, predominately Black, marginalized community that has the reputation of being a dangerous place. Young White female students walked down the street with older Black males as the community members shared stories of pain and struggle, as well as victory and power. Different stops on our walking tour became storytelling stations where emotion pierced everyone who listened. "This is where the bodies of two Black men were brought, after they had been lynched and dragged through town . . ." A couple of blocks east, "Here is a church building where the pastor wanted to clean up the drug traffic and violence, not by pushing the criminals out, but by bringing them in, so the church purchased the liquor license of the popular bar and dance hall and transformed those spaces into food pantries, children and youth centers, and a Cop Shop [a gathering place for bridging the gap between law enforcement and community members]." Then, a few blocks south and around the corner, "This is the very spot where a now nationally recognized tutoring program began in the home of a community member who was desperate to see our children succeed academically."

There is a popular quote by an unknown author that reads: "Before you judge my life, my past or my character, walk in my shoes, walk the path I have traveled, live my sorrow, my doubts, my fear, my pain and my laughter." We did not expect, nor did we want, these students to "walk in our shoes." What we appreciated was that they walked on our streets, looked in our eyes, listened to our stories, and recognized that we had something remarkable to say and something significant to teach them.

Many of our teacher candidates come from small, rural communities and have little prior exposure to racially diverse populations of children and families. Their ideas about race are uninformed, often deriving from popular media espousing an increasingly White nationalist ideology and agenda—an implicit bias and subconscious racism that Beverly Tatum (2017) coined as "smog in the air we breathe" (p. 6). Presenting with a deficit mindset about Black and Brown students and the communities in which they live, our candidates lack the contextual cognizance to deconstruct educational inequity, and instead, according to Bronfenbrenner (1979), often blame the victims of evil for the evil itself. With a sincere desire to counter this trend, our efforts were predicated on the development of relationships and grounded in an authentic desire to learn and experience the funds of knowledge (Moll et al., 1992) and community cultural wealth (Yosso, 2005)—the richness of children's lives outside of school. Setting our intentions on the long term, outside the realm of the time-limited, outcome-driven, semester-long, "one-off" world of the university, we were in uncharted territory and uneven ground.

We focused our efforts on situating candidates' learning entirely in the community in which they would eventually practice-teach, partnering with community colleagues who were uniquely qualified to impart the wisdom and expertise faculty and candidates could not learn absent authentic relationships. Rich in history, in faith, in revitalization activity, in reverence for children and elders, and in mobilization against oppression and injustice, the neighborhood was an exemplar of how traditionally marginalized and minoritized communities, often viewed from the perspective of what they "lack and need," persist and persevere, even in the face of untenable odds.

Anthropologist Wade Davis (2008) shared, "The world in which you live is just one model of reality. Other cultures are not failed attempts at being you. They are unique manifestations of the human spirit." Reaching out into the community, we sought to co-develop a structure that would illuminate this fundamental truth for our candidates, thereby increasing their capacity to not only understand, but to privilege children's experience *outside* of school as inseparable from their success *inside* of school.

WE ARE THE EXPERTS, BUT NOT BECAUSE THEY SAID SO

But it was more than walking and talking together. They wanted us to share in the creation of content, share in shaping curriculum, and give guidance on how to create a culture of care in their future classrooms. They wanted us to share at what I call "the experts' table." Parents, family members, and Whitely community members are experts! We were when we met this special group of campus professors and their students. We were experts all of the years we were previously probed, evaluated, and tested by many college departments, students, and professors. We were experts when they devalued us, silenced our authentic voices, and ignored us, when they were finished with us. We have ALWAYS been experts, we just never looked at it that way, and the rest of the world made sure that we knew our place. WE never thought of ourselves as such; not those of us who had merely a 3rd-grade education, like my mother-in-law who lived in Whitely when I met her. By this time, she and her husband had been married for 43 years and had raised 15 children, all in a little house that was only about 1,500 square feet. The Scaifes lived in Whitely for more than 50 years, nearly 65 years for Mrs. Scaife (since she outlived her husband by nearly 17 years). She would have never considered herself an "expert" on anything, just a hard-working mother who cleaned the homes of White folks and knew how to make neck-bones, green beans, and cornbread stretch. But her list above screams otherwise and validates her expertise on motherhood, family, and community.

According to Merriam-Webster Online Learner's Dictionary, an expert is . . .

1. A person who has special skill or knowledge relating to a particular subject;
2. Having or showing special skill or knowledge because of what you have been taught or what you have experienced.

This suggests that there is more than one way to be an expert. Expertise is as much about experience as it is about what one has been taught or trained in. Some might say it is more about experience . . . No one could watch Mrs. Scaife feed and raise 15 children, in a small house, where she, her husband, and children lived off a very limited income, connected with the local community church, and served her neighbors, and not call her an expert.

What could one learn from Mrs. Scaife? Do I even need to go into detail? How could her expertise support a teacher in the school? I hope there are many things that are obvious.

The magic here is that Mrs. Scaife's knowledge reached beyond her household, her 15 children, and more than 200 grand-, great-grand-, and great-great-grandchildren. Mrs. Scaife is just one example of family and community expertise. When you add her knowledge and experience to that of Otee Stills, who loved to swim, being denied that opportunity at the local downtown YMCA and at the public pool, or Cornelius Dollison, who remembers participating in the "sit-ins," or Ananias Thompson, who was one of the first Black men to be drafted by the Dodgers organization ("a heck of a pitcher," we're told), you find funds of knowledge flowing from every street and an abundance of community wealth waiting in the rich storehouse we love, called the Whitely community. This is why, when people ask me if I come from and live in a poor community, I proudly say, "You might call it that, but I can tell you that Whitely is RICH in what matters most."

   The reality is that within every community where children live, learn, and grow, there are experts: experts in homes, experts at local stores, experts cutting hair at the local barbershops (as well as customers there to receive a fresh cut), and experts sitting on their porches who know the last names of every child that walks by. People from poor communities often have to leave to go see their doctors and others who carry expert titles and degrees; we understand that these people are experts. Even schoolteachers who work in our communities are valued as experts and professionals. Principals and other school administrators have the reputation of knowing more than parents and families, but we were learning something in this process. We were learning that we (parents, families, and community members) brought an extraordinary wealth of knowledge to the academic table—a wealth of knowledge that the professionals needed. It made sense, once this revelation set in. Of course, absolutely, we ARE experts! Maybe more than any of the professionals who work in our schools—we are the ones who live with children every day, we are the ones who watch them grow, year after year. We are the ones who see them in their most natural state (I don't know that traditional school/classrooms can be considered natural spaces for children). We watch them in the front yard where they allow their imagination to soar and sometimes play alone. We watch them in the church yard mimicking adults they have studied in the Sunday worship experience, with hands clapping, feet tapping, and shouts of pretend praise. We watch them on the cracked concrete of the outside basketball court working on that jump shot and dreaming of the NBA. We are the ones who are there to wipe the tears after nightmares, give a spoon of cough medicine in the middle of the night, and decide if we can miss a day of work because that dose of cough medicine didn't settle the cold. We begin to recognize that if educators would truly ever be able to make the kind of impact education was intended to make, educators would need us!

   I am not savvy with numbers and honestly have never been a good math student. Anything above simple multiplication paralyzes me, so I was not much help to my three children when they were charged with successfully completing Algebra II, Calculus, and Geometry (although they kept telling me "Geometry is not really math"—NO! It's worse than math because you are adding letters . . . everyone knows that letters were not created to be calculated!). Anyway, the point is, although I did not have much to offer them, mathematically, I am the one who knew just how much math homework they could handle in one setting. I am the one who knew what extrinsic and intrinsic motivators worked for them. I am the one who knew that Jauwan needed a 20-minute break during long spans of homework, that Jayla would shut down and feel like a total failure if concepts were not clicking for her, and that Jasi cried herself into a frustrated frenzy. Most importantly, I knew how to meet the needs of them all—to comfort them,

encourage them, and recharge them. Their classroom teachers needed
to know what I knew if they would be as successful as possible in not
merely teaching but *reaching* my children! That's the goal—REACHING our
children, not merely teaching them, which unfortunately too often amounts
to dumping irrelevant curriculum that is not ever culturally responsive
and hoping they remember it for the test. Education means connecting; it
suggests shaping the curriculum content based on what the educator knows
about their students This "knowing the student" happens as the educator
seeks to know that student's culture, community, and family. This has
been one of the greatest revelations shared between university professors,
teacher candidates, and community members.

   The university professors and students were not merely on assignment;
their inquiries were authentic, and their desire to learn and grow was
genuine. They recognized that they needed us. They realized that we had
the answers to many of the questions that educators don't ask because
they have yet to admit that they simply "don't know." When you think you
know what you really don't know, you fail every time, and in the service of
educating children, this can be tragic. Connecting with family members and
community folks opens the eyes of educators to realities and resources that
will serve them for years to come. We were always experts. They recognized
that and treated us as such.

Many of our candidates, without expressed consent, have been enculpur-
ated into a narrative that informs them that children from low-income,
minoritized backgrounds exist within spaces where families and communities have forfeited responsibility for their physical, psychological, and
educational well-being. That families and communities are the "problem"
instead of integral to the solution is a popular precept that not only com-
promises but indeed thwarts the very pedagogical practices that are integral to changing the systems that persist in the propagation of inequity.

   In a paradigm of authentic community engagement, candidates are
introduced to a new narrative for their consideration: a narrative that
invites them to develop relationships with families whose love of their
children and whose dedication to their education is without question.
Candidates are additionally invited to consider how spaces of learning,
when *not* affirming of families and community, can be not only irrelevant
but also threatening to children's psychological survival, that in lieu of
surrendering their culture at the door, they choose actively *not* to learn,
lest they become barren of the strengths that inform who they are and
what they can become (Kohl, 1992). Bettina Love (2019) discusses an
"educational survival complex" where marginalized and minoritized students are forced to endure "spirit murdering," sacrificing who they are
and from where they come. Love (2016) defines spirit murdering as "the

denial of inclusion, protection, safety, and nurturance" (p. 2), all of which brain science support as requisite to the conditions that engender authentic learning (Darling-Hammond et al., 2020).

Exposed to the work of Ladson-Billings (1995), Emdin (2016), and Paris and Alim (2017) as viable alternatives through which to engage students in spaces that are intentionally built upon both content and pedagogy that are culturally affirming and sustaining, candidates begin to understand the imperative of looking toward sources outside those traditionally privileged in the education of teachers in order to achieve the overarching goal of equity in education.

There exists a traditional hierarchy of knowledge that elevates the institutional wisdom of universities and schools over community expertise. Candidates' authentic experiences developing relationships with community experts challenges that hierarchy, leading them to question the nature of its construction, as well as for whose benefit it has been sustained.

TELLING OUR STORIES AND HELPING THEM COME ALIVE THROUGH CONTENT AND CURRICULUM

One of the most powerful forms of listening and learning has come through storytelling. Storytelling is a natural phenomenon in the Black community, and a vibrant tool in the Whitely neighborhood. As powerful, authentic, and readily available as storytelling is, community members were rarely (if ever) asked to come into the community school to share this gift and their living words of inspiration and education. Our partnership with the university gave space and place for this; it made storytelling a priority. Through listening to the stories of community members, candidates learned the power of our community, desires of community members, and the needs of families and children. One of the first lessons learned came as community members repeatedly related stories of classrooms that were devoid of any images that looked like them. They despaired over the absence of teachers of color, the lack of textbooks that told the stories of heroes and sheroes who looked like them, and bookshelves that had no children's books reflecting their families or culture.

Together, we turned the art of storytelling into projects, curriculum, and content. The "Books Like Me" event was the first formal opportunity for community members, educators, and teacher candidates to sit, read authentic African American–authored books, and hear stories from the folks present, in a formal setting. Community members made themselves heard: "We need Black books and Black stories in our children's school and classrooms." The university students and professors came alongside by researching books that might be sufficient. Although they did some initial research, they did not assume they were the right people to make the final decision of which books would be good for our children. Instead, they asked if we could meet with them, review the books together, and as community members make the final decision on books to be gifted to our school and community spaces. This was an exciting and historical event. As we began, energy was high with great expectation. Soon, that expectation turned to enthusiasm, and heartfelt emotion filled the place, as each book kindled a memory soon shared through a community member's own story set to the backdrop of laughter, joy, tears, or sadness. This may have been the inaugural moment of our collective awareness of our expertise and acceptance of our role as community educators. We knew, without a doubt, that these teacher candidates needed us; and if they needed us (as educators who were not yet responsible for a classroom of students), how desperately did the current, veteran teachers need us?

Storytelling and shared book projects continued between the university and the Whitely community. Soon, the stories of leaders, activists, professional athletes, educators, all from Whitely, gripped the minds and hearts of the students and professors. A museum was birthed in a historical church that was once a schoolhouse; erected in 1893, it is currently the oldest standing public school building in Muncie. The brick and mortar told its own story of faith and Black pride, and now the interior walls tell the stories of many Black heroes of Whitely, the city of Muncie, and beyond. We decided that our children needed to learn from the stories, from books like *Who Was Martin Luther King Jr.?* They needed to read *A Girl Named Rosa* by the beautiful Denise Lewis Patrick. But how powerful and life-giving for students to see, hear, and read the stories of lay people and leaders from their own neighborhood on the walls of the Shaffer Chapel Historical Museum. Yes! The historical landmark, once a schoolhouse and now a church house, became a STORYBOOK of a different kind, to be read regularly by the children and families that live two houses away, three blocks down the road, and, as my Mama used to say, "only a hop, skip and a jump away." Some of their very own family members were memorialized on the museum walls; some of the children even see themselves there: "I am a great leader right NOW?" with reluctant disbelief, whispered from the lips of a child who authored a book that found national recognition a few years prior. He was 6 years old when his book about gun violence was published.

The real-life stories of community members who lived through the 1950s, 1960s, and 1970s drew further attention to the value of their experiences and expertise. Theirs were voices that the university students knew they needed to privilege as they created their Civil Rights Unit for the after-school classroom. This is yet another example of community folks being called upon as educators. We were invited once again to review books and materials to be considered for multiple lessons in a Civil Rights Unit. I remember books that were moving and told true stories but used language that, in some cases and classrooms, our children weren't ready for. I recall sharing that those same lessons, although not appropriate for a younger audience, were absolutely vital for older students. "Use this book and lesson and yes, please say the 'N' word because our children are using it, and the way they are using it reveals that they are not aware of the weight of the word." I continued, "My father-in-law was born in 1921; he told his sons not to ever use that word . . . He knew they had not had his experience but hoped they would respect the painful memories and intense anger it sent through him, whenever he heard the word, even after more than 50 years." These were lessons the university students could not tell quite as passionately, without hearing them flow through the hearts, minds, and mouths of those closest to the experience. They needed us to help them shape the content for best presentation. They decided, on more than one occasion, to bring community members into the classroom to tell their own stories, to hold courageous conversations, and to honestly share their concerns. Talk about community members as experts and educators!

We already had the content—our experiences, our struggles, our joys, our pains, our successes—so this did not need to be created: we had lived it and were ready to share it. Our partnership with the university team and students helped provide the platform for sharing them in a way that would prepare teacher candidates for learning from, working with, and even imitating teaching techniques that would be relevant, responsive, and restorative. The community has not only influenced what teachers teach (culturally relevant books and curriculum used in the classroom, along with our accompanying stories), but also the way they teach. Our community values faith; this is most obvious by the number of churches in a relatively small neighborhood. We have 10 churches on 12 square blocks. Of course, this doesn't mean that all of the community children attend church regularly, but it does mean that most have been exposed to some aspect of faith, and even attended church at least once with a parent, family member, or neighbor. Because of this, university students frequently visit the local churches. They usually attend with their community mentors, as a way of "doing life together," but as an added benefit, these teacher candidates almost always see elementary students at church who attend the community school. This means they see many of these children during the school day and in the after-school classroom (during the week), as well as at church (on the weekend). This is significant for the children, who are first surprised and always excited to see their "Ball State student" in a space outside of the school building. Parents, families, and community members are also delighted that future teachers would think so much of our children and community that they would want to spend time with us, in our own spaces (although the schools are often set in a community, they are not always viewed as being a true part of the community).

But the benefit of teacher candidates showing up at local churches not only impacts the families and students; the experience also affects the teacher candidates in significant ways. First, candidates are amazed by the love and warm welcome they experience from the first visit to the last. So overwhelming is the welcome that, in some cases, teacher candidates have joined the neighborhood church, and others have met their life partner there. Many students express that they have never experienced such a reception, even in their home churches. A second benefit of church attendance is what the candidates learn from the energetic atmosphere that cultivates interaction, participation, and involvement. The candidates witness children who seem not to have enough self-control to sit still for 20 minutes in the school-day classroom, now sitting quietly engaged in the church experience for more than an hour (sometimes closer to 2!). This experience causes students to pose a few questions: What is happening in this space that is not happening in the traditional classroom space? Why are 1st-graders happy and connected here but bored and disruptive in the school-day classroom? Well, the answer lies in a simple lesson taught and learned as you watch the preacher. In these Black churches, the preacher is expressive, mobile, and intentional in his or her engagement of the entire congregation. The preacher is empowered, not only by the words of God (which he or she is committed to teaching with passion), but also by the responses of the congregants. It's called "call and response," and it is a wonderful lesson that teachers should learn and apply in their school-day classrooms.

The preacher in the church is the "teacher" in the congregational classroom. The preacher makes the content come alive through stories, examples, illustrations, and demonstrations all strategically placed throughout the sermon. Everything that the preacher does in the church house, the teacher can do in the schoolhouse. The content and curriculum will necessarily differ, but the creativity, enthusiasm, and interaction are the difference-makers. As the teacher candidates witness all of this, they are learning, once again, from community members. The preacher has become an important educator for the preservice teachers, and the preacher's Sunday teaching methods/lessons can change the outcomes for children who meet in classrooms during the week. This is yet another powerful example of community partnership.

One final lesson from the church and seen through the example of a pastor and congregation is this: the pastor-preacher is like a father (or mother) figure in the community church. He or she makes it a priority to know every family in order to meet their needs and remain relevant in preaching and counseling. These vital connections and conversations come in brief but regular conversations after Sunday morning service, mid-week gatherings for the weekly Bible Studies (a time when longer conversations can take place), and during special events that always include food, fun, and fellowship (dinners, picnics, holiday parties, special anniversaries). Church paints a beautiful picture of authentic community and proves what can be done when we enthusiastically share in the process.

A university faculty member once shared with me, "As I consider my decade of engagement in this powerful space, I truly believe that the Whitely neighborhood embodies the 'it takes a village' message. While I can list many examples, what has impressed me appreciably is the respect that children are shown and how they are truly held in esteem. As I have observed members of the neighborhood over the years, I see how they look at children as the embodiment of their future selves—who they are now, but also what they envision and believe they will become. I am moved by the fact that I am often uncertain who the parent(s) is/are, because there is a communal commitment to the children. What I observe, as well, is that children, in the spaces where this adoration is patent, know they are celebrated, not in a 'I am so special' way, but with an understanding that they are loved and cherished beyond measure. I think of them as 'glowing' in these spaces where their lights shine so brightly—and it is beyond apparent that their light and joy is then reflected back on those in their presence." She went on to share her thoughts on the experiences of these same children in school—children whose physical prowess, verbal dexterity, or circuitous storytelling is discarded as superfluous at best, and more often a bothersome barrier to the real work of school. My heart hurts for the teachers who do not look past textbook manuals or district memorandums for the answers on how to truly reach and teach, but it aches more for the children whose greatness is unrecognized. We simply must do and be better.

The question of "whose voice matters" in the education of teachers has been previously pondered (Guillen, 2016; Zeichner, 2010), and arguably, scholars have worked to articulate aspirations for the knowledge, skills, and dispositions of teachers authentically grounded in community wisdom and expertise. Murrell (2001) defined the "community teacher" as one who works to understand the cultural knowledge traditions of the children, families, and community being served, and uses these traditions to make meaningful connections for and with children and families. Zeichner (2010) elaborates that such work "shifts the epistemology of teacher education from a situation where academic knowledge is seen as the authoritative source of knowledge about teaching to one where different aspects of expertise that exist in schools and communities are brought into teacher education and coexist on a more equal plane with academic knowledge" (p. 95). Further clarifying this construct, Kretchmar and Zeichner (2016) offer "teacher education 3.0" as an approach that requires a willingness to shift ingrained beliefs within universities about "whose knowledge counts in the education of teachers" (p. 153). While the literature includes examples of programs of educator preparation that have worked toward authentic community engagement (Lee et al., 2013; Lees, 2016; Zeichner, 2010; Zeichner et al., 2016; Zygmunt & Clark, 2016), how such programs are sustained in the long term, and, more importantly, how community members engage (or are engaged) as teacher educators, why they make this commitment, the level of control they have (or lack thereof) in co-creating the program of educator preparation, and how their roles evolve and change is much less well documented.

As we enter our 12th year of partnership in the Whitely neighborhood, a preponderance of the community mentors with whom we currently partner have been our colleagues and friends for now over a decade. While faculty members have come and gone, and institutional priorities have been defined and redefined, Whitely's identity, ownership, and agency in the education of future teachers has been sustained through their concerted commitment to their children and through patterns of persistence and perseverance informed by a historical and continued struggle for survival.

A poem by Nayyirah Waheed (2013) reads:

If we
wanted
to.
people of color
could
burn the world down.
for what we
have experienced.
are experiencing.
but
we don't.
—how stunningly beautiful that our sacred respect
for the earth. for life. is deeper than our rage.

In sacred respect for their children, *all* children, and for the world they will collectively continue to inhabit, members of the Whitely community have forged a path of liberation and empowerment, of agency and action, and by doing so are sharing their light, illuminating a way forward for others.

CROSSING BACK OVER THE BRIDGE
FOR THE BENEFIT OF THE REAL "UNDERPRIVILEGED"

It is not uncommon for colleges and universities to bring students into a local school; we have covered that, and we know what that looks like in traditional settings (an unfortunate one-sided benefit that leaves a community feeling used and abused). It is rare to see a university do what this program of educator preparation did in the Whitely community—ask permission, build relationships, gain trust, ask questions, and come alongside, sharing in the journey and work while allowing the community to lead, share their expertise, and educate. As if this experience has not been mind-blowing enough, the university took one bolder and unheard-of step. They not only said, "We need our teacher-candidates to go in and LEARN from the experts and educators who live in the Whitely community," they also realized that many preservice teacher candidates on campus were not getting the community-engaged experience. Some students on campus were being trained the traditional way, neglecting real community experiences that foster culturally responsive and sustaining practices, family engagement, privileging community values, and challenging their deficit lens. Rather than only bringing students into the community to learn from community members, they hired me, a community member, to take my experience to the campus to teach students there. It was my honor not only to share my stories but to carry the stories of our elders and advocates across the bridge, from community to campus.

What an honor! I was privileged to reach over 300 elementary education and early childhood students with the stories of our neighborhood and lessons for connecting with children, families, and communities, no matter where their teaching career takes them. I mean, they needed me (and others like me) on campus. I knew that I might have been viewed as "underprivileged," coming from a poor community, but in reality, these poor students I stood before, on campus, were truly the underprivileged ones. Why? How?, you might ask. Because they did not have the privilege of knowing the Whitely community and being transformed by the power of the warmth, friendship, and unconditional love poured out by this poor community that is RICH in what matters most.

Is this work about reaching Black children or marginalized families? Well, yes and no; we cannot deny that these families are treated as the "least of these." But it's more than that. I believe that when you make reaching society's "least of these" your priority, you will capture all in your reach. Truth is, Black families, poor families, marginalized children and families do not need something different than other families; we just need to be prioritized like other families have always been. Because we have been neglected for so long, there are lessons that must be learned if teachers will be successful in meeting us, reaching us, and teaching our children. As the poem says, "You must come to me . . . see me, know me, because I AM MY COMMUNITY."

AN INVITATION

In reference to contemporary schools and schooling, Bettina Love (2019) emphasizes, "we need spaces that not only protect those who are most vulnerable, but also heal them" (p. 98). Toward this end, in this chapter, we have shared community-engaged teacher preparation, accomplished in solidarity with members of historically marginalized populations, as a promising model for educator preparation (Cipollone et al., 2018; Zygmunt, Cipollone, Tancock, & Clark, 2018; Zygmunt, Cipollone, Tancock, Clark, et al., 2018; Zygmunt & Clark, 2016). This model, achieved through privileging community funds of knowledge (Moll et al., 1992) and cultural wealth (Yosso, 2005), creates classrooms "aimed at facilitating interactions where people matter to each other, fight together in the pursuit of creating 'homeplaces' that represent their hopes and dreams, and resist oppression, all while building a new future" (Love, 2019, p. 68). It is the future that Love describes to which we together aspire.

This piece is offered as an invitation to imagine how the work of preparing teachers can be both transformed and transformative—if only we *all* have the will to make it so. This requires careful consideration of the radical shifts required to engender education as a more equitable endeavor for all children, and the policies and practices that must be enacted toward this end. How we hope that what we have shared here collectively calls us and compels us, as well as those with whom we must join hands, to accept the challenge.

REFERENCES

Bronfenbrenner, U. (1979). *The ecology of human development.* Harvard University Press.

Buber, M. (2013). *The way of man: Ten rungs.* Kensington Publishing Company.

Cipollone, K., Zygmunt, E., & Tancock, S. (2018). "A paradigm of possibility": Community mentors and teacher preparation. *Policy Futures in Education, 16*(6), 709–728. https://doi.org/10.1177%2F1478210317751270

Darling-Hammond, L., Flook, L., Cook-Harvey, C., Barron, B., & Osher, D. (2020). Implications for educational practice of the science of learning and development. *Applied Developmental Science, 24*(2), 97–140.

Davis, W. (2008). *The worldwide web of belief and ritual.* http://www.ted.com/talks/wade_davis_on_the_worldwide_web_of_belief_and_ritual

Duncan-Andrade, J. (2009). Note to educators: Hope required when growing roses in concrete. *Harvard Educational Review, 79*(2), 181–194.

Emdin, C. (2016). *For White folks who teach in the hood . . . and the rest of y'all too: Reality pedagogy and urban education.* Beacon Press.

Freire, P. (1972). *Pedagogy of the oppressed.* Continuum.

Freire, P. (1997). *Pedagogy of hope.* Continuum.

Guillen, L. (2016). *Partnering with teacher education programs: The community mentor experience* [Unpublished doctoral dissertation]. University of Washington, Seattle.

hooks, b. (2003). *Teaching community: A pedagogy of hope.* Routledge.

Kohl, H. (1992). I won't learn from you: Thoughts on the role of assent in learning. *Rethinking Schools, 7*(1), 16–19.

Kretchmar, K., & Zeichner, K. (2016). Teacher prep 3.0: A vision for teacher education to impact social transformation. *Journal of Education for Teaching, 42*(4), 417–433.

Ladson-Billings, G. (1995). Toward a theory of culturally relevant pedagogy. *American Educational Research Journal, 32*(3), 465–491.

Lee, R., Showalter, B., & Eckrich, L. (2013). Beyond the ivory tower: The role of contextually based course redesign in a community-embedded urban teacher preparation model. In J. Noel (Ed.), *Moving teacher education into urban schools and communities* (pp. 56–72). Routledge.

Lees, A. (2016). Roles of urban indigenous community members in collaborative field-based teacher preparation. *Journal of Teacher Education, 67*(5), 363–378.

Love, B. L. (2019). *We want to do more than survive: Abolitionist teaching and the pursuit of educational freedom.* Beacon.

Love, B. L (2016). Anti-Black state violence, classroom edition: The spirit murdering of Black children. *Journal of Curriculum and Pedagogy, 13*(1), 22–25.

Moll, L. C., Amanti, C., Neff, D., & González, N. (1992). Funds of knowledge for teaching: Using a qualitative approach to connect homes and classrooms. *Theory into Practice, 31*(2), 132–141.

Murrell, P. C., Jr. (2001). *The community teacher: A new framework for effective urban teaching.* Teachers College Press.

Paris, D., & Alim, H. S. (Eds.) (2017). *Culturally sustaining pedagogies: Teaching and learning for justice in a changing world.* Teachers College Press.

Schorr, L. (1997). *Common purpose: Strengthening families and neighborhoods to rebuild America.* Anchor Books Doubleday.

Tatum, B. (2017). *"Why are all the Black kids sitting together in the cafeteria?" and other conversations about race* (20th anniversary ed.). Basic Books.

Waheed, N. (2013). *Salt.* CreateSpace.

Yosso, T. J. (2005). Whose culture has capital? A critical race theory discussion of community cultural wealth. *Race, Ethnicity, and Education, 8*(1), 69–91.

Zeichner, K. (2010). Rethinking the connections between campus courses and field experiences in college- and university-based teacher education. *Journal of Teacher Education, 61*(1–2), 89–99.

Zeichner, K., Bowman, M., Guillen, L., & Napolitan, K. (2016). Engaging and working in solidarity with local communities in preparing the teachers of their children. *Journal of Teacher Education, 67*(4), 277–290.

Zygmunt, E., Cipollone, K., Tancock, S., & Clark, P. (2018). Community-engaged teacher preparation. In J. Lampert (Ed.), *Oxford encyclopedia of global perspectives on teacher education.* Oxford University Press. https://doi.org/10.1093/acrefore/9780190264093.013.476

Zygmunt, E., Cipollone, K., Tancock, S., Clausen, J., Clark, P., & Mucherah, W. (2018). Loving out loud: Community mentors, teacher candidates, and transformative learning through a pedagogy of care and connection. *Journal of Teacher Education, 69*(2), 127–139.

Zygmunt, E., & Clark, P. (2016). *Transforming teacher education for social justice.* Teachers College Press.

CHAPTER 2

Community Mentoring

Seeking Cultural Dexterity Through a Process-Oriented Approach to Teaching

Candance Doerr-Stevens, Joëlle Worm, and Kelly R. Allen

I think when I came to Milwaukee, I came with the idea that I would teach, that I had something to impart or share. Afterall, I was the one with a college education, and had been prepared by a teacher education program. But in reality I have never been more wrong. I knew very little. My students taught me constantly . . . They showed me real grit and how ingenuity can impact every piece of your life. . . . My students' ingenuity and creativity was constantly on display in the classroom. What Milwaukee really showed me is that I didn't know it all, and maybe there is something to be said for realizing you actually know very little.

—Participant voiceover from digital story

In the excerpt above, from a digital story created by a teacher candidate upon completing his student teaching and community mentor program experience, we hear the voice of a young teacher reflecting on his student teaching experience in a midsized Midwestern urban school district. The voice is layered atop a series of images showing the skyscrapers and landmarks that visually define the city to him. Paired with the words are scenes of an empty classroom, a teacher's desk with a half-full cup of coffee, and an open grade book. The images collectively build a contrast of the big, bustling city against the small, lone teacher, a common storyline that positions teachers as cultural heroes and/or change agents who make a difference.

In some cases, this narrative can lead to insight that allows early-career teachers to forge a cultural positioning that opens up avenues for creating classrooms that build on students' multiple knowledge sets and cultural assets. Indeed, we see this to some extent in the words and images of the digital story excerpted above. Layered alongside the voice-over, which conveys a growing awareness of the teacher's own power and privilege, are several images of student artwork and social critique writing. In other cases, however, the teacher-as-hero story can reaffirm deficit narratives that firmly plant teachers as cultural authority, bestow-er of knowledge, and helper. All of these narratives may present teachers as a potential force for good. Coincidentally, these narratives also po-sition teachers as "outsider" and students as "other," stances that can inhibit cultural understanding.

Hoping to promote teacher positioning that was generative in its ap-proach to culture and not affirming of deficit narratives was one of our many aims when we set out to conduct our community mentoring pro-gram in the fall of 2017. We wanted to promote cultural competence and greater awareness of personal biases through relationship-building with community mentors. With some participants, we were successful in fur-thering new perspectives and teacher stances toward teaching and learn-ing. In other areas, we have much to learn. We share here what we did, what worked, and what did not. In particular, we share the varied teacher positionings that we observed throughout the program and how these cultural stances allowed different pathways for preservice and early-career teachers to negotiate their roles as community members in the classroom, the school, and beyond.

We have organized this chapter into four sections. In the first part, we offer a brief review of the literature on community-engaged learning. Here we focus on the limitations and potentials of community-engaged learning for teachers as it relates to cultural understanding and teacher practice. We next move into a detailed description of the community mentoring program as it was offered during the 2017–2018 academic year. In this section we focus on the different programming events offered and how the events connected to the teacher preparation coursework, as well as our usage of digital storytelling as a multimodal form of reflection and critique. We then move into a critical analysis of our program, focusing on what worked and what did not work. In this section we address areas where we fell short of our goals in terms of teacher support and program implementation as well as areas of curious surprise, where teachers and mentors redefined what community mentoring could look like. The final section provides a summary and discussion of the next steps we see for community mentoring and how we feel such efforts can be used to shift culture away from being an object of study to being an ongoing process and project of our teaching.

COMMUNITY-ENGAGED LEARNING AND CRITICAL INQUIRY

Research has shown that school and classroom practices are often misaligned with the cultural norms and lived realities of minoritized and marginalized students, leading to calls for pedagogical strategies that reflect the cultures and communities of students (Gay, 2002; Ladson-Billings, 1995; Paris & Alim, 2017). Yet, inclusive definitions of culture and community are not readily available, making it difficult for some groups of people, Whites in particular, to see themselves as cultural beings (Sleeter, 2016; Zygmunt-Fillwalk & Clark, 2007). These limited understandings of culture contribute to "narrow conceptions of learning" (Paris & Alim, 2017, p. 249), which have detrimental effects on students.

Culturally sustaining pedagogies (Paris & Alim, 2014) encourage educators to approach culture not as static and absolute, but as dynamic and varied in outcomes. This relational positioning toward culture requires what Paris and Alim call "cultural dexterity," the capacity to wear multiple identities within complex situations (2014, p. 91). Seeking to embrace this cultural dexterity, we align ourselves with Hammond's (2015) definition of culture as the "way that every brain makes sense of the world" (p. 22). This definition goes beyond ethnicity and language to include everything from the way people dress to their lived experiences and their overall worldviews. In addition to limiting definitions of culture, research also shows that educators struggle to implement culturally responsive and sustaining practices (Gay & Howard, 2000; Ladson-Billings, 2014), largely because they lack an understanding of the cultural practices of their students and communities (Kinloch & Dixon, 2018).

Alongside pedagogy, teacher education has been called upon to recruit and retain teachers of color, as well as to prepare White teachers for working with diverse student populations (Liu & Ball, 2019). To recruit and retain future teachers of color, as well as to effectively prepare candidates whose exposure to diverse populations of children and families have been significantly limited, community-engaged teacher preparation has been suggested as an avenue for enacting social justice education by connecting preservice teachers to the home communities of their students (Zygmunt & Cipollone, 2019). Similarly, community-engaged teacher preparation could provide a way for educators to better understand students, especially for "teachers who have a very foreign understanding of who their students are" (Clark et al., 2016, p. 270).

In the *Oxford Encyclopedia of Global Perspectives on Teacher Education* (Zygmunt et al., 2018), community-engaged teacher preparation is defined as a paradigm grounded in the concerted cultivation of relationships between universities, schools, and communities through which funds of knowledge (Moll et al., 1992) and community cultural wealth (Yosso, 2005) are elevated toward the end of ensuring a more equitable and socially just approach to teaching and learning. Situated in traditionally marginalized and minoritized spaces, community-engaged teacher preparation, according to Zygmunt and colleagues (2018a), positions community members as experts and is predicated on equalizing the power structures that traditionally privilege the expertise of the university and the school over the wisdom of the community.

While some programs of educator preparation are *based* at least partially off campus and in the community, they often can fall short of incorporating the criteria outlined above and can evidence impact that belies their intention. Absent authentic relationships and a commitment to equalizing power, such community-based initiatives, although attempting to address issues of equity and social justice, may reproduce and further entrench deficit perspectives of marginalized communities (Barnes, 2017a; Bortolin, 2011; De Leon, 2014; Flower, 2002; Haddix, 2015; Kozma, 2015; Mitchell, 2008). In particular, when preservice educators are engaged in short-term community-based programs, future educators can perceive themselves as doing a service to the community they are engaged with (Bortolin, 2011), thus emerging with an ethic of charity instead of critical consciousness. To this point, when time is not made for educators to engage in critical reflections that allow them to discuss their experiences and broader societal injustices and inequities, longitudinal change in educators' practice is less likely (Barnes, 2017). While some short-term programs have shown changes in teacher dispositions, shifts in teaching practice are less evident, an issue that Smolcic and Katunich note "reflect[s] the lack of longitudinal work and challenges involved in following program participants over longer periods of time after program conclusion" (2017, p. 54).

Community-engaged teacher preparation programs are intended to be "grounded in reciprocal relationships that bridge the university and neighborhood" (Zygmunt & Cipollone, 2019, p. 16), yet in some cases, programs that are community based may unintentionally exacerbate inequitable power dynamics between the university and community (Barnes, 2017a; Bortolin, 2011; De Leon, 2014; Flower, 2002; Haddix, 2015; Kozma, 2015; Mitchell, 2008). Smolcic and Katunich (2017) in particular found that in research focused on such programs, the voices of community members engaged in this work were often absent, a serious concern when attempting to redefine community partnerships.

Some attempts have been made to mitigate such concerns regarding equity in programs of educator preparation situated in communities, such as the implementation of longer-term programs (Bortolin, 2011; Smolcic

& Katunich, 2017) and incorporating intentional time for critical reflection and discussion (Barnes, 2017a). Other research suggests that the role of teacher educators and program facilitators is essential in ensuring that the critical aspect of community-engaged teacher preparation is not lost. For example, Barnes (2017b) cautions teacher education programs to be mindful of the sociopolitical context in which they are creating community-engaged programs. Barnes (2017b) encourages teacher educators and program facilitators to be conscious of *how* they frame partnerships and to articulate the purpose for being in the community, so that program aims do not "reify deficit or stereotypical beliefs about others" (p. 13). Of concern is how programs unintentionally position communities as "objects of study" for preservice teachers. Instead, Barnes (2017a) urges preservice teachers to "view themselves as involved in relationships with other people and places and relationships" (p. 229), as through these relationships they will gain a deeper understanding of reciprocity and how it emerges differently across settings.

Community mentors can play an important role in this positioning. Mentors work alongside preservice teachers to interrupt deficit perspectives and help understand and interpret the experiences the preservice teachers are having (Zygmunt & Cipollone, 2019; Zygmunt & Clark, 2016). However, the critical role of the mentor in community-engaged programs brings into question, once again, the power dynamics of community-engaged programs and how they are often disproportionately positioned to favor the interests of the university. In considering this, Zygmunt and colleagues (2018b) question "the implications of an education preparation program predicated upon members of a minoritized neighborhood educating predominantly White candidates" (p. 136). They note that the experiences of the mentors engaged in this work continue to be absent in research on community-engaged programs.

Questions and concerns related to equity, power, and voice within university and community partnerships persist across a variety of contexts. Teacher education partnerships in Milwaukee, Wisconsin, are no exception. Like many other universities situated in urban contexts, the University of Wisconsin-Milwaukee (UWM) offers teacher education preparation with a focus on urban contexts. Milwaukee, Wisconsin's largest urban center, could be described using Milner's (2012) *urban emergent* category in terms of its education systems. Milner ascribes this category to cities of less than one million people. While these cities "do not experience the magnitude of the challenges" that larger *urban intensive* cities face, they do confront similar education challenges related to "resources, qualification of teachers, and academic development of students" (p. 560).

The teacher education programs at UWM have formed several close partnerships with Milwaukee Public Schools (MPS). In addition to being the state's largest school district, MPS is also greatly affected by Milwaukee's ongoing economic and racial segregation, as well as state-wide conservative backing of school choice/voucher programming. As with other urban emergent districts, 87% of MPS students identify as Black or African American, Hispanic or Latino, Asian, two or more races, or American Indian/Alaska Native (MPS Office of Finance, 2019), while approximately 70% of MPS teachers identify as White (Powell, 2018). This trend is mirrored in teacher preparation in Milwaukee. The major-ity of teacher candidates at UWM are not only White but also hail from suburban and rural environments, with little personal experience in urban settings.

Seeking to redress some of the deficit narratives perpetuated within tra-ditional teacher preparation and student teaching experiences, UWM, in partnership with various local agencies and religious nonprofits, designed and implemented the Community Mentor program. The program was in-formed by work from Ball State University's community-engaged teacher preparation model, yet also drew upon programmatic innovations already in place from the grant-funded UWM ArtsECO and UW System Institute for Urban Education (IUE) programs. UWM ArtsECO is a professional development and support program for art and art-interested teachers with particular emphasis on early-career educators from preservice to 5 years in the profession. In 2017–2018, IUE was a UW System program where teacher candidates from state of Wisconsin university education programs came to Milwaukee for urban student teaching placements in Milwaukee Public Schools. The community mentor programming took place during the 2017–2018 academic year.

COMMUNITY-ENGAGED MENTORING

The UWM Community Mentor program was conceived in the spring of 2016 when the directors of UWM ArtsECO and the UW System Institute for Urban Education (IUE) met. Both programs espoused a commitment to social justice and culturally relevant pedagogies. In the spring of 2016, the IUE director at the time was interested in experimenting with add-ing community mentoring into its program, and ArtsECO director Joëlle Worm (second author) was looking at ways to continue an early-career mentor program it had recently begun. The initial conversations centered on a grant-writing opportunity from a local foundation.

The IUE and ArtsECO directors attended the Ball State Summer Institute on Community-Engaged Teacher Preparation in the spring of 2017 to glean more from this model. This experience was, in fact, where the project's title, "I Am My Community," came from, after they heard

Wilisha Scaife's performance of her poem by the same name. Additional visioning and conception was provided by Candance Doerr-Stevens (first author) from UWM's School of Education, who introduced digital story-telling (DSt) as a modality for program participants to critically reflect on their teaching identities and experiences within the program (cf. Bishop, 2009; Brownell & Wargo, 2017; Coggin et al., 2019). Building on notions of critical digital literacies (Avila & Zacher Pandya, 2013) and participatory culture (Jenkins et al., 2016), the production of digital stories was framed as a creative social practice for writing and rewriting cultural spaces and community practices (Lambert, 2009). Doerr-Stevens also provided critical insight into survey development for the program: the pre-questionnaire and the post-program retrospective survey. Planning for the program continued through the summer of 2017, and implementation began in August. Table 2.1 provides an overview of the programming events and activities provided during the academic year.

Recruitment for the program was shared between ArtsECO and IUE programs. IUE mentee participants were recruited by the IUE director. All were preservice education majors who agreed to include community mentoring along with their one-semester student teaching placements in Milwaukee Public Schools. ArtsECO mentee participants were recruited by ArtsECO director. All were early-career (0–5 years) educators who had interfaced with the UWM ArtsECO program during their preservice licensure at UWM. Community mentors were teachers from the district with an explicit focus on community work, as well as small business owners and representatives from faith-based organizations who worked with the IUE and ArtsECO directors. In some cases, these community mentors lived or worked in the communities of the schools where the mentees were teaching. In other cases, their affiliation was connected to a community neighboring or near the mentees' school sites. In all cases the mentors lived and/or worked in Milwaukee.

Expectations for the program were communicated through a flier shared with mentor and mentee participants at recruitment and introductory program events (kickoff and mid-program meetings). Participants also signed IRB consent forms to participate in the program's affiliated research components (surveys, focus groups, and artifact creation—including digital stories). The introductory materials included expectations for both mentors and mentees, such as:

- Attendance and participation in cohort-wide meetings (kickoff, mid-program, and year-end)
- Attendance and participation in 1–2 cohort-wide "Planned Community Outings"
- Mentor visit to the teacher's / teacher candidate's classroom

- Weekly or biweekly connections between mentors and mentees (face-to-face, email, phone)
- Digital story creation and presentation (mentees only)

The program incorporated both single-semester and year-long participants and provided programmatic (mentor) and research (mentee) stipends upon completion.

Table 2.1. Community Mentoring Programming at a Glance

Program Event	Participants	Month of Programming
Kickoff	Program Leaders Preservice & Early Career Teachers (Mentees) Mentors	August
IUE Seminar	Preservice Teachers	September–December
	IUE Staff	February–May
Mentor/Mentee Meetings	Mentees Mentors	September–May
Mentor Meeting	Program Leaders Mentors	October
Community Outings	Program Leaders	October–November
	Mentors/Mentees	April–March
Digital Storytelling (DSt) Workshops	Program Leaders Mentors/Mentees	December & March
Midpoint Transition Event (DSt Presentations)	Program Leaders Mentors/Mentees	January
Final Program Event (DSt presentations)	Program Leaders Mentors/Mentees	May

A program kickoff meeting for first-semester and year-long mentor and mentee participants was held in August. This meeting included icebreaker and introductory activities, a presentation on the program, and an introduction to digital storytelling. A mid-program meeting in January allowed year-long and incoming spring mentor and mentee participants to learn about the program and experience the digital stories of the outgoing fall mentee participants. In addition to regular touchpoints between mentors and mentees, two digital storytelling workshops were offered to promote storytelling as a mode of reflection and critique and to assist with the technical and communicative aspects of the digital storytelling format.

Alongside the program-specific activities related to community mentoring, the mentee participants attended regular sessions for coursework or professional development specific to their professional needs. For example, the preservice IUE mentee participants gathered for weekly seminars, to connect theory to practice through related readings, and for written reflections and discussions on culturally relevant pedagogy/practices. The credit-bearing seminars gave participants the opportunity to debrief their experiences in their cooperating classrooms/schools. Early-career ArtsECO mentee participants had access to ArtsECO Teacher MeetUps, monthly networking, and professional development events with alternating art-education related themes and locations.

Threaded throughout the various program events was a focus on the teachers' and teacher candidates' stories. At the program kickoff, mentee participants were asked to pay attention to their own journeys into the teaching profession both as emerging professionals and adults negotiating access into a new city, school, and neighborhood. By the end of the program, mentee participants were asked to compose a digital story to share some aspect of their journey. This invitation was revisited informally in the IUE seminar setting and explicitly through the digital storytelling workshops that focused on multimodal expression and storytelling. Mentors were also expected to support the reflective and storytelling aspects of the program through their regular interactions with their assigned mentees. In this sense, the digital storytelling component was positioned as an ongoing project, a possible topic of discussion with their mentors.

DIGITAL STORYTELLING FOR CULTURAL REFLECTION

Across the two semesters of the community mentoring program, 15 mentees, teachers, or teacher candidates participated in creating digital stories (for ease of discussion, we will refer to the teachers and teacher candidates as "teachers" throughout this narrative). The final digital stories exhibited a variety of ideas and narrative structures relating to teaching experiences and positioning.

Broadly speaking, we found that teachers viewed themselves as either taking a position *within* the community of their school and/or students' neighborhood, or as being outside the community in the role of *helper*. These differing positions afforded distinct perspectives for representing themselves and their students, which we will further explain below. Within these teacher positions, we observed a variety of themes across all of the stories. Some of the most common themes evident in the stories included the ideas of journey and personal transformation. These stories often focused on the idea of "home" and "work" and the distances traveled between the two. The distances were represented as both physical in terms of miles traveled and metaphorical in terms of culture and worldviews experienced and extended. Another theme was that of reciprocity in learning, where both students and teachers were benefactors of learning. These stories positioned teachers as lifelong learners and growing with and alongside their students. A third theme of interest among the digital stories was that of cultural learning about self and another. In some cases, this cultural learning was described in the stories as "cultural enhancement" or "cultural exposure." In other cases, the learning was described as gaining "cultural humility."

Within each of the themes, there were varied representations of teacher positioning in relation to their students and school cultures. In some cases, the stories reproduced stereotypical positionings of teachers, students, learners, and leaders. In other cases, the stories revealed a more complex understanding of teacher position, student agency, and school culture. In addition to the creation of the digital stories, mentees were tasked with presenting their work to their peer colleagues within the mid-year and end-of-year events. Several of the participants expressed nervousness related to this task. The semi-public performance of the teachers' stories required them to consider how their stories might be read by a wider audience. They were also able to witness the range of cultural inquiry and reflective capacities of their peers, which they wouldn't have experienced had the stories remained "hidden" between teacher participant and university instructor.

While the final digital stories do not represent comprehensively the teachers' learning about self and community, they do offer windows into the storylines and discourse resources that early teachers have access to when describing their emerging practice. In the section below we describe the different types of narratives represented in the digital stories shared by the participants. The two main types of stories were "teacher as helper" and "teacher as within community." While all of the digital stories did not fall cleanly into these distinct categories, the distinct types help to illustrate the distinct positionings. We discuss these narrative features alongside key programming events and features of the community mentoring program.

Teacher as Outside Helper

One of the most common storylines evidenced in the digital stories was that of the teachers' perspective as being *outside* the community as a helper or servant. In some cases, this was the dominant storyline shaping the organization of images and progression of events throughout the story. In others, it was less central but evident in small ways. In the excerpt below, taken from the voiceover of Marcus's* digital story, we see the outsider perspective most clearly.

> To me, Milwaukee was a fantastical place full of bustling crowds, fun attractions, and high spirits. It was a place you go when you are looking for something to do. Festivals, restaurants, sporting events, museums, you name it the city has it. It wasn't until I began working in MKE and explored the full 414 zip code that I witnessed firsthand the lesser known tenets that define the city. Milwaukee is the most segregated metro area in the United States. MKE has the most Black students in the state and is the biggest contributor to WI's achievement gap and just so happens to be the worst in the country. . . . These are the realities that my students and their families face daily . . . Problems in urban cities are not better or worse than others. . . . They are just different. I have come to see the value of urban education and am so grateful.

In the voiceover excerpt above we see a sampling of a common story pattern we noticed among our participants: that of outsider fulfilling or reaffirming the teacher-as-helper narrative. Phrases such as "teach the teacher," "explore more communities and see their charm," and "grateful to serve" were common in this group of narratives. This narrative of teacher-as-helper is a common discourse readily available within popular messages used to support public education—a message often used to recruit teachers to the profession. It is not surprising that beginning teachers would be drawn to this helper narrative as a way to make sense of their yearling overtures into the profession.

This narrative of helping a community is not wrong or damaging in itself. When presented as the goal or endpoint of teacher learning, however, it has the potential to promote deficit narratives that present school

---

*Pseudonyms are used for proper names to protect identities of project participants.

communities as lacking and/or needing the help of a teacher. At first glance these narratives may present a sharing of knowledge and power between student and teacher, that of a reciprocity of learning where teachers become learners, and students become experts on their culture and, in turn, "teach the teacher." Unfortunately, these same narratives also position teachers as benefactors or patrons to school communities. They assume that teachers "do good" or improve the school community. Yet, in this "doing good" and "cultural improvement" they imply that the school culture or community is in need of help or lacking in some way. These helper narratives reinstate deficit discourses, which limit novice teachers' access to alternative discourses that present school communities and student cultures as fluid and pluralistic. In turn, teachers become situated as "outsiders" and their students as "others," rather than co-creators *within* and *of* the students' community. Paris and Alim (2014) caution that these dichotomous positionings can limit the flow of cultural, linguistic, and community practices in the classroom in ways that oversimplify learning and ultimately promote assimilation.

In reflecting on our program, we attribute some of these deficit narratives—*teacher as savior* and *students and school community as lacking*—to the varied levels of fidelity when implementing the program goals and practices, especially when it comes to working with the mentors. To begin, the program drew on the commitments of various community mentors, each operating within their own definitions of community and cultural positioning. The guiding principles for selecting community mentors were varied and perhaps a bit broad. Attempting to combine the missions of the two collaborating programs, community mentors were defined as individuals engaged with and connected to different communities and cultures within the city of Milwaukee. In some cases, the mentors were connected to communities closely aligned with the schools the teachers worked in. In other cases, they were not. They were assigned to mentees based on how we thought their life experiences and circles of engagement would support the teachers within their school assignments. For example, one of our male community mentors preferred to work only with male teachers. Another mentor had extensive experience working in schools and designing community art events and thus was paired with mentees who voiced a desire to complete larger, project-based learning goals. Considering the 1:3 mentor-to-mentee ratio, however, the pairings were not always specific to the teacher candidates' context. Additionally, some mentors were incredibly proactive in scheduling their connect time with their mentees, while others played a more passive role, waiting for mentees to initiate. Unfortunately, one mentor had to exit the program midyear, leaving some mentees without the relationship-building experience that the program intended.

When possible, the mentors enjoyed talking with one another to discuss ideas and share experiences. Throughout the program, the mentors met as a group only one time. The agenda for this session included hearing updates on the mentor/mentee interactions and reviewing and discussing the program requirements, especially in the context of support needed from the university and sharing upcoming events and the updated program calendar.

For some mentors, the time was spent sharing what they had done with their mentees, with a focus on the conversations exchanged and additional planned activities. One mentor, Jessica—a self-described "foodie"—always took her mentees for a meal and referred to "soul food" as her teaching tool. This same mentor shared a story about the innocence of one of her White mentees who, after hearing friends say there was no reason to go to Milwaukee's north side, asked if she could take him there. Jessica shared how this mentee admitted that he was unable to tell her about his own heritage, demonstrating his acceptance of not seeing himself as a cultural being (Sleeter, 2016; Zygmunt-Fillwalk & Clark, 2007). After their trip to the north side, this mentor gave the mentee homework to watch the documentary *Milwaukee 53206* (McQuirter, 2016) as a way of contextualizing the sociopolitical representations he was hearing from friends and what he experienced in their drive through the neighborhood.

In many ways Jessica was enacting what some call the "cultural ambassador" of community mentoring, providing a warm welcome for unknowing newcomers, while at the same time disrupting common narratives (Catapano & Huisman, 2010; Zygmunt & Clark, 2016). Not only did Jessica expose her mentee to new cultural perspectives, she also intervened to promote more complex understandings of place by requiring her mentee to view the *Milwaukee 53206* documentary. Many might say that Jessica enacted the critical caring (Noddings, 2002) necessary to invite teachers to embrace more complicated understandings of community knowledge. For some mentees this approach was effective. For others, however, the cultural ambassador approach, without a meaningful relationship, was not enough to shift preconceived notions and instead reified insider/outsider positionings.

Another mentor, David, shared in the same mentor meeting how he was addressing the cultural deficits articulated by his mentees. One of his mentees identified a language barrier between her and her Spanish-speaking families, as well as difficulty connecting curriculum to students' lived experiences. David suggested that she take the students on outings around the community of the school. When the teacher voiced hesitation and administrative limitations, David suggested that she instead enter into cultural spaces of her students' Latinx community, including a local Latinx art gallery and performance space and local Dia de Los Muertos celebrations. He also suggested that she use technology (Google Translate) to attempt to create communication patterns with her students' families in their home language. David often used technology himself to connect with his mentees, creating and updating a shared Google Doc with events that he thought were pertinent to the areas of inquiry expressed by his mentees. For David, community mentoring was about blurring self-imposed boundaries between "self" and "other." Instead of positioning himself as cultural ambassador, he facilitated activities of cultural engagement as a way to disrupt cultural routines that may cement and codify perceptions of self and others.

This meeting among the mentors was an important touchpoint for the mentors' participation, giving them the opportunity to share how they were interacting with their mentees and to critically reflect on the role they could potentially play in their mentees' development as new and future teachers. Mentors gained new insights and ideas from one another that they could take back into their work with their mentee teachers. Due to difficulties of scheduling and shifting leadership within the programs, the mentor meeting was held only once during the fall semester. In looking back on the critical reflection and knowledge-sharing on the part of the mentors, it behooves us to consider the resources and time devoted to mentors and their own needs for exploring cultural positioning. While the mentors may have been well established and competent in their professional domains, facilitating additional time for them to co-create their mentoring practice would have given them the opportunity to find clarity and focus within their mentoring.

In addition to mentor and mentee pairing, the program also included cohort-wide community events referred to as "Planned Community Outings." These events invited the mentors and mentees to gather in different parts of the city for large pre-planned events. Some were service oriented, such as volunteering at a food pantry and cooking breakfast at a homeless shelter for men. Other engagements invited participants to reflect on their own racial positioning as well as the history of race in America, such as the film screening and discussion for James Baldwin's *I Am Not Your Negro* (Peck, 2016).

These events were received with mixed reviews from participants. On open-ended questionnaires that asked participants to describe a moment in the program where they felt they had learned the most about community, one participant described the service-oriented community outings as "eye-opening" yet at the same time feeling an "inauthentic connection to the space." Another participant felt that the community outings further highlighted the depth of cultural understanding needed. As this participant stated,

I think it would be incorrect to explain/state that I truly "understand" someone else's culture. I believe that part of the process was understanding that I can never fully understand, I can only continue to learn.

In reviewing the execution and participant responses to these planned community outings, we realize that some of the community outings may have reinforced the teacher-as-helper positioning that is common upon entering teacher education programs. Even though some of the community mentors had relationships with the sites that were chosen, the events lacked a deeper framing of the sociopolitical histories of the places visited and the activities of serving that were being enacted. For example, in gathering at the food pantry and men's shelter, the community was positioned as lacking and in need and the teachers as those able to help and serve. While some of the participants described the experiences as "informative" related to how important the service agencies are for certain communities, the events did little to deepen the participant's understanding of current race relations surrounding the places, events, and practice of serving in Milwaukee. A more critical framing of the outings by program faculty, focusing on community assets and innovation, could have offered inroads for the teachers to position themselves as insiders and co-creators of the communities, helping them to see communities and cultures as dynamic entities.

Teacher as Within Community

Not all programming implementations reinforced deficit narratives. In fact, we observed multiple situations in which the teachers created classroom meaning alongside their students. This type of prolonged teacher interaction led to nuanced understandings of culture. For one student teacher it was the process of making and remixing music with students that opened doors into becoming part of the community. Pat positioned culture and community as projects in the making. Pat describes this role as one of "offering up":

When I moved to Milwaukee to student teach, community was my biggest project. I knew that I wanted to be a part of the Milwaukee community, the Crossroads High School community, and I also knew that I wanted to build communities in my classroom. I knew that as an individual, to become part of Milwaukee I'd need to offer up some skills. For me that meant finding and accepting invitations to play music or sing locally.

52   Community Members as Colleagues

In the voiceover narrative above, Pat describes their student teaching experience as a project of "building community," a practice that involves a continual showing up and working to become part of a community or create community with students. This focus on building *within* or contributing *to* the already existing communities was evident in some digital stories produced by the program participants. Phrases such as "forge a bridge with community" and "Milwaukee has become my home" were common in this group of narratives.

In Pat's case, as with the other participants who worked with the same mentor, we observed a distinct teacher positioning *within* community. Instead of being an observer (*outside the community*) of an established school or student culture, we have the teacher as a co-creator of classroom and/or learning community. We attribute much of this positioning to a specific mentor's commitment to student experiences. This mentor, David, promoted teacher growth by having his mentees view themselves as part of the community and by encouraging them to make community within the classroom. In fact, when one of his mentees asked him to take him on a tour of his part of the city, David instead encouraged the mentee to visit the many displays of street art throughout the city, asking the mentee to note how each mural represents various histories and cultural assets in the city. In many ways, David resisted the role of cultural ambassador. A practicing artist himself, David gravitated toward community-based art projects as a cohesive set of activities to define and build communities. David preferred to sit with the teachers and create lesson plans in which he would ask them to get to know their students. This approach often led to the teachers centering the students, their schoolwork, their insights, and their artwork as the cultural assets to be shared.

This focus on the students and the community inside the classroom was evident in all of the digital stories of the mentees who worked with David. In these videos, teachers focused on student work completed throughout the semester and student views on the classroom, their schools, and their city. This focus on the students and student work positioned curriculum as a set of practices to enact and revise communities within the classroom. Similar to Paris and Alim's (2017) emphasis on "heritage practices" and "community practices" (p. 90), David invited his mentees to view culture and community as a collaborative project, one in which people with diverse aims show up and create culture and community together through shared practices. A focus on practices in progress over past-oriented traditions in need of study allows for participation and mobility within culture and communities in ways that promote "complex, fluid relationships among race, culture, and language" (p. 91). Complex relations break down binaries of teacher and student as well as self and other. In turn, the identity bindings toward deficit narratives of "savior" and "helper" are loosened, allowing teachers and students to position themselves as continually in flux, in progress.

MOVING FORWARD:
TEACHING AS ONGOING CULTURAL PROJECT

In moving forward to design and implement more informed community mentoring programs, we would reallocate our time and resources to deliberately invert the cultural gaze that was unintentionally encouraged through some of our programming. These efforts toward inversion would begin first with working more closely with community mentors to further integrate their perspectives into the programming and extend the professional development opportunities for facilitating adult learning and interrogating culture. Second, we would prolong the time and space that teachers have with their community mentors and the programming. And, third, we would make intentional and deliberate a process-oriented mindset for creating community, one in which teachers position themselves as co-creators of community and ultimately active insiders of classroom culture.

To begin, we would work more closely with the mentors, inviting them in to co-create definitions and practices of culture. In subsequent mentor initiatives in other teacher education programming, we have learned that monthly or biweekly gatherings are essential to co-producing programming with the mentors and ensure it is responsive to mentees' experiences and needs. An additional intervention would be to more intentionally discuss and deliberate conceptions of culture among the mentors. We find that this is necessary because when pre-service teachers' deficit perspectives continue to persist without being interrogated, a community-engaged experience could further perpetuate inequities within partnerships (Barnes, 2017b; Zygmunt & Cipollone, 2019; Zygmunt & Clark, 2016).

Another way to deepen mentor participation would be to invite mentors into the design process of the program. A space especially poised for mentor input would be in the design and framing of the Planned Community Outings. These outings, as executed in our program, revealed a missed opportunity to enact an asset-based approach to community engagement, which Barnes (2017) urges is essential for promoting equitable relations among community partners. With input and selection suggestions from the mentors, the outings could explicitly focus on the strengths and relationships embedded within these community spaces. In this case, the outings would not reinforce service narratives but instead showcase the resilience and grassroots activism at work within these communities, which could in turn serve as potential models for community learning within classrooms.

A final opportunity to deepen connections with community members would be to invite mentors to join the teachers in making digital stories, to share aspects of their culture and represent how they actively contribute to their communities. One mentor attended one of the digital storytelling workshops and found the event to be an additional space for dialogue with the teachers about their own homes and backgrounds. Interested in the intersections of story and teaching, this mentor wanted to learn more about the digital storytelling process. Similar to how digital storytelling has been used in various community contexts to give voice to members and define community values (Lambert, 2009), this media-composing practice could be further framed as a shared practice for both mentors and mentees to explore together the various routes of cultural understanding.

If funding allowed, we would extend the community mentoring to a 2-to-3-year format beginning in student teaching and extending into the first 2 years of teaching. This extended approach could involve more focused and critical attention to place and relational aspects of learning while also allowing mentors and mentees the opportunity to explore their perceptions of self, positionality, and community over time. We understand that grant-funded initiatives often necessitate short-term interventions that must be completed in limited periods of time. One way to work within these grant cycles could be to use short-term, grant-funded cycles as an opportunity to embed programming within districts or professional support organizations.

In addition to intentional efforts to problematize deficit narratives across programming activities and deliberate cultural work with mentors, we also suggest a dynamic engagement with the notion of culture and how it is discussed and operationalized within programming. Upon completing our year of community mentoring, we realized that all parties involved held distinct understandings of culture. While having multiple understandings of culture can be productive and even preferred to promote the "cultural and linguistic flexibility" necessary for culturally sustaining pedagogies (Paris & Alim, 2014, p. 90), this multiplicity was not explicitly communicated as a shared goal.

Within our collection of cultural understandings, we would emphasize the *practices* of culture. These practices may be based in one's heritage and/or community. As we observed in the teachers paired with David, where collaborative meaning-making occurred through various classroom and community projects, cultures and communities are also ongoing projects. These community practices co-produced new cultural spaces that granted the teachers fluidity to position themselves as both teacher and insider to the students' lives. We hope that by embracing a multiplicity of practices we will encourage within teachers, and students as well, a cultural flexibility to move in and across multiple contexts, a dexterity to position themselves *outside* of deficit narratives and *into* spaces of confidence, resilience, and abundance.

CONCLUSION

We appreciated the opportunity to experiment with a community mentor model, yet we were challenged by the complexity of meshing the aims of different programs and assuming alignment in the definitions and perceptions of the individuals involved. Given the opportunity to do it all again, we would recommend allocating resources toward the establishment of shared definitions among program leads and key implementation staff (such as community mentors). While perhaps time-consuming at the outset, we believe this has the potential to improve fidelity of implementation across the program. Additionally, we agree with Barnes (2017a) that building in intentional time for critical reflection and discussion at regular intervals throughout the programming is key to the continued development of the group and to ensuring the program stays responsive to those involved. Finally, we question what is possible in short-term (single-semester or even single-year) programs to truly shift teacher stance and inform classroom practice. Instead, we suggest multi-year formats that allow teachers to grow in their understanding of themselves, their classrooms, and their teaching practices in ways that embrace classroom communities and cultures as ongoing projects.

REFERENCES

Avila, J., & Zacher Pandya, J. (2013). *Critical digital literacies as social praxis: Intersections and challenges.* Peter Lang.

Barnes, M. (2017a). Encouraging interaction and striving for reciprocity: The challenges of community-engaged projects in teacher education. *Teaching and Teacher Education, 68,* 220–231.

Barnes, M. (2017b). Practicing what we preach in teacher education: A critical whiteness studies analysis of experiential education. *Studying Teacher Education, 13*(3), 294–311.

Bishop, J. (2009). Preservice teacher discourses: Authoring selves through multimodal compositions. *Digital Culture & Education, 1*(1), 31–50.

Bortolin, K. (2011). Serving ourselves: How the discourse on community engagement privileges the university over the community. *Michigan Journal of Community Service Learning, 18*(1), 49–58.

Brownell, C., & Wargo, J. (2017). (Re)educating the senses to multicultural communities: Prospective teachers using digital media and sonic cartography to listen for culture. *Multicultural Education Review, 9*(3), 201–214.

Catapano, S., & Huisman, S. (2010). Preparing teachers for urban schools: Evaluation of a community-based model. *Perspectives on Urban Education, 7*(1), 80–90.

Clark, P., Zygmunt, E., & Howard, T. C. (2016). Why race and culture matter in schools, and why we need to get this right: A conversation with Dr. Tyrone Howard. *The Teacher Educator, 51*(4), 268–276.

Coggin, S. K., Daley, S., Sydnor, J., & Davis, T. R. (2019). Imagining my ideal: A critical case study of digital storytelling as reflective practice. *Reflective Practice, 20*(2), 143–159.

De Leon, N. (2014). Developing intercultural competence by participating in intensive intercultural service-learning. *Michigan Journal of Community Service Learning, 21*(1), 17–30.

Flower, L. (2002). Intercultural inquiry and the transformation of service. *College English, 65*(2), 181–201.

Gay, G., & Howard, T. C. (2000). Multicultural teacher education for the 21st century. *The Teacher Educator, 36*(1), 1–16.

Gay, G. (2002). Preparing for culturally responsive teaching. *Journal of Teacher Education, 53*, 106–116.

Haddix, M. (2015). Preparing community-engaged teachers. *Theory into Practice, 54*(1), 63–70.

Hammond, Z. (2015). *Culturally responsive teaching and the brain: Promoting authentic engagement and rigor among culturally and linguistically diverse students.* Corwin.

Jenkins, H., Ito, M., & boyd, d. (2016). *Participatory culture in a networked era: A conversation on youth, learning, commerce and politics.* Polity Press.

Kinloch, V., & Dixon, K. (2018). Professional development as publicly engaged scholarship in urban schools: Implications for educational justice, equity, and humanization. *English Education, 50*(2), 147–171.

Kozma, C. (2015). Intercultural inquiry as a framework for service-learning course design. *Journal for Civic Commitment, 23*, 1–19.

Ladson-Billings, G. (1995). But that's just good teaching! The case for culturally relevant pedagogy. *Theory into Practice, 34*(3), 159–165.

Ladson-Billings, G. (2006). It's not the culture of poverty, it's the poverty of culture: The problem with teacher education. *Anthropology and Education Quarterly, 37*(2), 104–109.

Ladson-Billings, G. (2014). Culturally relevant pedagogy 2.0: a.k.a. the remix. *Harvard Educational Review, 84*(1), 74–135.

Lambert, J. (2009). *Digital storytelling: Capturing lives, creating community* (3rd ed.). Digital Diner Press.

Liu, K., & Ball, A. (2019). Critical reflection and generativity: Toward a framework of transformative teacher education for diverse learners. *Review of Research in Education 43*(1), 68–105.

McQuirter, K. (Director). (2016). *Milwaukee 53206* [Film]. Transform Films.

Milner, H. R. (2012). But what is urban? *Urban Education, 47*(3), 556–561.

Mitchell, T. (2008). Traditional vs. critical service learning: Engaging the literature to differentiate two different models. *Michigan Journal of Community Service Learning, 14,* 50–65.

Moll, L. C., Amanti, C., Neff, D., & González, N. (1992). Funds of knowledge for teaching: Using a qualitative approach to connect homes and classrooms. *Theory into Practice, 31*(2), 132–141.

MPS Office of Finance. (2019). *2019–2020 superintendent's proposed budget.* Milwaukee Public Schools. https://mps.milwaukee.k12.wi.us/MPS-English/CFO/Budget--Finance/Informational.pdf

Noddings, N. (2002). *Educating moral people: A caring alternative to character education.* Teachers College Press.

Paris, D., & Alim, H. S. (2014). What are we seeking to sustain through culturally sustaining pedagogy? A loving critique forward. *Harvard Educational Review 84*(1), 85–100.

Paris, D., & Alim, H. S. (2017). *Culturally sustaining pedagogies: Teaching and learning for justice in a changing world.* Teachers College Press.

Peck, R. (Director), & Baldwin, J. (Author). (2016). *I am not your Negro.* [Film]. Independent Lens.

Powell, T. (2018, September 24). Same race teachers: MPS students & teachers weigh in. *WUMW Lake Effect.* https://www.wuwm.com/post/same-race-teachers-mps-students-teachers-weigh#stream/0

Sleeter, C. E. (2016). Critical family history: Situating family within contexts of power relationships. *Journal of Multidisciplinary Research, 8*(1), 11–23.

Smolcic, E., & Katunich, J. (2017). Teachers crossing borders: A review of the research into cultural immersion field experiences for teachers. *Teaching and Teacher Education, 62,* 47–59.

Yosso, T. J. (2005). Whose culture has capital? A critical race theory discussion of community cultural wealth. *Race, Ethnicity, and Education, 8*(1), 69–91.

Zygmunt, E., & Cipollone, K. (2019). Community-engaged teacher education and the work of social justice. *Journal of Family and Consumer Sciences, 111*(1), 15–23.

Zygmunt, E., Cipollone, K., Tancock, S., & Clark, P. (2018a). Community-engaged teacher preparation. In J. Lampert (Ed.), *Oxford encyclopedia of global perspectives on teacher education.* Oxford University Press. https://doi.org/10.1093/acrefore/9780190264093.013.476

Zygmunt, E., Cipollone, K., Tancock, S., Clausen, J., Clark, P., & Mucherah, W. (2018b). Loving out loud: Community mentors, teacher candidates, and transformational learning through a pedagogy of care and connection. *Journal of Teacher Education*, 69(2), 127–139.

Zygmunt, E., & Clark, P. (2016). *Transforming teacher education for social justice*. Teachers College Press.

Zygmunt-Fillwalk, E., & Clark, P. (2007). Becoming multicultural: Raising awareness and supporting change in teacher education. *Childhood Education*, 83(5), 288–293.

CHAPTER 3

Whose Voices Matter?

Intentionality and Shared Vision

April L. Mustian, Jennifer O'Malley, Gynger Garcia,
Carlos Millan, and Maria Luisa Zamudio-Mainou

Today's PK–12 public school landscape is changing, yet many elements remain the same. Despite a growing racially, ethnically, and linguistically diverse student population, the teaching force remains statically White and female (U.S. Department of Education, Office of Planning, Evaluation and Policy Development, Policy and Program Studies Service, 2016). And, despite the growing grassroots efforts to challenge high-stakes testing (United Opt Out National, n.d.), there remains persistent pressure on educators to meet state-mandated initiatives that leaves them feeling as if little time remains for much else besides rigid curricular implementation.

These constraints (i.e., cultural mismatch and high-stakes mandates) limit teachers' willingness and abilities to venture "beyond the walls" of the classroom so as to recognize the value of learning *from* their students and the communities they serve (González et al., 2005). What often results is culturally oppressive curricular implementation in which teachers fail to be anything more than the gatekeepers of knowledge (Freire, 1970). This myopic approach to teaching and learning prevents students from utilizing their own knowledge funds to question and construct new and relevant meaning that can be applied to their daily lives, and diminishes students' beliefs that their education is valuable (Moll et al.,1992; Villegas & Lucas, 2002). There is no greater evidence of this than the growing education debt that continues to separate Black, Latinx, and Indigenous students from their White counterparts (Ladson-Billings, 2006), accompanied by the persistent call for educational equity by families, communities, and scholars alike.

THE CASE FOR CULTURALLY RESPONSIVE TEACHERS

On the other end of this very complex issue is a growing body of research that emphasizes the benefits of a *culturally responsive teacher* whose pedagogical identity is centered on (a) cultural reciprocity; (b) affirmation of student, family, and community identities; and (c) a deep understanding that teaching and learning are multidirectional (e.g., Au, 2009; Gay, 1995; Ladson-Billings, 1994). When teachers engage in culturally responsive practice (CRP), students benefit in a multitude of ways. For example, Aronson and Laughter (2016) conducted a research synthesis of 38 studies utilizing CRP in math, science, social studies, and literacy, and found that CRP not only improved students' academic success by standardized achievement standards but also increased students' motivation, interest in content, abilities to engage in content-area discourses, self-efficacy as learners, and confidence when taking standardized tests.

Knowing the positive impacts of CRP, much of the responsibility for the development of this kind of teacher has solely been assumed by the academic institutions preparing the next generation of K–12 educators, with little thought about the contributions communities also have in this development. Specifically, a complicated and marred history persists between institutions of higher education (IHEs) and the communities that have often been subject to cultural excavation in the name of educational advancement (Smagorinsky et al., 2003; Zeichner, 2010). In fact, IHEs have long been viewed as "ivory towers" by those outside their walls, often as a result of the perception by those on the inside that monopolies of knowledge reside *only* there (Buckley, 2012). Because knowledge creation is one of the core functions of IHEs, many academics have held tightly to the notion that "knowledge is power" rather than "knowledge *sharing* is power" (Skyrme, 2012). The difference between those two phrases is only one word, but it makes a significant difference in the ways in which IHEs have traditionally gained, or rather, forced, entrance into communities.

COMMUNITY-ENGAGED CULTURALLY RESPONSIVE TEACHERS

Traditional teacher preparation, specifically, has focused on school–university partnerships often largely absent of community voice and representation. Rather, the partnerships have been limited to field placements and the reliance on master teachers to serve as mentors for teacher candidates in need of clinical teaching experiences. Further, teacher preparation curriculum has often lacked the intentional interrogation of candidates' identities, implicit biases, and preconceived notions about urban communities. This is a significant disservice to all community types but is especially so for urban schools and classrooms, which are often much more racially diverse but still comprise primarily White, middle-class teachers who are not from those same communities.

Recent research, however, affirms the need for teacher education to embrace community-based practices as a significant component in the preparation of urban teachers (Waddell, 2013). Extending the work on CRP, scholars have begun to place greater emphasis on the critical need for *community-engaged* teachers (Haddix, 2015). Haddix states:

> The goals of teacher education must evolve beyond the teaching of strategies and methods for implementation in a school vacuum toward a process for beginning teachers' critical interrogation of their social locations and the ways in which they engage with and honor their students' lives and histories. (p. 64)

Thus, our urban teacher model has morphed over time as we have reenvisioned what it means to be a community-engaged teacher, recognizing how critical it is to include the voices of our community partners and equalizing their power across all of our programming supports for our urban teacher candidates. Because of this, we were intentional about whose voices should comprise the co-authorship of this chapter. As such, two community partners (Gynger and Carlos) and three faculty/staff (April, Jennifer, Maria) worked together to create a shared vision for and the resulting written contributions of the chapter that is now before you. This chapter serves as a bit of a roadmap from our own work in hopes that it might speak to any institutions or communities grappling with some of these same issues. To anchor the chapter, we believe it is important to provide a brief overview of our origins so as to contextualize lessons learned and recommendations to others.

OUR PROGRAM'S CONTEXT:
ORIGINS OF THE NATIONAL CENTER FOR URBAN EDUCATION

Our program, founded as the Chicago Teacher Education Pipeline (CTEP), began in 2004 as a collaboration between Illinois State University (ISU), the largest preparer of teachers in the state, and Chicago Public Schools (CPS), the largest school district in Illinois. The inaugural executive director, Dr. Robert Lee, set out to create a bi-directional partnership, supporting Chicago teacher candidates to pursue postsecondary education at ISU while improving the preparation of ISU preservice teachers for urban schools. In pursuit of these goals, a critical third stakeholder was brought into the partnership design: the community. In 2005, ISU, together with CPS and several local and national funding sources, identified Little Village (a predominantly Latinx community in Chicago) and its local schools as its lead community-based partner to work together under the New Communities Program (NCP) initiative to support comprehensive community development. As a participant in the NCP, the lead community-based organization had developed a comprehensive quality-of-life plan with education as a top priority, allowing ISU and CPS to begin the partnership with an asset-based framework and work alongside community members toward common goals of improving educational outcomes for its residents.

Understanding the human and capital costs of high teacher attrition rates as well as the necessity of preparing culturally informed and responsive teachers to authentically serve the changing demographics of K–12 students, CTEP recognized the value of community-engaged partnerships to anchor our shared educational goals. The mission has always been grounded in social justice and works to cultivate and sustain innovative, resilient, and effective educators for urban schools and their communities.

As the community–university–school partnership developed and strengthened over the past 15 years, CTEP secured three U.S. Department of Education Teacher Quality Partnership grants to further cultivate and expand this best practice model for urban teacher preparation, extending its model to five Chicago communities (i.e., Little Village, 2005; Auburn Gresham, 2010; Albany Park, 2012; East Garfield Park, 2014; and Pilsen, 2015; see Figure 3.1). As shown in Table 3.1, expansion to each subsequent Chicago community was guided by a desire to authentically reflect the student population in CPS, geographically, demographically, and linguistically.

In keeping with the original partnership model, each expansion included the identification of a lead community-engaged partner who prioritized education, could connect ISU CTEP to educational initiatives already in place, and employ the new partnership relationship to push improvements collectively. Obtaining final approval by the Illinois Board of Higher Education (IBHE), CTEP became the National Center for Urban Education (NCUE) in 2016, extending its partnership model to two other urban sites in Illinois: Decatur (2015) and Peoria (2016). See Figure 3.2 for a map of Illinois State University and all satellite teacher pipeline locations.

Figure 3.1. Partner Communities in Chicago

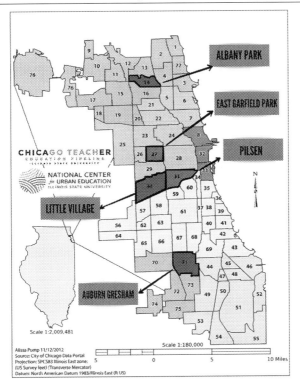

Figure 3.2. Illinois State University National Center for Urban Education Sites

Table 3.1. Partner Community Demographic & School Partnerships Information

NCUE Partner Community	Initial Year Partnership	Community Demographics	School Partnerships at a Glance
Little Village	2005	75,000 residents 84% Latinx 70% low-income*	22 schools (13 elementary, 1 middle school, 8 high school)
Auburn Gresham	2010	46,000 residents 96% Black 67% low-income*	8 schools (5 elementary, 3 high school)
Albany Park	2012	52,000 residents 40+ languages spoken 43% low-income*	14 schools (8 elementary, 1 middle school, 5 high school)
East Garfield Park	2014	20,000 residents 88% Black 73% low-income*	6 schools (2 elementary, 3 high school, 1 specialty K–12)
Pilsen	2015	33,000 residents 76% Latinx 57% low-income*	7 schools (4 elementary, 1 middle school, 2 high school)

*Low-income = the percentage of households reporting income below $50,000.
Sources: CMAP (n.d.); U.S. Census Bureau (n.d.).

NATIONAL CENTER FOR URBAN EDUCATION
CURRENT MISSION AND CHARGE

Throughout its development and growth, the National Center for Urban Education has striven to center its work within each particular community of practice. This means bringing together parents, teachers, principals, district personnel, community members, university teacher candidates, staff, and faculty to develop, guide, and execute work and programming in true collaboration. As a university community, and alongside our partners, we recognize that we can be agents and advocates of social justice only if we stand in solidarity with schools and communities to confront challenges encountered locally and to help leverage resources toward that end (Zeichner et al., 2016). Our collective work must not only benefit our teacher candidates as they study to become teachers in Chicago, Decatur, and Peoria, but must also contribute to the strengthening of communities, schools, teachers, children, and families. This requires having stakeholders from the community participate in the design and implementation of programs as well as structuring feedback loops that authentically honor their voices.

The NCUE programs reflect the mindset of intentional reciprocity and begin with supports to schools and communities. The Teacher Education and Access to College for Highschoolers (TEACH) program was established in neighborhood high schools in our partner communities to engage students as they pursue higher education with a focus on those interested in a teaching career. Once on campus, ISU students can select from over 100 redesigned courses that have been fundamentally revised to focus on urban education through immersive clinical experiences in urban partner schools and communities.

Our faculty themselves go through a professional learning program as part of their redesign requirements in order to fully engage with our partner schools and community organizations. This preparation occurs within a cohort professional learning community format, and faculty receive ongoing support throughout the year. Perhaps what makes this professional learning program stand apart from other professional learning opportunities for faculty are the required immersions within our communities. Faculty "live" in Chicago for 5 days and visit Peoria and Decatur for 1 day each, where they learn about each community *from* community members. They spend time in partner schools, visit various community assets, and engage in meaningful dialogue with various stakeholders (e.g., families, teachers, community leaders). Though many of our affiliated faculty who go through this professional learning process have been connected to urban communities in some way, we are intentional that each community is unique and must be known by faculty before they can even begin to prepare teacher candidates to understand the sociocultural contexts integrated into urban redeveloped courses. We believe that faculty members' intentionality behind and enthusiasm in developing authentic relationships with the community are what lay the initial groundwork in our teacher candidates' desires to pursue urban and community-engaged teaching.

After taking coursework specific to the urban education program, ISU teacher candidates can apply to participate in the unique and selective Summer Teacher Education Program for Urban Preparation (STEP-UP) program prior to student teaching. Born from a recognition by our community partners that there was a need for an additional immersive experience to bridge the gap between campus coursework and urban student teaching, STEP-UP provides preservice teachers with an intensive summer fellowship where they co-teach in district summer school, intern at community organizations, and receive targeted professional development and reflective seminars while living with host families in partner communities. Next, teacher candidates can choose a semester or year-long student teaching experience within schools in partner communities. Last, NCUE graduates receive support when they begin their careers in our partner districts, following the best practice highly structured in-building mentoring model (e.g., Carr et al., 2017; Hong & Matsko, 2019) with supplemental specialized professional development seminars to improve instruction and better meet the needs of their students.

At each program level, community, school, and university, stakeholders are at the table to ensure an authentic experience that pushes student growth while keeping the model accountable to each of its stakeholders. Throughout our urban teacher prep journey, we have hit snags, made missteps, learned hard lessons, and celebrated tremendous success. We feel it is important to sit in our vulnerability in order to more transparently share with anyone reading this that the achievement of a truly authentic shared vision with the communities we work alongside takes time, trust, intentionality, and accountability.

MISSTEPS AND RESULTING SHIFTS

As described earlier, a critical component to our model includes early community exposure and engagement in our urban partner neighborhoods. One primary way we do that is when a faculty member works with a NCUE liaison and a community-engaged partner to create at least one experiential opportunity in a given semester that is tied to the major outcomes of the courses, which were redesigned for the urban teacher education program. A second way we do this is through our STEP-UP summer fellowship for interested teacher candidates. Over time, what both of these kinds of experiences look and feel like have changed because 16 years of this work has allowed us tremendous opportunity to continue in our growth and commitment to urban school and community partners. We would be remiss, however, if we highlighted only the growth that has brought us to this point. Thus, we would like to share some of our missteps, several of which we believe might have been necessary learning points to evolve and deepen our collective work. Along with our missteps, we do want to provide you with the shifts we made as we learned what it means to truly center community knowledge, leverage collective power, and work toward an authentically shared vision for urban teacher preparation.

Who Holds the Power?

Early Missteps. We have had community partners at the table since the inception of our work in 2004, but for many years the decisionmaking power tilted in the direction of those of us at ISU who held administrative or faculty positions in this work. Though we have always funded our lead community partners, they often connect us to parents and community scholars to provide workshops or to share their rich knowledge as panelists during clinical visits. At first this work was done voluntarily by community members with an implied assumption that they would be happy to be invited to the table to share their stories and wisdom with our future teachers. We quickly recognized this horrific misstep for what it was: classist, elitist, and plagued with a lens of Whiteness in which we were further marginalizing communities of color (Leonardo, 2009) with whom we claimed to be in a relational partnership.

Resulting Shift—Compensating for and Honoring Community Knowledge. This significant misstep was a wake-up call for us around the notion that, just as we value faculty when they provide professional development and compensate them for their time and knowledge, we must value community scholars to equally honor their impact on our preservice teachers. To make this an intentional practice, we built our cultural and community funding line into our budgets for programming. We also created an equitable rate of compensation to be used for presenters from the academy or community. Far from being purely transactional, this intentional funding model ensured that value was placed on community knowledge by design.

Though community scholars have always been professional development providers during our STEP-UP summer fellowship, described earlier in the chapter, we realized we were still relying too heavily on ISU faculty members to provide professional development each weekend of the 4-week experience and were *underutilizing* the community funds of knowledge at our fingertips. Thus, the pendulum has shifted in the direction of community scholars and practicing urban teachers as the primary conduits of knowledge for our STEP-UP fellows about urban community engagement and what it truly means to be a *community teacher* in Chicago (Murrell, 2001).

Preparation for Entrance into the Community

Early Missteps. When teacher candidates and professors alike are visiting an urban community for the first time, their preparation, or lack thereof, for entrance into the community makes a significant impact on what the community will experience with their presence and what professors and teacher candidates will take away from the time they spend there. When a professor has done little to lay the groundwork for who makes up that community or what the expectations are for the experience, this establishes a particularly negative and disengaged energy before the experience even begins.

Further, when we fail to properly prepare our faculty in the interrogation of their own deficit-based ideologies, it has often tainted the lens with which our teacher candidates viewed our urban community partners. For instance, we had a faculty member make a statement about how pleasantly surprised they were at how well behaved students were in the classrooms they visited, and many teacher candidates echoed that same sentiment. The interrogation fell on the shoulders of our community liaison, who said, "Why were you so surprised? Why is it surprising to find great students and high-quality instruction in our community?" In another instance, a faculty member minimized the cultural importance of the term "soul food" by saying it was "just comfort food." This kind of statement contributes to the continued attempted erasure of a term symbolic of food traditions preserved by enslaved Africans in the Deep South.

Just these examples alone can cause great harm to the relationship between a university and urban partner communities because the burden to push back against these stereotypes and microaggressions often falls on the community instead of better preparation on our part to challenge our own and our colleagues' ideologies through intentional professional development and ongoing support. This also speaks to the misguided assumption that professors engaged in urban teacher preparation have already "arrived" at some final destination of sociocultural competence and do not have their own identity work to do. These examples indicate that such an assumption could not be further from the truth.

Resulting Shift—Intentional and Ongoing Preparation. We have several recommendations for better preparing teacher candidates and faculty for ethical immersion into partner communities. One of them is to have community input and voice in intentionally integrated ways. For instance, when NCUE's Director of Faculty Development (April Mustian) begins preparation for new professors to redesign their courses for urban integration each summer, community partners contribute to and approve the list of recommended readings; provide resources that give honorable and legitimized context to each of our partner communities; work collaboratively with all NCUE staff to plan the residency agenda when the new faculty cohort engages in 7 days of immersive experiences in Chicago, Decatur, and Peoria; and engage in critical discourse with faculty throughout the residency experience.

Another way we center community voice for a shared vision is when faculty begin to prepare the immersive experiences for their teacher candidates. Since each community has a primary educational liaison, they work with the faculty member and an NCUE program coordinator assigned to that community to collaboratively plan the experience. Online tools (e.g., Google Drive) are used for shared planning documents, multiple planning calls are held, checklists are created that delineate assigned tasks, and multiple accountability checks are made to ensure that everyone is following through with their assigned roles and responsibilities. This process often begins before the semester even starts so that quality time is given to the planning of each experience.

We also support faculty in how to better prepare their teacher candidates for the experiential part of the course. Faculty now embed preparation components into the content of their coursework. Our candidates begin researching the community ahead of time, immerse themselves in various experiences while in the community, meet residents to hear their stories, ask thoughtful and informed questions (often prepared in advance), and have purposeful discussions that help build their exposure and deepen the understanding of the sociocultural context of a particular community. What we have found is that this will either excite candidates about becoming invested in our communities in the future, or it will confirm that this type of work is not for them.

We believe that it is better and less harmful for our communities, and K–12 children especially, for a teacher candidate to realize earlier in their preparation than later that they do not see themselves as urban educators. We already know the impacts of ill-informed and naive newly licensed teachers taking jobs in communities for which they were not prepared to teach. Thus, this work is as important in supporting candidates who want to serve in and learn from urban communities as it is in supporting those candidates who realize this is not where they should be. Critical reflection is also a part of most teacher candidates' experiences. Faculty engage candidates in post-trip surveys, journals, and peace circle discussions to unpack and debrief on the experiences in which candidates engaged. Additionally, the faculty member, community liaison, and program coordinator hold a debrief call to discuss what went well and what might be considered differently for the next experience.

Finally, we see our STEP-UP fellowship as the pinnacle of our shared vision and the equalizing power dynamics we have worked incredibly hard to achieve. Each spring, we convene a review panel for STEP-UP candidate interviews, which last an entire weekend. The panel consists of a liaison from each of our partner communities, one faculty member, the STEP-UP director, and the NCUE director. We all share in the questions we ask each candidate; we discuss our thoughts on each candidate, and then we are intentional about the community liaisons providing their preferences on which candidates they believe would be good fits for their communities. One of the most intriguing features of STEP-UP is that our fellows live with host families in each of our partner communities. We have a systematic vetting process for who becomes a host family, but many of our host families have served in this capacity for years. We select one weekend for a "speed-meeting" session where host families get to meet the new fellows. Host families are able to pick their top three fellows, and the fellows pick their top three families. It always amazes us how much fellows' and host families' choices match! This is but another way we are intentional in carrying out shared vision and power in our work.

Authentic Community Engagement

Early Missteps. Early iterations of our community experiences for teacher candidates resulted in more of an "observation style" immersion where candidates just watched, took notes, and left. For instance, in the East Garfield Park (EGP) community, teacher candidates would visit schools, passively observe in classrooms, engage in a community walk and tour through the Breakthrough Urban Ministries (our primary community-engaged partner in EGP) FamilyPlex, visit the Garfield Park Conservatory, eat lunch and/or dinner, and possibly hear from parents or students in informal ways. In Pilsen, these visits often included classroom visits, after which the community liaison has been traditionally tasked with identifying several interactive ways to introduce the community and its members to our candidates. These have included visits to community museums like the National Museum of Mexican Art or interaction with community members during a community mural walk/tour through Pilsen.

What our teacher candidates took from these kinds of experiences was rich, but left much to be desired for the community. In fact, this "zoo tripping" impact is felt throughout the community because "outside guests" come into a space to learn information about an urban setting and take that information away with them for their personal agenda (e.g., to challenge candidates' preconceived notions of how urban communities function). This leaves community residents feeling used and unvalued and is exactly the "cultural excavation" for which IHEs have long been criticized.

Our First Shift—Reciprocity. Recognizing the shortcomings of those earlier surface-level experiences, we realized that a missing component was *reciprocity*. We knew that our faculty and teacher candidates benefited greatly from community immersions, but where was the benefit to the community? How could we work to foster a more authentic bi- or multidirectional partnership? We knew that many faculty and teacher candidates held a sincere desire to engage in service as part of their clinical experience. So we began working together more intentionally about the ways in which faculty and candidates engaged in this notion of reciprocity within our partner community spaces. Though this aspiration may be laudable, it was not long before we realized that the "service" projects were conceived primarily from the perspective of the university faculty and teacher candidates. One example was when a faculty member teaching a behavior supports course worked with our community partner in Auburn Gresham to survey the schools they would be visiting to determine what needs they may have around School-Wide Positive Behavior Support (SWPBS) incentives so that her class could work together to purchase some needed supplies. This was something the faculty member designed because it matched the outcomes of her course, but it wasn't something that organically emerged as an authentic need in the partner schools at the time. In other instances, during the planning process, the question would be posed to our community partners, "What project can we help with on a Tuesday from 1 o'clock to 2:30?"

As we analyzed our attempts at "reciprocity," we realized we were doing little more than "feel-good volunteer work" that actually perpetuated, rather than challenged, notions of White saviorism among our teacher candidates. We then began to shift our efforts to service-learning in the hopes that this would move us into a more deeply connected partnership with our faculty, teacher candidates, and community partners. What we learned is that, though well-intended and with positive short-term outcomes, we were creating more work for our community partners and our partner schools that was not sustainable. For example, in a literacy supports course, one faculty member worked with two community liaisons, one from our northwest community partner and another from one of our southwest community partners, to create a pen-pal project that would allow students from those two very different communities to get to know one another and learn about where each one lived. Our teacher candidates worked with the students in our northwest partner community to write the initial letters and supported them by teaching them to use graphic organizers to aid in the writing process (this was a connection to the outcomes of the literacy applications course). Students were excited to take part in this project, but it resulted in only one pen-pal exchange and could not be sustained.

Final Resulting Shift—Authentic Reciprocity Grounded in Grassroots Efforts. Over the last few years especially, our community partners have wielded critical voice and power to help nudge us to better center the community in the planning and shift the perspective to what is happening in the neighborhood or at a partner school that needs support from our teacher candidates, will give our candidates more authentic experiences, and can be sustained. The guiding question about service and reciprocity has now become, "*How can we plan our experience around a specific community need so that the service is authentic and not an artificial event created for the sole purpose of our teacher candidates' savioristic need to 'give back'?*"

And because our collaboration stems from relationships, community liaisons leverage their relationships with school leadership and other community businesses/organizations to learn at the outset which need/event teacher candidates can come alongside to support during a visit. Whether the need be investing in the community through donations of time, talent, or finances, we now base our efforts on what is already happening in the community and how candidates and schools can support and learn from one another for mutual growth. This has helped us shift the ways in which we engage our candidates in our communities so that reciprocity is more authentic and naturally integrated into existing grassroots efforts.

Further, by joining existing projects, we can help build capacity and speed up the goals for the community partner hosting the project. By building capacity within our community partner organizations, we can help sustain projects for a longer time and create a reciprocal and continual tradition of supporting them. Our teacher candidates, in turn, are able to interact more authentically with community members as opposed to the "zoo trip volunteering events" of the past where candidates were just scratching the surface of the community due to the proverbial glass window separating them from authentic relationship-building. Now these authentic connections are more easily made as part of the grassroots collective vision within community, which allows our candidates opportunities to break their own misconceptions of a neighborhood and its residents.

Actualized Examples

We would like to share just a few examples of the ways in which we now engage university–community partnerships more authentically and critically, as a testament to the way the previously described *shifts* have yielded more authentic interconnectedness and bidirectional learning.

East Garfield Park. Our primary community partner in East Garfield Park is Breakthrough Urban Ministries. After 20 years working together with the residents of East Garfield Park, Breakthrough's "people first" focus helps to unite the community. We have seen how the concept of community partnerships, relationships, and collaboration can produce lasting change. The Breakthrough FamilyPlex is a product of this concept.

Students from the community helped conceptualize the facility many years ago. Today, the FamilyPlex is a 42,000–square-foot complex in the heart of East Garfield Park on the West Side of Chicago. It holds classrooms, a fitness center, the Bridge Cafe, a gymnasium, and a medical clinic. It has quickly become a community hub filled with parents, students, elders, and many other stakeholders, all collaborating together with a shared vision for the community.

Another one of Breakthrough's key concepts is our Network Model. The concept of this model builds networks of support for individuals of all ages by providing mentorship, access, exposure, and accountability while helping them gain resources and opportunities. This happens through an array of people supporting a single individual. A perfect example of this was seen through the 2019 Chicago Public Schools teacher strike. This citywide dilemma required our East Garfield Park community to mobilize. As the strike continued for days, Breakthrough provided daylong programming for displaced children on the West Side of Chicago. Local students had access to hot meals, safe spaces to play, various opportunities to learn, and abundant adult support. We could not have hosted an all-day, everyday "strike school" for children without the aid of our ISU teacher candidates. They took initiative, asked questions, jumped in, taught lessons, played games, took kids roller skating, served food, and more. They knew the expectation in this situation was to be part of our children's Network Model and be that "network of support." One of Breakthrough's amazing and dedicated youth staff, Tqunish Hamilton, summed up this kind of effort and our overall mission quite well: "It's a beautiful thing for preservice teachers to work alongside of this community to help and learn for themselves. This will develop better teachers."

Our authentic community-engagement opportunities have also included setting up and helping with Breakthrough's Community Christmas Store and Community Trunk Party, aiding youth in our afterschool programs, sorting clothing at our shelters' women's boutiques, preparing meals at our shelter kitchens, stocking our Fresh Market food pantry shelves, and increasing our physical presence and support at our summer block parties, called HomeCourt. These are all needs/events already happening in our community that depend on the aid of community members and supporters for sustainability. Our teacher candidates come alongside to support these efforts as contributing future members of such a community.

One specific example of such support is the annual Family Math & Literacy Night held at one of our partner elementary schools. Our school partner wanted to invite families into the school space after school and create fun and engaging math and literacy activities for students. For 3 years now, a faculty member and their teacher candidates have partnered with this school. In the first year, candidates supported students and families with games and activities provided by the school. For the last 2 years, candidates have worked in small groups to create homemade, engaging, standards-based math and literacy games; worked with their professor to purchase prizes for students and their families for the event; and led the activities on Family Math & Literacy Night. All the materials created by the teacher candidates were donated to the school so that teachers could continue using the activities throughout the school year.

Pilsen. The Resurrection Project (TRP), our primary community partner in Pilsen, was founded as a grassroots community organization nonprofit in 1990 with $30,000 in seed capital. TRP's mission is to build relationships and challenge individuals to act on their faith and values by creating community ownership, building community wealth, and serving as stewards of community assets. TRP has engaged in issue-specific organizing, mobilization, and grassroots activism for 30 years. The systems change efforts of TRP that anchor its base-building work have local, citywide, statewide, and national impact. For example, TRP has a long history of base-building around immigration reform, which is a national effort, while also mobilizing around education issues impacting the State of Illinois and advocating around ordinances that impact Chicago (e.g., Sanctuary City ordinances, such as limits on sharing of information to federal immigration agents, and issuing driver's licenses for undocumented immigrants).

The central premise of TRP is that base-building strategies lead to community-level health, equity, and well-being through action at the individual and social network level. A unique asset and value of this organization is the leadership of Latinx individuals and other people of color, immigrants, women, and people whose characteristics reflect TRP's constituency. TRP has a history of developing leaders and, when opportunity arises, hiring leaders from its participants. TRP unequivocally builds power with and for Latinx individuals and other people of color, immigrants, women, and people from low-income backgrounds. The organization understands the need to center stories that too often are untold. TRP serves families and individuals across the Chicago metropolitan region with a focus on Chicago's Southwest Side in the mostly low-income, first- and second-generation Mexican communities of Pilsen, Little Village, Back of the Yards, and suburban Cicero and Melrose Park in Cook County, Illinois. These communities include an estimated 35,000 undocumented immigrants.

In the spring of 2019, one professor brought his teacher candidates to Pilsen, where they spent the first part of the morning in four partner elementary schools. Afterward, the teacher candidates assisted with ELLAS (*En La Lucha A Sobrevivir*, or *In the Fight to Survive*). ELLAS is a community-engaged, peer-to-peer approach that has proven effective in reducing barriers for under- and uninsured Latinx. The peer-to-peer approach in ELLAS is a critical component of its success, as it hinges on the notion that people are often more willing to accept or are more receptive to information given when it comes from someone they trust (Victor et al., 2018). To raise money to support their mission, ELLAS had begun a project to create a thrift store/pop-up shop and had been collecting donations from the community and the city. The teacher candidates on this particular trip came in and assisted with the sorting project and helped expedite the timeline of the opening of the store by several weeks.

In this community-engagement work, teacher candidates interacted with ELLAS members and took part in organic conversations with community members. During these conversations, candidates learned how these volunteers got involved with ELLAS, discovered more about the impact of their work, and learned about the medical studies and articles in which they had participated and helped write. Araceli Lucio, Health Organizer for The Resurrection Project and founder of ELLAS, said, "Our volunteers get excited when the students [fellows] come because they feel that they can share their values and their work with a new group of people." This disrupts the misconception that knowledge is cultivated only in institutions of higher learning and, instead, creates authentic counternarratives that community members have valuable knowledge that too often goes unnoticed or underappreciated. In fact, one of the fellows, who had learned a great deal from ELLAS members, actually called his mother one evening during the fellowship to ask if she'd had her mammogram completed within what he'd learned was an appropriate time frame.

The grand-opening date of the ELLAS pop-up store was in May 2019, and this grassroots effort resulted in extensive positive media coverage. Due to the news reports, ELLAS was flooded with donations from all over the city, which then opened up continued opportunity for our STEP-UP fellows to support the ELLAS store during the summer of 2019. Since the opening of the ELLAS pop-up shop, more teacher candidates and faculty members have continued to support the ongoing needs of this grassroots initiative. Araceli also added, "*Lo mejor es que ellos regresan cada año y vienen con mucha curiosidad de lo que estamos haciendo en la comunidad*" ("The best thing is that they return every year and they bring curiosity about our work in the community"). Araceli's words speak to the success that ensues when we engage our candidates in community work that is organic and mission oriented.

IMPACTS OF THIS WORK ON URBAN TEACHER RETENTION

Everything shared here is important and meaningful, but it means even more when we look at the impact of our collective work over time. To date, more than 200 of our teacher candidates have taken part in our one-of-a-kind STEP-UP fellowship. And the STEP-UP fellows who have gone on to teach in our partner schools have a three-year retention rate of 70%, which surpasses the 3-year retention rate in CPS by 15%. Moreover, in 2015, we created a full course sequence called INFUSE (Innovative Network of Future Urban Special Educators) within our special education program at ISU to better meet the continued need to fill hundreds of special education teaching positions that remain vacant in Chicago year after year. Since INFUSE's inception, 90% of our special education teacher candidates hired by CPS are still teaching there. This represents 20% of the 310 special education teacher vacancies in CPS in 2019, which is half of all teacher vacancies in the entire district.

FINAL THOUGHTS FOR OTHERS
WHO ARE INTENTIONAL ABOUT THIS WORK

Sustaining community–university partnerships is critical if we intend to prepare community-engaged, culturally responsive teachers. Because communities and higher education typically operate with very different structures and ways of being, creating a truly reciprocal relationship takes a commitment to honor each other's ways of knowing and a willingness to be open to interrogating those long-held beliefs and biases, especially on the university's side. One of the keys to our partnership has been the inclusion and integration of community voices in the design and delivery of *every* aspect of our urban teacher preparation work. Community experiences cannot be just "added on"; community knowledge must be honored and compensated. Our work has evolved over many years, yet there remains so much more that we should and must do to sustain our shared vision for urban teacher preparation. We thus recognize the need for intentional, ongoing, deep self-reflection, evaluation, and action-oriented shifts to remain rooted in our collective mission and encourage anyone doing similar work to engage in the same.

REFERENCES

Aronson, B., & Laughter, J. (2016). The theory and practice of culturally relevant education: A synthesis of research across content areas. *Review of Educational Research*, 86, 163–206. https://doi. org/10.3102/0034654315582066

Au, K. (2009). Isn't culturally responsive instruction just good teaching? *Social Education*, 73(4), 179–183.

Buckley, S. (2012). Higher education and knowledge sharing: From ivory tower to twenty-first century. *Innovations in Education and Teaching International*, 49, 333–344.

Carr, M., Holmes, W., & Flynn, K. (2017). Using mentoring, coaching, and self-mentoring to support public school educators. *The Clearing House*, 90(4), 116–124.

CMAP. (n.d.). *Community data snapshots, Chicago community areas, June 2019*. https://www.cmap.illinois.gov/data/community-snapshots

Freire, P. (1970). *Pedagogy of the oppressed*. Continuum.

Gay, G. (1995). *Culturally responsive teaching: Theory, research, and practice*. Teachers College Press.

González, N., Moll, L., & Amanti, C. (Eds.). (2005). *Funds of knowledge: Theorizing practices in households, communities, and classrooms*. Lawrence Erlbaum.

Haddix, M. (2015). Preparing community-engaged teachers. *Theory into Practice*, 54, 63–70.

Hong, Y., & Matsko, K. K. (2019). Looking inside and outside of mentoring: Effects on new teachers' organizational commitment. *American Educational Research Journal*, 56(6), 2368–2407.

Ladson-Billings, G. (1994). *The dreamkeepers: Successful teachers of African American children*. Jossey-Bass.

Ladson-Billings, G. (2006). From the achievement gap to the education debt: Understanding achievement in U.S. schools. *Educational Researcher*, 35(7), 3–12.

Leonardo, Z. (2009). *Race, whiteness, and education*. Routledge.

Moll, L. C., Amanti, C., Neff, D., & González, N. (1992). Funds of knowledge for teaching: Using a qualitative approach to connect homes and classrooms. *Theory into Practice*, 31(2), 132–141.

Murrell, P. C., Jr. (2001). *The community teacher: A new framework for effective urban teaching*. Teachers College Press.

Skyrme, D. (2012). *Knowledge management: Making sense of an oxymoron*. www.skyrme.com/insights/22km.htm

Smagorinsky, P., Cook, L.S., & Johnson, T.S. (2003). The twisting path of concept development in learning to teach. *Teachers College Record*, 105(8), 1399–1436.

United Opt Out National. (n.d.). Retrieved from http://unitedoptoutnational.org

U.S. Census Bureau. (n.d.). *2013–2017 American community survey (ACS) 5-year estimates*. https://www.census.gov/programs-surveys/acs

U.S. Department of Education, Office of Planning, Evaluation and Policy Development, Policy and Program Studies Service. (2016). *The state of racial diversity in the educator workforce*. https://www2.ed.gov/rschstat/eval/highered/racial-diversity/state-racial-diversity-workforce.pdf

Victor, R. G., Lynch, K., Li, N., Blyler, C., Muhammad, E., Handler, J., . . . Elashoff, R. M. (2018). A cluster-randomized trial of blood-pressure reduction in Black barbershops. *New England Journal of Medicine, 378*, 1291–1301.

Villegas, A. M., & Lucas, T. (2002). Preparing culturally responsive teachers: Reshaping the curriculum. *Journal of Teacher Education, 53*(1), 20–32.

Waddell, J. H. (2013). Communities as critical partners in teacher education: The impact of community immersion on teacher candidates' understanding of self and teaching in urban schools. *Current Issues in Education, 16*(2), 15. http://cie.asu.edu/ojs/index.php/cieatasu/article/view/1198/505

Zeichner, K. (2010). Rethinking the connections between campus courses and field experiences in college and university-based teacher education. *Educação, 35*(3), 479–501. https://www.redalyc.org/pdf/1171/117116968010.pdf

Zeichner, K., Bowman, M., Guillen, L., & Napolitan, K. (2016). Engaging and working in solidarity with local communities in preparing the teachers of their children. *Journal of Teacher Education, 67*(4), 277–290.

Part I Reflection

In *Letter from the Birmingham Jail* (1963), Martin Luther King Jr. wrote, "We know through painful experience that freedom is never voluntarily given by the oppressor; it must be demanded by the oppressed" (p. 5). In these first three chapters, we see this precept righteously roused by members of communities, who, emboldened with both voice and vision, exercise power in defining a future relationship with the academy: one in which listening instead of lecturing can guide teaching and learning, and in which honor of community cultural wealth can replace exploitation of social circumstance. In the same document, King says, "I am cognizant of the interrelatedness of all communities . . . whatever affects one directly, affects all indirectly. I can never be what I ought to be until you are what you ought to be, and you can never be what you ought to be until I am what I ought to be" (p. 2). King's words are animated by powerful passages in these first chapters, which provide evidence of members of communities rejecting an antiquated convention of expertise, and who, by doing so, unapologetically, "taught" the "ought" to those who so desperately needed to learn.

In *The Tempest*, William Shakespeare wrote, "What is past is prologue" (1958). Indeed, it would appear that everything that came before these new beginnings between the university and these communities—the longstanding self-interest of the university coupled with neighborhoods' offense at this unbalanced affiliation—sets the stage for the synergy that would unfold, and the mutuality of its evolution. Ironically, *The Tempest* is a story of betrayal, love, and forgiveness, and so, it appears, is the story told in these first chapters. Therein, authors reference the timing of their alliance and their mutual mentorship, which was ultimately reparative of past betrayal. In all three chapters, at great risk of the repetition of past rhythms, members of communities bestowed fervent grace upon the academy, embodying compassionate clemency and tentative trust for the sake of their children's future. This posture of fierce love in times of trial, as referenced in Nayyirah Waheed's poem presented in Chapter 1, is illustrative of marginalized communities' continued struggle to survive, and indeed thrive, despite systemic oppression that impedes this intention. Through such redemption, university–community reconciliation is being realized as a bridge to new futures forged.

The documented benevolence and tenacity of communities in these first chapters, while exerted with passion and purpose for community children, neither absolves the academy from accountability for past practice, nor excuses its members from engaging in reparative regenesis. How programs of educator preparation find their way to troubling the traditional model of teacher training and transcend borders into the spaces and places where candidates can authentically learn the richness of students' experience outside of schools is articulated uniquely in each of the three narratives. It also goes without saying that intention does not always equate with impact, and there are missteps from which to learn along even the most purposeful paths. In *The Courage to Teach: Exploring the Inner Landscape of a Teacher's Life*, Parker Palmer (2007) writes, "Humility is the only lens through which great things can be seen—and once we have seen them, humility is the only posture possible" (p. 108). Unfortunately, humility is not frequently found among the ranks of the professoriate—those whose directive to "create knowledge and generate truth" perceptibly distances them and their scholarly pursuits both socially and intellectually from those outside of the academy. James Comer (1995) suggests that "no significant learning happens outside of a significant relationship." From the stories in these first chapters, we divine that the success of community-engaged experiences are predicated on the longstanding and ever-emerging relationships that unfold when a common commitment is sanctioned and supported by members of the university and community: relationships that reposition members of the community as the experts from whom members of the academy are charged to learn. Should we endeavor to engender education as a socially just and equitable experience for all children, a stance of humility on the part of the academy is, thus, the only posture possible. It is imperative, as programs of community-engaged teacher preparation move forward, that they do so not from an "outside-in" perspective, but rather that they intentionally invest in the process of co-constructing experiences in solidarity and parity with members of traditionally marginalized communities. By ceding responsibility for doing so, teacher education risks reproducing both the omissions and commissions of the past whereby faculty and candidates hear, but don't *listen*, and view, but don't really *see*, retreating to campus with a sense of self-gratifying servitude, absent personal transformation. We could do nothing worse than reinforce this righteousness.

Authentic community engagement in the preparation of teachers speaks to the imperative of elevating and engaging voices too often silenced. In doing so, we argue that acute attention must be exercised in privileging these voices as they are, not as teacher educators would have them be, lest we reify a traditional narrative of colonizing community concern for candidate consumption—an act antithetical to the true nature of the alliances we aim to nourish. We assert the imperative of teacher educators' presence in the community spaces in which candidates' learning is newly situated, so that teacher candidates can effectively negotiate the social, emotional, cognitive, and sometimes spiritual disequilibrium such learning instigates. Our presence can further contextualize these experiences within broader constructs of equity and social justice. This is the work of teacher education in these spaces, and a responsibility we must enthusiastically embrace.

These chapters also underscore a collective obligation to honor those who have bestowed upon "outsiders" the gift of a new orientation toward teaching and learning, as well as a mandate to institute practices that equalize power. Furthermore, a fervent focus on the language we use to articulate university–community partnership in a fashion that privileges cultural wealth and steers clear of suggestions of saviorism requires vigilance to avoid reinforcing a traditional narrative of the academy's benevolence upon the "disadvantaged." Alternatively, the articulation of a collaborative and mutually agreed-on vision can translate to an equitable endeavor through which responsibilities can be negotiated and miscalculations mediated. As these first chapters equally celebrate success and concede culpability in unique journeys in community-engaged teacher preparation, the authors recommit to a concurrent charge to continue the work and to evolve in concert to transcend tradition and repave a path of purpose. Only in doing so will the ultimate goal of the development of "community teachers" (Murrell, 2001) who engender an equitable and socially just education for *all* children be realized.

REFERENCES

Comer, J. (1995). Lecture given at Education Service Center, Region IV, Houston, Texas.

King, M. (1963). *Letter from the Birmingham jail*. http://okra.stanford.edu/transcription/document_images/undecided/630416-019.pdf

Murrell, P. C., Jr. (2001). *The community teacher: A new framework for effective urban teaching*. Teachers College Press.

Palmer, P. (2007). *The courage to teach: Exploring the inner landscape of a teacher's life*. Jossey-Bass.

Shakespeare, W. (1958). *The tempest*. Harvard University Press.

COLLABORATIVE RELATIONSHIPS AND EQUALIZING POWER

A community-engaged approach to educator preparation is predicated on university, school, and community constituencies developing ongoing relationships through which partnership goals inform a collective agenda and a framework of supportive and sustaining structures for children. It should be understood that this takes time, patience, and consistent representation of individuals from all parties so that strengths are identified, trust established, and accountability measures articulated and monitored. Moreover, it is through these conversations that a commitment to educational success for all children can be decreed and an allegiance to a united vision sustained.

Traditional teacher preparation programs typically arrange for the mechanics of their participation in schools and communities with little input from teachers in the schools and rarely with any attention to community concerns. A model of authentic community-engaged teacher preparation removes silos, instead weaving a fabric of connection among the universities that prepare teachers, the schools that teach children, and the communities that inform how children make meaning of the world. This connection, surrounding a united vision for children's success, redefines educator preparation as a more purposeful and powerful force in the development of community teachers equipped to make teaching and learning more socially just and equitable for all teachers and children.

As authentic and reciprocal relationships are forged, a true community of practice emerges, wherein mutually agreed-on strategies are developed to achieve a united vision. The specific strengths possessed by members of the community, exercised through principles of mutuality, reciprocity, and genuine regard for authentic collaboration, are the tools through which the vision can be realized.

Universities, schools, and communities possess independent and unique cultures, systems of organization, and structures of power, and, traditionally, these are not held in equal regard. Schools typically enjoy power over children and families in both the content delivered and the pedagogy through which the content is communicated. Similarly, the academy, as a community of scholars, traditionally postures itself as the keeper of knowledge and generator of new truths. The knowledge of the community, incongruously, is frequently left out—commonly dismissed as irrelevant in the equation of educational success for children.

Authentic community-engaged teacher preparation embraces as a principle precept the strengths inherent in each of the three contexts. It acknowledges the unique contribution to children's success that can be realized when the rich cultural capital of communities is privileged, alongside the knowledge base of schools and the expertise and resources available from the university. When all three strands are equally elevated, outcomes can be exponentially achieved. The equalization of power in community-engaged teacher preparation requires resolute humility on the part of both schools and the university. Community-engaged teacher preparation refutes the self-importance of traditionally recognized sources of wisdom, dismantling institutional barriers and personal pieties, and forging a new structure through which previously un- or underrecognized sources of expertise can be heard, recognized, and valued in the preparation of teachers.*

The chapters in this second section represent diverse examples of how communities, schools, and universities have united around a common vision to prepare future teachers and to ensure that those teachers have the understanding and ability to provide students with an education that is relevant and meaningful, and that builds on the cultural wealth of the community. In all cases, the collaborative

---

*This material is excerpted from "Community-Engaged Teacher Preparation," by E. Zygmunt, K. Cipollone, S. Tancock, and P. Clark, 2018, in *The Oxford Encyclopedia of Global Perspectives on Teacher Education*, edited by Jo Lampert. Reproduced by permission of Oxford University Press. http://global.oup.com/academic. For permission to reuse this material, please visit http://global.oup.com/academic/rights.

relationship among the university, school, and community evolved over time and continues to change as those involved confront new challenges and opportunities. The one factor that remains steady throughout all of these programs is an ongoing commitment to valuing each other's knowledge and expertise in pursuit of a common goal.

REFERENCES

Zygmunt, E., Cipollone, K., Tancock, S., & Clark, P. (2018). Community-engaged teacher preparation. In J. Lampert (Ed.), *Oxford encyclopedia of global perspectives on teacher education.* Oxford University Press. https://doi.org/10.1093/acrefore/9780190264093.013.476

Shared Power in Teacher Preparation

University, School, and Community

Nadine McHenry, Janet Baldwin, Hilda Campbell,
Anonymous Contributor, Essence Allen-Presley,
Bretton Alvaré, and Taylor Borgstrom

THE TRUE MEANING OF PARTNERSHIP

As teacher educators, community members, and school staff who have taken this journey toward full immersion into community-engaged teacher preparation, we are often asked what key elements are necessary for implementation. This is a critical question that demands careful examination in order to identify what is necessary for success. Outcomes are important measures, but we should not lose sight of what conditions must be in place to establish and sustain a viable partnership among local schools, universities, and communities.

In education, we are driven to look at replicating success and reassure ourselves when we finally find a practice that can both be duplicated and make a difference. While we have been asked repeatedly to come up with a "formula for success," it wasn't until we were tasked with putting our thoughts in writing that we began to see what was at the core of our being: shared power.

Bringing two educational institutions together to share power is no easy task. The university rests on academic autonomy and documents the results of its own programs through careful research. The school district seeks increases in achievement, but public schools must follow a carefully prescribed path that allows little autonomy. Considering that educational organizations are susceptible to shifting priorities, leadership changes, outside influences and mandates, the political climate, and market forces, it is challenging to identify a common course that will lead to sustainable structural change. Sharing power necessitates a shift to a common focus:

meeting the needs of the children who are meant to benefit from our efforts. Integral to this mandate is that all partners align themselves with this focus and share power in a way that is authentic. When all stakeholders share this singular purpose, it is not a matter of dividing up power but rather of aligning and harnessing our efforts to improve our craft and learn from one another. All stakeholders must have a seat at the table.

In the evolution of our collaborative process, it was critical that we identify the "why" of our partnership. What are the drivers that influence our organizations? Are we likeminded? What is our ultimate goal? Can we stay on course in spite of resistance from our larger organizations? Can we stay true to our philosophy while meeting the needs of our organizational stakeholders? We were guided by the firm belief that if we continue to focus on what is good and right for children, results would come, but we were also aware that those results need to be expressed in terms that meet the diverse priorities set by our university and our school district.

The bedrock of this partnership is equalizing power among stakeholders: the university, the community, and the school. People often do not recognize the importance of power-sharing, and, frankly, we were guilty of this ourselves. It wasn't until we were asked to select a topic that would speak to our partnership that we began to recognize its importance. Daily conversations were critical to the initiation, formation, operation, retooling, evaluation, and sustainability of our partnership. This partnership seeks to transform the way we educate children and aspiring teachers, promote cultural proficiency for all partners, enhance community connections through sharing and honoring its wealth of knowledge, and develop a partnership in which all members have a voice that is elevated and heard.

DYSFUNCTION

As we examined the coming-together of our two institutions, the university and the school district, we had to contend with a history marked by negative interactions, misconceptions, misinterpretations, and dysfunction. Who would select an elementary school in a district that had been under receivership for substandard academic performance and financial difficulties for over 26 years? And who could trust a university that designed its own charter school that had very little relationship with the education division at the university? Compounding this potential conflict was the school district's and university's frequent changes in administration, the latest of which had recently brought in a new university administration with a different perspective on community engagement than that held by the preceding administration.

Historically, a great deal of tension has persisted between the university and school district. Little interaction occurred between the two organizations, and when it did occur, it was often contentious, laced with distrust and disrespect. The school district was failing, but any overtures from the university were interpreted as condescending and further reinforced the images and stereotypes held by both organizations. When the university reached out for field placements, it was solely for the purpose of meeting course requirements, with little thought about continuity, disruption, or tangible benefits for students. When given a choice, teachers routinely declined accepting university students because they were serving no useful purpose for their children and most often sat and "observed" while teachers worked hard to meet the needs of children with no assistance. When more formal approaches were made at the district level for potential collaboration, requests were dismissed, rebuffed, or most often ignored. As a result, the university established its own charter school, and the relationship with the school district continued to languish. A university liaison was finally able to gain access to both the university and the school district and persuaded/suggested that they consider a partnership that would be mutually beneficial. Conversations were arranged, and slowly a nucleus of likeminded people emerged who were willing to investigate a way to develop a meaningful partnership.

PROGRAM DESCRIPTION

The community-engaged teacher preparation program presented in this chapter is made up of components that include daily immersion in a local elementary school, supported by a block of university courses and a selection of community events. This combination of experiences helps teacher candidates develop a mindset based in culturally responsive pedagogy viewed through lenses of empathy and perspective-taking. The fieldwork, course content, and community engagement represent an equal partnership among school, community, and university representatives, utilizing their varied assets and expertise.

Fieldwork occurs every morning, and classroom teachers provide modeling and supervision as teacher candidates interact with elementary-aged students. University faculty are on hand each morning as well; they observe and provide timely feedback to teacher candidates using the Charlotte Danielson teaching evaluation model (Danielson, 2014), which is embedded with criteria for cultural proficiency and culturally responsive practice. Teacher candidates and their assigned community mentors are expected to attend regularly scheduled community events and have ongoing conversations to learn about the community.

Coursework includes literacy education, special education, science methods, urban anthropology, and a course entitled "The Community Teacher." All class meetings are held at a local church to keep teacher candidates immersed in the community. Their coursework and relationships with community mentors help teacher candidates realize the importance of building/establishing authentic connections with their students, families, and the community. Teacher candidates learn the history of their city while recognizing the roles that race, class, and culture play in its evolution through urban anthropology. Teacher candidates design intervention strategies for the development of strong reading skills within the context of culturally responsive practice in their special education and literacy courses. They develop and teach a robust science unit using inquiry-based teaching methods and hold a science fair for the elementary school and the community, with many university partners in attendance. In the Community Teacher course, they dig deeper into the importance of relationship-building as they examine their own mindsets and the effects of their own perspectives on their teaching through reflective conversations.

The most distinctive feature in our community is race. We explore the unshared history of race and racism in the city, identify ongoing discriminatory practices and policies, and consider ways to apply this knowledge to how we teach children in our school. The director of the program attends all classes to help teacher candidates make connections among the program components. The university recognizes the time and effort required and generously allows for one course release for the director, with the remainder of her course load dedicated to the program, school, and community.

In order to build a program based in participatory leadership, members of our learning community took part in regularly scheduled reflection meetings that allowed all members to provide support for those program features that worked, offer suggestions to strengthen the features that did not work so well, and identify goals for the following year. The purpose of this learning community is to "create, expand, and exchange knowledge and to develop individual capabilities" (Wenger et al., 2002, p. 42), bringing together new voices and experienced voices so that, as time progresses, the novice becomes the expert and ushers in the next class of new voices. This learning community, consisting of university faculty and teaching candidates, school administrators and teachers, and community representatives acting as mentors, collaborates on research to discover the impact of this program on different members of the learning community. Members representing each of the stakeholder groups annually attend the Ball State University Summer Institute on Community-Engaged Teacher

Table 4.1. Members of the Partnership

Role	Affiliation	Years With Program
Program Coordinator/Professor (Science Methods)	University	5
School Principal/Adjunct Professor (The Community Teacher)	Elementary School and University	5
Community Mentor/Adjunct Professor (The Community Teacher)	City and University	4
Classroom Teacher/Adjunct Professor (Literacy Education)	Elementary School and University	5
Professor (Special Education)	University	2
Professor (Urban Anthropology)	University	5
Classroom Teacher	Elementary School (former University Teacher Candidate)	2

Preparation as presenters. The professional development provided for all members of our learning community is co-constructed and focuses on everyone learning about the community and school.

In the pages that follow, we will share our stories. We will discuss our Courageous Conversations (Singleton, 2015), shared power, and each person's role within our partnership. Each story will show how the emphasis on "we all must have a seat at the table" evolved over time. Our team members and their affiliations are listed in Table 4.1.

BECOMING AN INSIDER (PROGRAM COORDINATOR/PROFESSOR)

The university program coordinator has been connected with our partnership from its inception. She is a university faculty member teaching one of the five required courses and oversees all aspects of this unique approach to teacher education. This involves interfacing with the school district; acting as a liaison between the university, school, school district, and the city; coordinating community mentors; communicating with all stakeholders; and facilitating all events. These events include community activities, professional development, relationship-building, program development, sharing results, encouraging partners, funding, and growth. All of this is in the interest of encouraging everyone's voice and ensuring that all collaborators are fully engaged with our partnership.

I came to this partnership as a professor with a background in both K–12 schooling and higher education who valued community engagement. My mindset was grounded in a K–12 / higher education distinction, in which my advanced degrees could provide the much-needed knowledge base to "fix" the myriad of problems that I perceived to be perplexing those in the K–12 arena. As I tried to implement programs in schools around the city, I began to realize that my job was not to "save" children of color and their teachers. Rather, I should share my background and partner with educators to discover answers together and develop programs to meet their needs. I evolved from a mindset of "White hope" to one of "participatory leadership," one where all members of our alliance have equal voice in decisionmaking and problem solving.

When I began teaching in 1977, the ideas in vogue at the time included multicultural education, environmental education, drug education, and other programs designed to redress social ills through public schooling. Multicultural education, in its infancy, was a call from the Civil Rights Movement to address inequity in schools. From my vantage point as an environmental educator, I viewed this new movement as excess baggage for an already overcrowded curriculum. I saw multicultural education as a curricular contestant vying for the same time slots and curriculum spaces that we, who were saving the planet, were competing for in schools. I navigated the linkages between universities and school districts by bringing forward *my* research/experience and building programs based on that background for all of the teachers to accept and adopt, without critical inquiry into why they should do this or how it suited the needs of the community. I worked so hard to make *my* programs fit into schools. When teachers and administrators would or could not meet my expectations for implementing these research-based programs, I left and looked for another, more fertile context for program and professional development. Over time, I began to understand that civic engagement grounded in service-learning had to start with the community. This new way of doing things shifted the power dynamic—rather than the university leading the way with no real buy-in from affiliated institutions, all members of the partnership entered the relationship with their respective areas of expertise valued and honored with equal import.

As our learning community crystalized and people began to accept and support the concept of participatory leadership, in that all ideas were considered and vetted by everyone, the dynamic changed toward one of equalization of power. When we first started this program, I understood the idea from a theoretical perspective, but now I can see the idea in praxis. We are a community of practice in which learning is situated within relationships between and among people. We are a community of people who care about a common set of issues, and we share practices that are developing in response to the needs of the community. Members of our community of practice believe in participatory leadership and orient individuals to the center, working toward a shared goal.

As I reflect back on our journey over the past 5 years, I can see that the structure of our community of practice based in participatory leadership is a good fit for 21st-century teacher preparation programs and also an exemplar of equalized power. Placing new teachers alongside practicing teachers, university faculty, and community members solidifies the strength of each and every member of this team. We worked together to develop our program, from its philosophy to its structure (schedule, logistics, etc.). We held courageous conversations between administrators and teachers on the university, school district, and community level, allowing everyone's voice to be heard. This is where the rubber hit the road, and the theory became a living and breathing practice. There were planning teams that brought together ideas from representative teachers, administrators, university faculty, community members, and teacher candidates. This co-design process has continued as we have evolved into our 5th year together.

I had to *un*learn in order to relearn my notions of the relationship between the university and K–12 education. Should higher education professionals dictate change based on their research? Or should there be a synergistic system of sharing? I had to relearn my positionality in the partnership and place equity of voice at the forefront of our thinking toward participatory leadership.

KINDRED SPIRITS (SCHOOL PRINCIPAL/ADJUNCT PROFESSOR)

The school principal has been involved with the partnership since its initiation and shares responsibility with the university program coordinator for planning and implementing all activities. There is significant overlap with the university coordinator's responsibilities, ensuring that they are synchronized and staying true to their mission and purpose. Responsibilities also include the design of school and community activities that bring all stakeholders together, as well as exposing teacher candidates to and engaging them with families and school-based personnel. Carving out time and getting approval for appropriate professional development for all partners within district constraints is critical. All of this occurs within a context of being accountable for all school district expectations, which often translates into partnership tasks becoming additional to normal job responsibilities.

As a principal in an urban school that was a part of a district under receivership by the state, there were always competing pressures to implement new directives and adopt new partners to address the academic needs of our students. Severe financial distress had reduced our staff by almost 60%, and our lack of resources made us dependent on support from outside our school district. Our school is located directly across the street from the university, and thanks to the vision of the university administration, a number of positive partnerships developed. The continuing financial turmoil of the school district brought us to the point at which the elementary school was going to be closed. The university offered to purchase our building and lease it back to the school district for $1 per year for a 5-year term. This brought some temporary relief; however, the constant changes in school district administration led to repeated bouts of uncertainty and mistrust.

Against this backdrop, a community/district liaison from the university suggested a new partnership with our school that was focused on a university–school collaboration. My role as principal has always been the gatekeeper for our school, making sure that there was value for our children when anyone proposed to come through our doors. The dean from the university's School of Education suggested I attend the first annual Summer Institute on Community-Engaged Teacher Preparation at Ball State University. Our team, which also initially included the dean of the School of Education, the university program coordinator, two university faculty members, and the school principal, took the plunge.

Exposure to the model at Ball State, extensive conversations, and planning during our trip led to the emergence of a likeminded philosophy and a strong commitment to a partnership. I was seen as a full partner, which laid the foundation for equalization of power. Strong rapport existed between the coordinator of our emerging program and myself in my role as principal of the school; this was essential to our work and our success. We recognized the need to pull in community mentors from the city and elementary school faculty as quickly as possible.

Our steering committee had representatives of all stakeholders, including community mentors, university faculty, elementary school faculty, the dean and assistant dean of the College of Education, the university's community liaison, the program coordinator, and myself. Frank conversation became the norm, and we all committed to a year of planning to address misconceptions and offer an opportunity to build trust. I felt the freedom to challenge the lack of diversity within the university's faculty and student body, request access to university facilities, and emphasize the primacy of creating an authentic experience that would benefit the elementary school students. Facilitated "Courageous Conversations" enabled us to learn how to listen and established the groundwork for sharing power as we eventually moved into the planning phase—developing syllabi, assigning responsibility for supervision, acquiring funding, building community support, and ironing out the specifics of our memorandum of understanding (MOU) between the university and the school district. Strong working relationships developed among the university faculty, school faculty, and community mentors. As our team coalesced, we sought to address the needs of the university and school district administrations, which had to be met in order to reach a formalized agreement that recognized our partnership.

The hallmark of our partnership is ongoing, frequent communication. School and university representatives prepared and interviewed the teacher candidates to make a match for placements in classrooms. We were certain of their need for cultural proficiency, and as we made those plans, we quickly realized that our professional development had to be jointly constructed, with all parties in attendance. Ongoing work on cultural proficiency was a must for all participants. In order to share equal power, we had to be "all in" both in planning, development, training, and execution.

One of the biggest triumphs for our partnership is having one of our elementary school faculty members appointed adjunct professor for the university literacy course. As a building principal, I was aware of the talent that existed within our staff and, in particular, that there was a master teacher who could easily fill this role and provide a strong link between the course-level content and expectations along with the pedagogy that drove the implementation of ideas developed in class. This master teacher is extremely successful in demonstrating best practices within her own classroom and incredibly skillful in relating to the needs of our teacher candidates who would launch into student teaching after their semester with us. She clearly communicates the "how" and the "why" of her pedagogy and took on the role of an expert liaison between university faculty, school faculty, and myself. It was clear to me that while we were building the university's brand in order to potentially increase their market share of education majors in a very competitive environment, we were also offering an opportunity to develop well-prepared teacher candidates within a successful school environment. In exchange, the elementary school was getting a boost in our student–teacher ratio, more opportunities for small-group and individual interventions, a "free look" at potential student teachers, and ultimately the possibility of hiring the best of them should an opening arise. Ultimately, we were able to offer a position to one of our best teacher candidates, which was again a great accomplishment, fulfilling one of our most important goals.

In the end, I would be remiss if I did not identify the impact this experience has had on my personal and professional development, and the encouragement it has provided me as an educator. I entered education as a profession to make a difference in the lives of children. This was easy to see in the classroom, but as I moved into administration, the competing forces and expectations made this goal much harder to achieve in tangible ways. I came into a school that had a very hard-working, dedicated staff that constantly faced difficult circumstances of being woefully underresourced, including continuous instability, lack of job security, and ceaseless financial crises and changes in district administration. Despite all of the obstacles, staff members remained unflappable in providing the very best for the children they serve. They have helped children to achieve remarkable gains on state assessments and have garnered recognition for establishing an extremely successful positive behavior support program. Throughout my tenure, the school district has been under receivership by the state, and there has been little recognition of the accomplishments of this remarkable group of educators. This remains a symptom of organizational dysfunction. The encouragement that has come from being a part of a culture that brings the university, the school, and the wider community together is uplifting beyond words. It is an opportunity to do work that focuses on what is good and right for our children and to carry it out with likeminded kindred spirits who share the same hopes and dreams and provide an oasis from the chaos that often surrounds us. For this I will be forever grateful.

BEING FIRST AIN'T EASY, BUT . . .
(COMMUNITY MENTOR/ADJUNCT PROFESSOR)

The community mentor's role is essential to the success of a community-engaged teacher preparation program. Mentors act as navigators for the teacher candidates as they explore the community and school, nurturing the candidates and providing access to open communication and sharing challenging issues. They build teacher candidates' comfort in asking difficult questions and establishing an intergenerational/interracial relationship with respected, long-term members of the community. Mentors act as advocates who speak on behalf of the community. Life experiences and cultural backgrounds are shared in an open, honest forum. Community mentors participate in all professional development, school programs, and activities with teacher candidates designed to be relationship-building. As an adjunct professor for the Community Teacher course, this mentor provides authentic experiences and her own life story to help teacher candidates see things from a real-life perspective. Her experiences and willingness to share are an asset to the program as she relates her life story as a Black female in a White, male-dominated career and as a pastor/police chaplain.

Many of my experiences have been life-altering since entering 1st grade at the elementary school in my hometown. I remember, in 1953, walking to school, big bow in my hair, crisply ironed dress, and a joy-filled heart about this new, exciting opportunity, having no idea how quickly my joy would be altered by a young child unknown to me. I was shocked when he spit on me.

Stopping immediately, looking up at who I believed to be his mother, I waited for some action, some form of discipline. *Nothing.* No "Why?" No "Stop, that's not right, you shouldn't do that!" Absolutely nothing. I thus felt compelled to stand up and respond on my own behalf. My ability to speak out has always been a part of who I am. Witnessing the child not getting what he deserved, after receiving what I didn't deserve, I quickly punched him. The adult then asked, "Why did you do that?"

I answered, "I waited for you to do something, you didn't, so I did"—and off to school I went.

My teachers were committed to educate their students. "Do your best, complete your work, and be respectful." Those commands were always the norm. I learned so much more than basic reading, writing, and arithmetic. Being selected to participate in plays and programs instilled pride; but giving me permission to do more talking was not needed. I went home year after year with report cards that stated, "Hilda is an excellent student, but she talks too much."

Remaining in this city was my conscious decision, driven by hope to make a difference. I grew up in the projects and lived in the same project again after being married. Within 2 years, good jobs, good goals, and saving produced a cash down-payment to purchase a home. My success has been possible due to parents, family, church, community members, and teachers, many of whom I still remember today.

I became a mentor to teacher candidates completing their field study at the school while obtaining my bachelor's degree through the university. Learning of this opportunity in teacher education, I felt compelled to inform mentees just how important it is for them to view their students as whole, valuable children, quite capable of being good students, even if many come from one-parent family homes. Some may live in neighborhoods impacted by violence and limited resources, but that is not their total being.

Equalizing power means not just being told what is needed but allowing input from parents regarding what would be beneficial. As educators, we must delve into what is good and best for each individual child we encounter. Like sponges, these young vessels absorb everything placed upon them, and they are affected by every adult decision made.

What drives me to be redirected instead of retired is the necessity to reveal to the self-appointed expert important facts often overlooked. Information, degrees, and positions alone are not competent gauges for students who require individual support. Educators must also be aware of issues and trauma caused by oppression in order to operate with genuine concern that empowers versus an approach of assumptions or pity.

Many children could enlighten their educators if they were recognized as important to the learning process. Considering the life experiences of children living and learning under the constraints of marginalization and oppression, a power shift is needed. In my own experience, equalizing power within the team permits those with lived experience to express the reality of daily challenges and issues that affect parenting and learning. Educators must be required to explore cultural differences outside of their own.

One of the guest speakers we invited to our Community Teacher class shared his story and described the determination that caused him to survive the unbelievable hardship he endured during his early life. According to him, support and motivation from educators and family sustained him during times of struggle and doubt. He decided that his doctoral degree was not optional. It was necessary to gain access to higher education instead of just K–12.

The entire community is empowered when they witness lives changed through intentional commitment and interaction. Training, role-modeling, and personal motivation impacts students and parents. Educators must realize they can't always recognize from the outside the diamond hidden inside every child. Therefore, teacher education yielding highly qualified teachers does not translate into a rubber stamp for every child's learning. True *equalizing* power will be experienced in marginalized communities only when we, as community members, have a recognized seat at the table with both teacher educators and school personnel.

MODELING EXCELLENCE IN TEACHING AND RELATIONSHIPS (CLASSROOM TEACHER/ADJUNCT PROFESSOR)

This pivotal member of our team is a full-time model teacher at the school for a class of low-incidence special needs children and the instructor of the anchor course in literacy for our program. She relates her experience in the classroom directly back to her literacy course. She was a member of our steering committee, a building representative for the teachers' union, a Student Support Teacher Leader overseeing all special education functions and leading the development and implementation of interventions for all students, and a new teacher mentor. She functions as the teacher representative for the program, sharing teachers' insights and concerns with others. Her role is in both worlds: She is able to walk beside her students (young and university age) and the faculty, and can pull herself out of her own perspective to see the views of others. She is willing to listen and offer alternative perspectives in a way that students can hear and understand; she is an excellent bridge between the practical level of the school and capturing the heart of teacher candidates and university personnel. She offers total credibility of a trusted voice for both the university and school faculty.

For as far back as I can remember, I had a strong desire to become a teacher. I can remember playing school in the summertime with the materials my teacher would give away at the end of the school year. I would teach the younger kids in the neighborhood. I wanted to make a difference.

Fast-forward 15 years. I am a special education teacher in the school district from which I graduated. I started my teaching career in the elementary school I attended. I was afforded the opportunity to work alongside teachers who taught me. Teaching in this district has not been easy. I have had multiple administrators (principals, superintendents, special education supervisors) along the way. With each new principal comes a new vision, a new preference, and new ability or inability to deal with parents, students, and teachers. With each new superintendent comes a new agenda, new curriculum, and new focus. With each new special education supervisor comes new special education policies and procedures.

I am a teacher, a community member, a teacher mentor, a parent, and now an adjunct professor. When I was invited to become part of a steering committee for yet another "experiment" in our school district, I have to admit, I was not thrilled. I felt it would be yet another responsibility piled on top of the ever-growing list of responsibilities that teachers have. I was worried that this partnership would turn into a dictatorship where the university would serve as the "expert" when they have no idea what goes into the day-to-day operations of our school. But most of all, I was tired: tired of people coming into our schools, using our students, our resources, and our expertise only to leave when they accomplished their goals.

Being on the steering committee was refreshing. Everyone had a say. No one really knew what the partnership was going to look like, so we were able to cultivate a relationship formed to meet all of our needs. Being able to listen to people voice their concerns, misgivings, and mistrusts through courageous conversations was amazing.

The 1st year was all about preparation and professional development. This was important so we could all be on the same page. If we keep the question, "Are we doing what's good and right for children?" at the forefront of our minds when making decisions, we will make the right decisions for our school and students.

As a parent and a community member, I needed to think about the school students: How are students benefiting from this partnership? The program has evolved over the years. The benefits to students of our school are more prevalent than in the earlier years of the program. The biggest advantage is increased support in the classroom. The school students are being exposed to different personalities and different styles of teaching. Research showed that we were having difficulties meeting the needs of students who were struggling academically at the school. This year, teacher candidates learned about Response to Intervention in my literacy course.

They were tasked with identifying a small group of students who were below basic, assessing students, providing interventions, and seeing how those students responded to the interventions implemented. The results look promising, and I look forward to seeing how this translates to student progress.

As an adjunct professor and mentor teacher, I needed to think about the university students: How are community-engaged teacher preparation students benefiting from this partnership? The community-engaged teacher preparation students are gaining invaluable experience. They are being provided authentic, hands-on experience in teaching prior to their student teaching. They are learning to build relationships with students, parents, and the community at large. I have to make sure teacher candidates are learning critical literacy skills/strategies, while at the same time teaching them to build relationships with students, classroom teachers, and families.

As a teacher, I needed to think about our teachers: How are teachers benefiting from this partnership? Having another teacher in the room can be beneficial for everyone. Teacher candidates are usually enthusiastic. They are eager to experiment and try new ideas. They demonstrate new strategies and techniques that may reinvigorate the veteran teachers' teaching. Having a teacher candidate can reaffirm the strengths in your teaching as you share your ideas and strategies with them. You help shape the next generation of teachers. No matter what your seat is "at the table," remember to always do what's good and right for students, and your program will thrive.

STILL I RISE (PROFESSOR)

This team member is a full-time professor in education and coordinator of the special education program at the university. She teaches the special education course that is one of the five courses in the community-engaged teacher preparation program. She works closely with the other two methods courses to ensure that all elementary students' needs are met through the use of Universal Design for Learning in both literacy and science lessons. She has experience as a school administrator, supervises and observes teacher candidates, and provides continuous feedback to teacher candidates on a weekly basis. She allows the team to be grounded with her personal experience navigating a nearly all-White university.

Prior to arriving at the university, I would consider my cultural perspective broad, diverse, and inclusive of all races. As a young Black woman who rose through the ranks and represented success from an impoverished neighborhood and a graduate of an urban school district, I believed I had a broad perspective of cultural differences, classism, and racism. When I arrived at the university as a full-time professor, I came face to face with "White privilege" and was "mouth-wide-open shocked" at how privilege looks in the 21st century at a predominately White higher education institution surrounded by a Black, low-income community. Several thoughts played over and over in my mind: *Why am I here? Are these people really going to be teaching students?* Most of all, I found myself saying, "You have to be kidding me" each and every day. Often I would say, "Did they really just say that aloud?" The reality of my answers was that this is real, this is my job, and how much I appreciated teachers I'd had who looked like me and pushed me to be my best. The day-to-day experiences, comments that were said to me, and the emotions I felt every day cannot be captured in my portion of this chapter, so I will condense my perspective into a few major themes.

Arriving on Campus: When I arrived at the university and completed my first 2 weeks of informal orientation, I noticed no other faculty of color in the Education Department. I asked a colleague, "How many minorities are in the department besides me?" They responded, "Just three of you, and you are the only African American." I remember thinking of the importance of students having images of people who look like them as teachers and role models. The thought of school students having teachers they could identify with was starting to resonate with me now more than ever. I had never thought much of it because I had attended my urban neighborhood high school and had several Black teachers during my K–12 education experience. On top of my daily experiences at work, I am living in a country where I believe "acceptable racism" is being handed down from national leadership. As I reflected on all the things occurring in the country, did I really want to work in a situation where I have to "prove myself equal" or, in other words, where I had to prove my abilities, talents, and expertise were good enough to be in higher education? As the semester approached, I attended the first "faculty welcome" given by the president, and found myself searching for other professors who looked like me. I found six in a room of over 100 professors. As I sat at this meeting, I felt the eyes, stares, looks, and whispering from my fellow White professors and remembered thinking, "I left K–12 education to come to higher education for another dose of proving myself and my skills." I thought to myself, "God, another test?"

The Beginning: The semester began, and I was excited and ready. I had been an adjunct for about 4 years, so I felt I was not a novice in the higher education arena. I knew the rules of being mindful of my words, facial expressions, nodding my head even when the answer is completely wrong, and smiling even when students are offensive and/or disrespectful. As a young Black woman in higher education, I knew to watch what I say, limit personal stories about myself, don't overshare about my life, keep all examples to the content, say "I don't know" if I don't know, make sure everything I say can be backed by research—along with 20 or so other unwritten rules about being a Black professor in higher education. Sometimes the stress of trying to get White college students to understand the many perspectives of Black culture and how to teach minority students was OVERWHELMING. Often I pondered how to teach from the perspective of "not ending up in the news" or losing my job due to a "perception difference" as opposed to focusing on the issues and trends in urban education. University teacher candidates were traditional White college students perceiving themselves as privileged and working with perceived "low-income students." I struggled with how to deliver the content in a meaningful way so they could give 300% to the students they would soon be teaching and not believe that "teaching Black students is hopeless."

Finding Balance: Is this community-engaged teacher preparation program merely a checklist to ensure meeting a diversity requirement? As I was finding my balance in the classroom (and I am still searching for it), I was still questioning the intent of the program coordinator. I was trying to keep an open mind and not judge anyone. I wondered if the program faculty was a group of "White individuals" trying to be the "great White hope," thinking they were doing "social justice" by saving the "poor Black kids." I questioned their motives, integrity, and character every day by their actions, relationships, responses to questions, and the content in their lessons. Doing this allowed me to assess if the professors' intentions were really about "cultural responsiveness" and "transformational thinking," or if this was a box to check off for their "own moral development" or "inclusion/diversity status." I wondered if I was hired for the Inclusion/Affirmative Action checkbox on Human Resources statistics, or if we really were implementing change so teacher candidates could implement culturally effective practices in the classroom. What I learned about halfway through my 1st semester was that the program coordinator really understood social justice and social reform and was implementing change at a grassroots level. The other program faculty and professors really cared about the health and well-being of the children from the community. The team's mentors were from the community and were experts on the community. They were fully active in shaping the teacher candidates and the program as it related to serving local children.

It's working out for my good: As my first semester of my 1st year concluded, I found that although our skin color is not the same, we care about the same issues. Our thoughts, goals, and perspectives on urban education are similar. At the core of who we were, the program faculty wanted to transform the narrative about the city and its residents. As faculty we created our safe space and could have the courageous conversations about difficult topics and be genuine. I found the program team to consist of "people who look like me from the inside out." My professional relationships developed into friendships through authentic, cultural, transformational thinking.

BRIDGING THE CAMPUS–CITY DIVIDE (PROFESSOR)

This member of our team is a professor in arts and science, in a discipline not typically connected to education. The course he teaches for the program focuses on urban anthropology and is organized around the local history and culture of the city, the community in which we work. He also offers professional development on these topics to the other stakeholders in the program. He acts as a critical friend who is at once a service-learning scholar who works closely with the community and an ethnographer who raises questions that provide valuable local historical and cultural context for our work. He offers critical tenets for learning and understanding cultural proficiency and reflects on the evidence of absorbing critical learning that he sees carried over to his class. He also serves as an outlet for students to turn to in moments of frustration or discomfort because he is not directly affiliated with their academic program.

One of the primary reasons I sought a position at this university was its mission "to contribute to the vitality and well-being of the communities we serve." This is also one of the core tenets of cultural anthropology: to serve as advocates promoting the well-being of the people we study. As I got acquainted with the institution, I learned that, despite its lofty commitment to community engagement, the university, like many well-intentioned urban institutions, has had a checkered relationship with the city in which it is located. Past mayors have, at times, praised the university for being a valuable "community partner" and "anchor institution" and, at others, referred to it as "a dragon" that buys up property and pays no real estate taxes. For their part, past university presidents have, at times, regarded the city as a gracious host and, at others, threatened to completely wall off the campus from surrounding neighborhoods. Local residents report experiencing trepidation when they have to traverse the campus, while many upperclassmen still warn 1st-year students not to "cross the bridge" that spans the adjacent interstate and separates the university campus from the rest of the city. Residents, especially those who live in the immediate vicinity, express gratitude for the benefits they derive from the university, such as added security and library access, while simultaneously harboring suspicions that the university may someday "take over" their neighborhoods and displace them.

As I worked to incorporate meaningful civic engagement into the anthropology curriculum and develop undergraduate-led research opportunities for my students, I discovered that the sometimes adversarial, sometimes collaborative relationship between the university and the city can undermine earnest attempts to equalize power. As a result of my training as an ethnographer, I was very conscious of the importance of conducting research "with" rather than "for" members of the local community. To this end, my anthropology students and I hosted a series of community listening sessions. The residents who attended these sessions used them as an opportunity to inform us that cooperating with other researchers over the years had failed to produce noticeable changes in their lives. They said they were sick of serving as the "guinea pigs" for university students and faculty who come and go as they please, publishing studies that improve their learning and advance their careers but do little to address residents' expressed concerns. This was articulated by a community activist who declared that she was "sick and tired of people getting their PhDs on the backs of our children."

I gradually built personal relationships with key community partners and then worked with them to identify research goals that my students could realistically accomplish as part of a new service-learning course I created called "Urban Anthropology." As my students produced a series of modest yet impactful research projects for our community partners, the suspicion and mistrust we initially encountered gave way to a spirit of community and collaboration. By giving our community partners the responsibility of establishing our research priorities and then evaluating our findings, I was able to reverse the typical power dynamics of the relationship between researchers and research subjects; we made it clear that we regarded our research subjects as true experts and ourselves as mere novices. After my urban anthropology course became part of the community-engaged teacher preparation program, I maintained this approach. The elementary school became our primary community partner, and I redesigned the course to focus specifically on urban education.

In spite of this progress, at the outset of the community-engaged teacher preparation program, the general suspicion and mistrust between the university and the city was at a fever pitch. The university had recently purchased a number of properties from the school district, including a middle school, their administration building, and the building housing the elementary school, the very school with whom we were partnering. The university administration disclosed little information about what it planned to do with the properties, allowing rumors to swirl about its intentions. When the university erected a sculpture of its logo on the elementary school's front lawn, it seemed to confirm what many believed was already a foregone conclusion.

So how did our program manage to not only survive but flourish in spite of these conditions? The first step involved securing a promise from the university administration that the school's future was not in jeopardy. The president graciously took the time to personally meet with the school's principal and quashed the rumors circulating about the school's closing. That the president made an effort to be available and accessible, and offered a personal guarantee to keep the school open, was a huge step in reestablishing trust.

The second step involved composing a steering committee in which everyone felt they deserved a seat at the table and felt comfortable speaking candidly with one another in an atmosphere of mutual respect and common interest. As co-equal members of the committee, the elementary school faculty and administrators had direct access not only to the university's directors and faculty but also to "higher-ups," such as the dean of the School of Education. The committee provided an invaluable forum for the direct exchange of ideas, comments, questions, and, most important, critiques among people who previously saw themselves as occupying different ranks and distinct spheres of influence.

Another important step was to invite all learning community constituents to participate in "courageous conversations," which provided an additional, informal space in which the boundaries that normally separate staff, faculty, and administrator could be transcended and standard power dynamics reversed. Power was further equalized by expanding the composition of the team that made the annual pilgrimage to Ball State University for professional development to include not just predominantly university representatives but also school faculty and community mentors. Welcoming elementary school faculty as adjunct professors further solidified their commitment to the program. As a result, an expanded sense of ownership and control grew that, in turn, deepened everyone's commitment to collaboration. In the end, shared power has led to a vibrant relationship that has penetrated institutional barriers and built a lasting trust to the benefit of the children, teacher candidates, faculties, families, and the community we serve.

NOTHING WORTH IT IS EVER EASY (CLASSROOM TEACHER)

As a graduate of our program, a student teacher in the school, and now a member of the school faculty, her story demonstrates the success of our partnership. During her time student teaching at the school, she was an articulate spokesperson at the university's Honors Forum and presented on the impacts of our community-engaged teacher preparation program. She also presented effectively to outside visitors who were considering the development of a version of our model. While other graduates of the program have been hired in the school district, she was the first hire at this elementary school. She built beneficial and long-lasting relationships with other teachers and staff at the school, which allowed her to work with and learn from veteran teachers from the very beginning through today. She demonstrates how to enlist parent support and understanding when trying to program effectively for children with incredibly diverse learning needs, and even several with severe behavioral challenges. She truly conveys high expectations for success and a positive, caring attitude in her classroom. She embodies the ability to effectively connect with families and the community to support positive outcomes for her children.

I come from a small, relatively rural town in New Jersey. In school, I was always a part of the majority—White and middle income. Then I went to the university where I was, yet again, part of the majority. It wasn't until my 1st day in the 4th-grade classroom as a part of the community-engaged teacher preparation program that I found myself to be in the minority as one of only three White people. It was the first time I was really aware that I was White.

My cooperating teachers were full of knowledge and wanted to see me succeed. We clicked so well that I was able to stay in that classroom for both the fall semester and student teaching. They were excellent models of what a teacher should be; they fostered a positive classroom culture, knew how to effectively teach the content, and understood how to keep students engaged by making the material relevant. The proof was in each student's success. Much of what I do today, I learned from them.

As the semester continued, my outlook on the community evolved. I did my best to dismantle and combat any personal bias I could identify. Without judgments, it became easier to go into the community and learn about my students and their culture in a meaningful way, which I could then embrace in the classroom.

The transition from the community-engaged teacher preparation program to student teaching was smooth. I had already developed relationships with the teachers and students. Being in the classroom all day during student teaching allowed me to deepen relationships and rapport with the students.

During my student teaching I was asked to give an Honors Week presentation about the community-engaged teacher preparation program. A few weeks before, a team from a university and school district in Texas came to investigate our program, as they wanted to apply it at their schools. We presented to the Texas team and answered their questions. I shared examples of how I incorporated the community and culture of the city into my work in the classroom and shared the positive reaction and results from the students. It was an honor to have an opportunity to share my love for the program and my core beliefs that it helped shape.

I genuinely believe it is what I learned about being culturally responsive and understanding that has taken me this far and sparked a passion for teaching and empathy for others.

Fast-forward a few months to September. I found out that there was an opening at the school, and within the week I was hired. On top of being a 1st-year teacher, I put a lot of pressure on myself. It is not easy to be a great, or even a good teacher. It requires a lot of time and energy. From the beginning, I have committed to making everything as relevant to the students as I can because I want every single student to be successful, not just most or some.

The transition from teacher candidate, to student teacher, to teacher was as smooth as it could be, thanks to the experiences I had under my belt. I understood the culture of the city, I knew some of the families, I knew the teachers that I would be leaning on for help and support, and I had many behavior and educational tricks I'd learned while working with my cooperating teachers. Having the honor of being a teacher in this school allows me the ability to continue to serve the community and students about whom I care so deeply.

Teaching is hard. Caring is draining. Seeing the children's faces light up when they see books with role models who look like them, the excitement when our call and response is to the tune of one of their favorite songs, and seeing them smile as hard as they can when they do well on their work— that is all the motivation I need. That is the proof that all of this time, effort, and stress is worth it. Each day I continue to build relationships with the students, so they know I am there for them, and that I value them.

By embracing the students, their city, and their culture, and by building lasting relationships, we empower the students. Each student knows that I value them the way they are, even if sometimes they make me crazy. As I grow as a teacher, my hope is that I can continue to empower students, and one day be able to help teacher candidates develop into the next generation of amazing teachers. My mission is to make young students feel empowered and valued now, so that they will be able to develop a voice to stand up for what they believe in and make a change in this world.

CONCLUSION

We must be clear about what we believe to be central to establishing a partnership that reflects an equalization of power and has the critical elements that will bring about a positive impact for children, prepare the next generation of teachers, and foster the growth of a community of learners engaged in a common endeavor.

We believe these elements to be necessary:

- A critical mass of university faculty, school principal, school faculty, and community mentors who are "likeminded" in their desire to enter into a partnership as equals and a desire to bring about continuous positive improvement for the school, the community, and the university
- A common vision of what is "good and right" for children
- Quality school faculty who can serve as strong role models for teacher candidates
- Community mentors representing a range of backgrounds, from city council members to retired teachers, who are dedicated to sharing the wealth of the community and investing in the lives of the teachers, teacher candidates, and children
- A university faculty member who can take on the role of program director to maintain momentum and ensure that all parts are working in concert—a role that requires resilience, drive, and perseverance in an ever-changing landscape of administrative institutional changes
- A university coordinator and school principal willing to communicate frequently and provide the checks and balances necessary to ensure that the partnership stays true to its mission
- A school faculty willing to invest the time necessary for planning, feedback, and serving as role models and mentors to teacher candidates
- Teacher candidates who understand the importance of being "all in," as demonstrated by all stakeholders within the partnership
- A commitment on the part of the university coordinator and the school principal to document and articulate the purpose, benefits, and results of the partnership and share effectively with university and school district administration to build their understanding and support of this important endeavor
- University faculty willing to become true partners by listening, sharing, supporting, and learning from school faculty and community mentors
- A commitment to recognize, celebrate, and share the "fruits of our labors" with the entire learning community
- A willingness to invest in the growth of others
- Continuous sharing, mentoring, and growing as full members committed to one another and the success of everyone, especially the children.

The core of our success is staying true to our commitment to equalize power. If we are to make a difference for the children we serve, we must constantly review and revisit what we are doing, including every decision that is made. Intertwined in this is the question of making a difference for the children we will serve in the future both at our school and the schools where teacher candidates will take their place in the professional ranks. If our beliefs are driving what we do, then all partners doing the work must be fully committed, and a loop of communication, planning, and improvement must be maintained. While we would like to present to others that they can count on unconditional support, we know the path is not that easy. Our governing organizations have much larger commitments, and maintain different views on our work. Winning their support often means putting forth extra effort to meet disparate expectations, while maintaining program integrity. Our partnership allows us to navigate those sometimes competing forces, while responding to concerns and helping others see the value of our work from their diverse perspectives. Power-sharing between the university, the elementary school, and the community has allowed us to stand firm in what we know will be sustainable and generate the change that leads to success.

REFERENCES

Danielson, C. (2014). *The framework for teaching evaluation instrument: Version 1.2.* www.danielsongroup.org.

Singleton, G. E. (2015). *Courageous conversations about race: A field guide for achieving equity in schools.* Sage.

Wenger, E., McDermott, R., & Snyder, W. M. (2002). *Cultivating communities of practice: A guide to managing knowledge.* Harvard Business School Press.

Designing a Community Engagement Strategy to Serve Historically Marginalized Urban Youth in Australia

Jo Lampert, Eric Dommers, Jaime de Loma-Osorio Ricón,
and Stevie Lebhers-Browne

INTRODUCTION

This chapter represents an emerging Australian partnership between an urban low socioeconomic cluster of schools in Melbourne, a community organization, and a new social justice–oriented initial teacher education program, Nexus. We track Project REAL as an example of how schools and one community organization have co-constructed a flexible learning option to better serve marginalized youth with a history of disengagement with school. Drawing on its early success, we then explain how that collaboration is now extending its reach to Nexus, which is developing transformative practices for preservice teachers preparing to work with marginalized youth. The programs explored in this chapter thus represent a three-way community engagement strategy involving a community organization, schools, and a teacher education program.

While we bring different theoretical paradigms to the table, we are united in utilizing social capital theory to explain inequities. This supports our main aim of doing education differently so that inequities are not reproduced. We begin the chapter by exploring how a critical pedagogy of engagement (Smyth et al., 2013) and the expanding field of community-engaged education can guide how teachers work. The next section of the chapter situates poverty and youth in the Australian urban context. This is followed by separate sections on Project REAL and the new teacher education program, Nexus, and one example of our partnership activities as it emerged during the COVID-19 crisis. We conclude by explaining our direction as we move into the future. Figure 5.1 illustrates the relationships between the schools, community services, and the teacher education program that we will describe in this chapter.

COMMUNITY ENGAGEMENT

Each of the authors of this chapter has had extensive, varied experience designing and coordinating educational programs for historically vulnerable or marginalized youth. Our community engagement strategies developed from a common commitment to looking for alternative ways to better serve the needs of young people historically excluded from mainstream school systems. Merging theory and practice, our initiatives explore the possibility of a community-engaged framework for teachers to recognize, understand, connect, and advocate more for young people from high-poverty or historically vulnerable urban communities.

Figure 5.1. Community Engagement Model

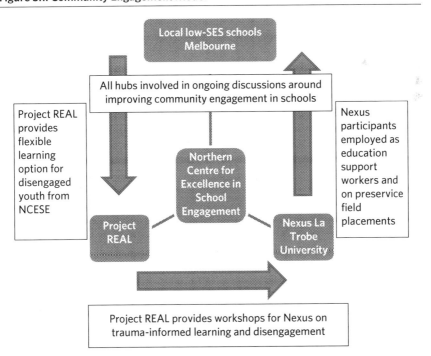

As an example of a critical pedagogy of engagement (Smyth et al., 2013), the call for community engagement in education responds to a concern that, while education can do good, we can also inadvertently re-traumatize, re-marginalize, and reproduce conditions that have been historically exclusionary (Zeichner et al., 2015). As strengths-based initiatives, we need first to understand young peoples' communities, and as Maxine Greene (1992) writes, "to open up our experiences (and yes, our curricula) to existential possibilities of multiple kinds is to extend and deepen what we think of when we speak of a community" (p. 254). While not exactly new, community-engaged partnerships are emerging as one key in advancing educational equity (Clark et al., 2016). Policy imperatives in Australia are increasingly encouraging community engagement, developing relationships with historically silenced communities, such as young people who are homeless or highly disengaged, which has not been mainstream practice (Zeichner et al., 2015).

Among other things, Australian youth from historically marginalized communities experience racism, discrimination, and disengagement from school. In addition, poor health and well-being impact academic achievement, attendance, and graduation (Australian Human Rights Commission, 2020). A significant issue for educators is how to equitably form authentic, ethical relationships with the most historically vulnerable groups, who have often had poor—even traumatic—experiences with schools and are disconnected from formal school systems. This is particularly important for initial teacher education because so little attention has been paid to community engagement for preservice teachers (Zeichner et al., 2016), and teachers so regularly feel unprepared to teach in communities different from the ones in which they grew up (Lampert & Burnett, 2016).

The theoretical framework for this project comes from the critical theory that considers the social, historical, and ideological forces and structures that produce and constrain how teacher education or schooling in general take place. Community-engaged teacher preparation entails situating teacher education in the cultural contexts in which young people grow and learn. This has meant physically embedding teachers within local communities and affording opportunities for place-based approaches that are context-specific and involve situated, immersive learning (Boylan & Woolsey, 2015). Differentiated from community-based initiatives, some of which simply take place at sites off campus, a community-engaged approach works toward more sustainable integration of educational programs in historically marginalized communities. The honoring of community expertise, their funds of knowledge (Moll, 2015; Moll et al., 1992; Yosso, 2005), is a decisive element in preparing preservice teachers to be equity-focused, democratic teachers (Murrell, 2007). While working in nonessentialist ways means there is no single method of engaging with community that works every time, or with every group, the research base for community-engaged teaching is an essential paradigm in advancing educational equity (Lee et al., 2013; Lees, 2016; Zeichner et al., 2015; Zygmunt & Clark, 2016).

Various terms, such as "disadvantaged," are used to describe communities most negatively affected by a mainstream school system. In this project we prefer the term "historically vulnerable" communities (Shim, 2012) because it overtly recognizes the sociohistorical circumstances that have led to the exclusion and marginalization that this project seeks to address.

Scholars and policymakers are calling for educators in schools to become transformational by working with and for the communities they serve. While policy imperatives are increasingly encouraging community engagement in education, developing relationships with historically marginalized families or the nongovernmental organizations (NGOs) that serve them has not been mainstream practice (Zeichner et al., 2015). Further, teachers often have little to no preparation for the social realities of the lives of their students and their students' families. Numerous education policies—including the blueprint Australian *Through Growth to Achievement* report (Gonski et al., 2018)—highlight that community engagement is often overlooked in educational policy and practice. According to Gonski and colleagues (2018), while many models of school–community engagement exist in Australia, school–community engagement to improve student learning is not common practice, and implementation can be ad hoc. Policy discourses of community engagement hypothesize that if schools are more engaged with local community organizations, students and their families will feel more included and will participate more in school practices. This is seen to lead to better student outcomes, including well-being and (though not always the aim) education and employment pathways. In the Australian State of Victoria's *Framework for Improving Student Outcomes*, building communities is a dimension of community engagement and identified as a learning priority (Victoria Department of Education and Training, 2020). The gap is both in how sporadically it is actioned and how little we know about the impact of community engagement strategies.

Though community engagement itself does not eradicate poverty, and teachers cannot be blamed for the historical social or political conditions that produce inequality, we argue that teachers can be better prepared both to make a difference and to positively impact students' experiences and outcomes. Merging theory and practice, the projects outlined in this chapter are examples of emerging pedagogies of hope (Freire, 1996). They are co-designed to recognize, understand, connect, and, most importantly, advocate for young people from historically marginalized communities.

THE AUSTRALIAN CONTEXT:
POVERTY AND MARGINALIZED YOUTH

Although Australians generally experience good health and high levels of social and economic prosperity, the Australian community experiences both cyclical and deep and persistent levels of poverty and social exclusion. Some recent research suggests that as many as 17% of Australian children live in households that experience poverty, and most of these children perform much worse in and out of school than their more advantaged counterparts (Davidson et al., 2018). While 6.5% of 5- to 6-year-old children living in Australia's wealthiest suburbs manifest two or more developmental delays, the figure for children who live in the most marginalized areas is much higher (Commissioner for Children and Young People, 2020). For Indigenous Australian children, the situation is concerning. Indigenous students are 2.3 times more likely to miss the Australian literacy benchmark for functional literacy at Year 7 than non-Indigenous learners (Mitchell Institute, 2016). The Australian Productivity Commission (2020) reports that gaps in academic learning outcomes between children from socioeconomically disadvantaged families and their more advantaged peers appear early in a child's life, and can "begin a cycle of disadvantage that sets a trajectory for poorer outcomes later in life" (McLachlan et al., 2013, p. 2).

The report notes that while most Australian families are able to provide support for their children, families dealing with complex problems such as poverty, poor physical and mental health, substance abuse, and domestic violence are under much greater stress (McLachlan et al., 2013) and, in turn, more likely to experience learning disengagement, behavioral problems, and poor educational outcomes (Australian Research Alliance for Children and Youth, 2009; McLachlan et al., 2013). Indeed, some 40% of children from the lowest socioeconomic status (SES) do not complete Year 12—compared with 25% noncompletion overall (Mitchell Institute, 2016). While there are many reasons for leaving school prior to graduation (including their need for paid employment to pay rent or survive), early school leavers are at markedly higher risk of experiencing deep and persistent disadvantage when compared with their peers who have completed Year 12 (McLachlan et al., 2013); this disadvantage manifests across multiple life domains, including economic participation, social connectedness, and health (OECD, 2008).

In Australia, the communities that bear the greatest burden of historical marginalization include Aboriginal and Torres Strait Islander peoples, communities of people who come from non-English-speaking backgrounds, people with low socioeconomic status, and refugee, rural, and remote communities (Australian Bureau of Statistics, 2016). The experiences of historical marginalization are often common across different social groups because poverty and poor health are common to many of these groups. These groups also have much in common with historically marginalized communities in other OECD countries, such as the United States, the UK, Canada, and much of Western Europe (Gale et al., 2017; Lampert et al., 2019; Organisation for Economic Co-operation and Development, 2017), and are especially comparable to other colonized countries.

Although education is the key to improving "life chances," employment and earnings prospects, health, social capital, and avoiding the justice system (Organisation for Economic Co-operation and Development, 2017), many schools located in historically marginalized areas struggle with challenges, such as racism, that are exacerbated by poverty and other factors. They also struggle more often with disruptive student behavior, a consequence of stress and trauma induced by poverty, disadvantage, and the factors named above, such as bullying and racism. Recent student disengagement research highlights that around 60% of staff in low-SES schools report several disruptions per class, compared with around 10% in high-SES schools (Goss et al., 2017). These disruptions can be unfairly attributed to deficit assumptions and stereotypes, rather than context. Teachers require a deep understanding of the real-life context to understand classroom incidents in schools that serve vulnerable young people and their families. Teachers also need strong, long-term relationships with their local communities in order to avoid deficit assumptions that might otherwise be used to explain student behavior (Zygmunt & Clark, 2016). Recognizing the effects of trauma is part of the community-informed learning that can come from partnering with community organizations. This became especially important in 2020–2021 during the COVID-19 pandemic. During this time, preservice teachers needed more than ever to understand what their most vulnerable students and their families might be experiencing.

The Northern Centre for Excellence in School Engagement (NCESE), situated in a historically diverse and poor community in Melbourne, sets the scene for community engagement in this chapter. The NCESE comprises 15 primary school principals who work together to build community links, networks, and programs to support the well-being, social capital, and learning needs of students and their families. The partnership formed between NCESE, Banksia Gardens Community Services (BGCS), and Nexus is an example of how communities and schools can work together to serve historically marginalized families and youth. The recent involvement of teacher education in this cluster means that a new generation of teachers can be prepared to understand disengaged young people from a community perspective. We hope this will work to overcome the limitations of traditional teacher education, which often exhibits a disconnect between theory, as offered in university coursework, and practice, as observed in mainstream classrooms. Nexus is seeking to include that hybrid, or third space, where university, school, community, and families can come together (Lee, 2018).

BANKSIA GARDENS COMMUNITY SERVICES (BGCS)

Banksia Gardens is a small community organization located in Broadmeadows, Victoria. Soon after the construction of the Banksia Gardens public housing estate, a group of public housing tenants developed the organization. They operated out of one of the public housing properties for over a decade. From the outset, the organization grew organically out of the landscape of this community. A community center, purpose-built in 1993, is where many of its programs are currently delivered.

Today, BGCS maintains a strong commitment to community development principles. Its programs are focused on the most pressing community needs: education and training, supporting local young people, environmental sustainability, community participation, and advocacy. Importantly, participation by children and young people in the BGCS programs enabled BGCS to gradually establish strong links with most local primary schools in Broadmeadows and surrounding areas. A significant proportion of these youth spent extended periods of time away from school, either as a result of absenteeism or suspensions, and many of them were also formally or informally banned from using local services such as the library, pool, and shopping center. Disengaged youth were welcomed and engaged with BGCS programs. However, our staff started to experience behavioral incidents that grew in frequency and severity. These escalated in violence and aggression toward staff, conflicts with parents following incidents, and situations where youth were unsafe (climbing on the roof, running across busy roads, etc.). This significantly impacted staff morale, and many staff members recall that period as a protracted crisis.

Despite many difficulties and challenges, most of these vulnerable children continued to attend our programs. BGCS began to understand that, without additional resources, we were missing an opportunity to turn their engagement with the center into tangible outcomes for their social, emotional, and physical development. To grow, some key questions needed to be answered: (1) How should BGCS respond to the needs of disengaged young people attending their programs, and the broader community? (2) How should BGCS develop a unified and coherent approach? The second question required an approach grounded in evidence and professional standards, signifying a move away from approaches motivated by staff compassion and energy levels or dependent on individual values (e.g., bleeding heart, tough love). As is often the case, some of the answers to these questions became apparent only in response to particular students and situations, thus reinforcing a belief that the young people who were hoped to benefit from community-engaged collaborations also informed the work at every stage.

Raymond*

One of the young people attending the program at the time was Raymond, a 12-year-old boy who lived with his father, clearly a very loving man despite several mental health and substance abuse challenges. Raymond was incredibly playful and witty, and always showed great compassion toward small children, animals, and anyone frail or vulnerable. Going to the local gym was one of his favorite things in the world.

At times, however, Raymond was also capable of extreme violence and aggression, and this eventually led to his expulsion from a nearby school with whom BGCS had a close working relationship. The behaviors through which Raymond expressed his unmet needs could also be extremely oppositional. In hindsight, many of BGSC's responses were not adequate, but the knowledge gained of his situation through close contact with him and his family enabled BGCS to advocate on his behalf. By the end of Term 3, and after several long conversations with the school principal, it became evident that Raymond would have to change schools. The principal was not prepared to reverse the expulsion. Unfortunately, his new school was only in a position to accept his enrollment in the new year, which left Raymond without a viable schooling alternative for several months.

Both BGCS and Raymond's current school were acutely aware of the protective role that school and his school friends played in Raymond's life, and of the detrimental effect that increased time spent at home could have on the family's dynamics. So BGCS came forward with a proposal: If the school agreed to provide financial resources, they would employ a teacher and an aide to support his learning at the community center. The school agreed, a Student Absence Learning Plan was developed, and Raymond started taking part in an individualized program at the community center 3 days per week. Raymond also spent half a day at his school in order to

---

*The story of Raymond told in this chapter is not any one person's actual story, but a composite. This fictional narrative merges the circumstances of many young people who have inspired Project REAL over the years.

maintain contact with his teachers and peers. In addition to this, a care team was formed comprising Raymond's father, school and BGCS representatives, and other support agencies (child protection, local council, family support agencies); a client support officer from BGCS was also allocated to support the family. This Student Absence Learning Plan was in place for approximately one term and was the seed for the next phase of the project, Project REAL.

Student Re-Engagement Working Group

Although the intervention with Raymond was positive, at least 20 more children were experiencing similar situations and engaging in school absenteeism, as well as antisocial behaviors. BGCS met with the Department of Education and Training (DET) and the local Principal Network to gauge their interest in establishing a broader intervention, knowing that many more young people would benefit from similar interventions. This demonstration of hope for better outcomes, and care and concern for the local young people, resulted in the creation of a Working Group of eight principals, BGCS staff, and DET representatives. One of the primary outcomes of the group was setting up a "Gateway School" for disengaged young learners at the BGCS center. This was achieved by the Working Group through establishing stronger links with a local secondary school, which continued to work together with BGCS on the establishment of Project REAL.

PROJECT REAL:
MEETING STUDENT NEEDS THROUGH COMMUNITY ENGAGEMENT

Project REAL was designed as a re-engagement program to meet the needs of students aged 9–12 years experiencing difficulties participating in mainstream education. Within a few months following the work with Raymond, 15 local schools had agreed to become partners in this community-led alliance and received financial backing from several philanthropic organizations. In February 2017, the doors of Project REAL were opened to the inaugural cohort of seven students. Banksia Gardens was also connected with an organization that plays a critical role in bringing trauma-informed practice to schools through trauma-informed positive education training (Brunzell et al., 2016). A commitment to reflective, evidence-based practice and continuous improvement became a foundational backbone of Project REAL, along with a trauma-informed lens.

The program accepted referrals from local primary schools, as well as from agencies, including the Department of Health and Human Services.

Students had typically demonstrated behaviors of significant concern (poor school attendance, poor educational performance) and had come from backgrounds of hardship and/or trauma. On acceptance, students attended Project REAL 3 days per week and received "supported participation" in a partner school for the other 2 days. The program was operating in a repurposed portable classroom provided by one of the partner schools. Sessions were included throughout the day to help prepare (calm, center, focus) students for academic work, including morning and afternoon circles, quiet activities, brain breaks, and calming activities.

While the objectives and the main structure of the program have remained intact, the initial stages of Project REAL saw a considerable amount of turmoil during what can only be described as a steep learning curve in relation to understanding trauma-informed practice both in theory and on the ground. This curve was evident in the lack of consensus about the practices, procedures, and structures to support the ongoing refinement of the program. Together with the inherent tensions derived from working with such vulnerable children and families, these conflicts were sources of instability that, at times, had an impact on the relationships between BGCS and the referring schools. In the initial stages, these partnerships were also relatively fragile, as "sharing students" forced BGCS and partner schools to recognize the gaps in our own expertise and knowledge and work together in new ways. Most of these difficulties were overcome by improving communication mechanisms between BGCS and referring schools, and by ensuring that all teachers and staff working with Project REAL students were in consensus regarding the main concepts of trauma-informed practice. Ultimately, these challenges resulted in several staff departures, but also the creative development of new approaches. By the end of 2017, a clear consolidation of thinking and practice had occurred among staff.

The Project REAL approach represented a local adaptation of theoretical and practice-based components derived from Trauma-Informed Positive Education and the Attachment, Regulation and Competency (ARC) Framework (Brunzell et al., 2016). It adopted a strengths-based approach that regards trust-building and overall well-being as preconditions to learning and represented interventions that were needs-based and flexible (Blaustein & Kinniburgh, 2010). In addition, Project REAL attends to socioemotional learning to develop greater social and emotional "literacy" (Oberle & Schonert-Reichl, 2016). Other strategies include regular engagement with and support for parents, such as assistance in collaborative and proactive problem-solving, parenting, and navigating bureaucracy and other services (Bowen, 1974).

Project REAL continues to operate as an alternative, flexible education setting for children who have been historically marginalized by mainstream schooling. In retrospect, it is clear that the response plan for Raymond shared many of the elements that ultimately made Project REAL successful. That is, it responded to a clear and urgent gap in locally available services; constituted a holistic intervention underpinned by a radical inclusion approach; and relied on strong relationships and respect, formed slowly and gained over time (between BGCS and the school, BGCS and Raymond, BGCS and Raymond's family). These relationships created a sufficiently safe environment for all stakeholders to be challenged enough for the intervention to produce different and better results.

Looking forward, identifying systemic integration points with initial teacher education, and with government and other community services, will strengthen our collective capacity to support highly vulnerable students. The consolidation and expansion of the NCESE community of practice will be a critical component of the project over the next 24 months. Establishing explicit links between trauma-informed practice, restorative justice, and existing systems and structures will be among our initial priorities. We have come a long way since we met Raymond, and our focus on family, community, and service continues to grow.

THE NEXUS PATHWAY INTO SECONDARY TEACHING: COMMUNITY ENGAGEMENT IN THE PREPARATION OF PRESERVICE TEACHERS

To extend the community engagement strategies outlined in the first section of this chapter, we now further discuss the partnership between Project REAL and Nexus. If new teachers are prepared from the beginning to work holistically with communities, new models can emerge that support the most vulnerable students. An emerging aim of this collaboration is to develop a community-engaged strategy by embedding the work of Banksia Gardens Community Services in the new Nexus pathway into teacher education.

La Trobe University's School of Education welcomed 40 commencing students into its first intake of the Nexus Program. The program aims to address teacher shortages in low-SES urban and regional locations in the State of Victoria, Australia. Nexus provides mentoring, a teacher aide salary, and support to university graduates while they train—on the job in schools experiencing teacher shortages—to become teachers. Nexus is delivered as part of the High-Achieving Teachers Program with the support of the Australian Government Department of Education and Training. La Trobe University also acknowledges the support of the Victorian Government.

We believe that teachers can and should be better prepared to understand and respond to community needs. The earlier preservice teachers can work in and with local communities, and the more opportunity they have for deep and critical reflection, the more likely they are to become agents of change (Strahley & D'Arpino, 2016). For teacher education, the challenge of engaging more deeply with local communities is about righting imbalances. This involves a shift in power and requires an institutionally embedded strategy to give historically marginalized communities a voice at the decisionmaking table in central, rather than tokenistic, ways (Gillan et al., 2017). We hope to develop a teacher education program where teachers deeply understand the communities in which they teach, see young people and their families as holding legitimate knowledge (Delgado & Villalpando, 2002), and are prepared to be knowledgeable agents of social change.

The Nexus teacher education program is designed as a reflective partnership among university, schools, and, most significantly, local communities. It is a new, place-based Master of Teaching (Secondary) program, with community engagement at its core. The program is designed to recruit, prepare, support, graduate, and track teachers through an alternative pathway into secondary teaching in low-socioeconomic-status Victorian schools. Teacher candidates are selected for the program using an equity-based points system (Howard & Rodriguez-Scheel, 2016), taking into account applicants' own backgrounds (i.e., whether from marginalized communities themselves), personal and professional histories, commitment to social justice, and discipline content knowledge. We recognize that teachers who come from local or low-SES communities, who are Indigenous, who have language backgrounds other than English, or who have experienced career interruptions or other barriers may have the experience, skills, knowledge, and dispositions to make a significant difference for disengaged young people (Sleeter, 2017).

Nexus is a highly mentored, scaffolded, employment-based teacher education program. We immerse our participants both in schools and local communities, slowly guiding them to independence as classroom teachers. On campus, in schools, and at selected community locations, they learn from teacher mentors. They are hosted by community families, working side by side as they reflect on critical theory and explore innovations in teaching for socially just practices that effect change for students and their communities. In this respect, Nexus engages in knowledge-building at all levels of teacher education, including the targeted selection of teacher candidates and the co-construction of a new model of teacher education informed by members of local communities to incorporate community perspectives. As Zyngier's (2017) work in community-engaged teacher education illustrates, when preservice teachers actively engage with communities outside of formal schooling, they learn that common deficit assumptions (e.g., that disengaged youth are poor learners or come from families who do not care about them or their education) are false. They come to see young people from historically vulnerable backgrounds as people with valid funds of knowledge, and with aspirations and goals that can be fulfilled (González et al., 2005).

NEXUS ENGAGEMENT WITH
COMMUNITIES AND SCHOOLS DURING COVID-19

The community engagement component of Nexus was designed to break down historical silos among university-based teacher education programs, schools, and local communities. Nexus participants complete their initial teacher education program while they work part-time as education support workers or teachers' aides in low-SES schools. Faced with new restrictions during the COVID-19 pandemic, we adopted "just-in-time" strategies for this community engagement. One realization during the crisis was the need for more training on trauma-informed learning. Our relationship with Banksia Gardens Community Services enabled us to offer this training quickly and from a community perspective.

In Nexus, each participant is entitled to a community mentor. The community mentoring program was designed for each preservice teacher to be paired with a community mentor (e.g., a parent, youth worker) who would be available for a safe and private conversation to help them understand students' home lives, behaviors, or challenges. This originally seemed difficult to arrange during these times when historically vulnerable communities were particularly stressed and understandably preoccupied with their own economic and health concerns. It emerged, however, that this was exactly the right time to consider community mentors, since understanding the experiences of the most minoritized communities was so crucial for our Nexus preservice teachers. Online discussion forums (using Zoom) proved highly successful and provided an informative and safe way for everyone to discuss the effects of hardship, equity issues, and ways forward.

For a period lasting several months, Nexus students participated in weekly online drop-ins hosted by community organizations, and run by Indigenous communities, youth organizations, LGBQTI groups, and others. Our weekly conversations became opportunities for the Nexus cohort to bring up questions; we could then respond by inviting other community groups, such as Banksia Gardens Community Services, to help them work through their concerns. Nexus participants were invited to communicate with BGCS staff to understand the seldom recognized funds of knowledge of their school communities. They were invited to email, phone, or visit face to face with more questions, to participate in an online community of practice set up by BGCS. We started planning for Nexus students to hear more from parents and young people themselves when things "normalized."

The unanticipated events of COVID-19 in 2020 shifted our ideas as we reflected on what teachers might need to know in times of crisis. On the one hand, there was a pause in what we could do as schools and community programs closed, went online, and grappled with the impact of the pandemic on vulnerable youth. On the other hand, the pandemic allowed us to concentrate on what seemed now to matter, which was preparing teachers for the urgency of supporting young people whose families were under increasing economic pressure and additional forms of trauma. It also required us to attend to our Nexus students' health and well-being, and to understand the health and well-being of teachers as well as students.

We knew Nexus preservice teachers would derive significant benefit from this new partnership, that the values and goals between Nexus and BGCS were shared, and that we wanted to work together. We always intended for community engagement to emerge organically depending on need and context, and through deeper relationships. Community engagement strategies for Nexus included:

- Involving local community organizations (and in some cases, families) on selection panels for Nexus candidates.
- Matching Nexus preservice teachers with community organizations depending on contexts. For instance, we connected them to Indigenous organizations, LBGQTI communities, and struggling rural communities still recovering from Australian bushfires.
- Providing opportunities for Nexus participants to study off campus in community spaces, such as in a room we rented from the Islamic community.
- Organizing potential practicum in alternative settings such as Project REAL.
- Encouraging Nexus participants to get to know community members as part of and outside of assessment, and to get to know students not from school records but from families, community members, and community organizations.

Planning for these activities is taking time, but this is mindfully purposeful. The engagement, however it unfolds, is designed to situate knowledge outside of its normative, sanctioned sources.

During our twice-weekly Nexus Zoom drop-ins, themes began to emerge. In particular, while they had just started their teaching degrees, how some students were disadvantaged by the school system was quickly visible. Placed in some of the 15 low-SES schools that make up NCESE, Nexus preservice teachers worked with students who were disengaged and had poor attendance at the best of times. In Australia, most teaching was offered online, but in the State of Victoria schools remained open for small numbers of students to attend if they were identified as at-risk, either because they were not safe at home or were children of essential workers. During this period, Nexus participants noted or heard from the teachers that some students were absent, falling even further behind, or exhibiting more challenging behaviors. This was no surprise given the isolation, physical and mental health issues, family hardship, and stresses exacerbated by the virus. However, very new to schools and teaching, it was hard for Nexus participants to understand their roles. They were generally being asked to "carry on" teaching academic skills, though they could see that the well-being of their students was a bigger issue. In our discussion forums, on Zoom and in emails, Nexus preservice teachers let us know they needed help:

> I did have an instance yesterday which I emailed M. K. and L. [other Nexus preservice teachers] about which was two students who seemed very disengaged and wondering if they had any suggestions for providing ways I could help them be engaged with their online work. Would you be able to provide any insight as well? These students were disengaged, distracting each other, refusing to do classwork, verbally aggressive (not to me, but to the other staff member) and were more than happy to be on their phones. —Participant X

> It's a challenging environment; there are only 9 secondary students, and some have learning difficulties. In fact, some have parents at home and access to remote learning, but the school has deemed them "at risk" for a variety of reasons if they stay home. —Participant Y

The schools took great care to mentor and support Nexus participants, but teachers were themselves stressed and overwhelmed. Our developing relationship with BGCS enabled us to call on Banksia Gardens to support Nexus students in their learning as future teachers. Nexus participants eagerly accepted offers from BGCS to (1) provide them with professional development trialing a new professional development package on disengagement; (2) engage in ongoing conversations with staff from BGCS about the needs of their students; and (3) develop opportunities for them to volunteer or participate in Project REAL, where they would meet young people outside of formal schooling. We are planning at least one panel where young people, families, and community members will talk to Nexus participants. This is an opportunity rarely offered in Initial Teacher Education. As our relationship deepens, and as things "normalize" post-COVID, our partnership will find new opportunities. We believe this is how community engagement within teacher education emerges: in small and genuine ways as trust develops.

CONCLUSION

Despite the relative prosperity enjoyed by many people in Australia prior to COVID-19, the country faces an ever-growing crisis involving deep and persistent levels of poverty and exclusion. Our education system has a critical role to play because schools are the first place where this disparity becomes manifest. It is therefore one of the first sites of potential intervention. The success of programs for vulnerable young people is, as Smyth and colleagues (2013, p. 316) write, "highly contingent on teachers engaging with the social and emotional lives of young people, in building a climate of trust, re-igniting young people's aspirations, creating opportunities for social learning, and developing supportive networks." In many historically marginalized communities, levels of school disengagement continue to be unacceptably high, despite the best intentions of principals and teachers, who often find themselves overwhelmed by the practical problems that persistent exclusion causes (behavioral incidents, low staff morale, high turnover, etc.). Numerous education policies reinforce community engagement as a gap in educational policy and practice (Gonski et al., 2018). The result of this is that all too often, schools struggle to understand community funds of knowledge (González et al., 2005) and respond to the circumstances of an individual student as if they were isolated from the rest of the community, and their responses often fail to take into consideration impacts on the student and their community (e.g., suspensions, expulsions), thereby potentially perpetuating the cycle of systemic disadvantage. Teachers must be reconnected to the lived social realities of students and their families.

This chapter documents the process of the "coming together" of a community organization, schools, and a teacher education program in the realization that the problem as described is much bigger than one single institution. It requires a whole-of-community response. Transforming complex and persistent historical and systemic disadvantage requires us to form strong, respectful, and constructive relationships holistically, not only with our students but with their families and communities as well.

REFERENCES

Australian Bureau of Statistics. (2016). *Socio-economic indexes for areas*. https://www.abs.gov.au/websitedbs/censushome.nsf/home/seifa

Australian Human Rights Commission (2020). *Education*. https://www.human rights.gov.au/education

Australian Productivity Commission. (2020). https://www.pc.gov.au

Australian Research Alliance for Children and Youth (2009). https://www.aracy.org.au

Blaustein, M., & Kinniburgh, K. M. (2010). *Treating traumatic stress in children and adolescents how to foster resilience through attachment, self-regulation, and competency*. Guilford Press.

Bowen, M. (1974). Alcoholism as viewed through family systems theory and family psychotherapy. *Annals of the New York Academy of Sciences*, *233*(1), 115–122.

Boylan, M., & Woolsey, I. (2015). Teacher education for social justice: Mapping identity spaces. *Teaching and Teacher Education*, *46*, 62–71.

Brunzell, T., Stokes, H., & Waters, L. (2016). Trauma-informed positive education: Using positive psychology to strengthen vulnerable students. *Contemporary School Psychology*, *20*(1), 63–83.

Clark, P., Zygmunt, E., & Howard, T. (2016). Why race and culture matter in schools, and why we need to get this right: A conversation with Dr. Tyrone Howard. *The Teacher Educator*, *51*(4), 268–276.

Commissioner for Children and Young People. (2020). *The poverty project*. https://www.ccyp.com.au/poverty-project

Davidson, P., Saunders, P., Bradbury, B., & Wong, M. (2018). *Poverty in Australia, 2018*. Australian Council of Social Service Poverty and Inequality Partnership Report No. 2, Australian Council of Social Service.

Delgado, D., & Villalpando, O. (2002). An apartheid of knowledge in academia: The struggle over the "legitimate" knowledge of faculty of color. *Equity and Excellence in Education*, *35*(2), 169–180.

Freire, P. (1996). *Pedagogy of the oppressed* (rev. ed.). Continuum.

Gale, T., Mills, C. & Cross, R. (2017). Socially inclusive teaching: Belief, design, action and pedagogic work. *Journal of Teacher Education*, *68*(3), 345–356.

Gillan, K., Mellor, S., & Krakouer, J. (2017). The case for urgency: Advocating an Indigenous voice in education. *Australian Education Review*, *62*. https://research.acer.edu.au/cgi/viewcontent.cgi?article=1027&context=aer

Gonski, D., Arcus, T., Boston, K., Gould, V., Johnson, W., O'Brien, L., Perry, L., & Roberts, M. (March 2018). *Through growth to achievement through growth to achievement*. Commonwealth of Australia.

González, N., Moll, L. C., & Amanti, C. (2005). *Funds of knowledge theorizing practice in households, communities, and classrooms*. Lawrence Erlbaum Associates.

Goss, P., Sonnemann, J., & Griffiths, K. (2017). *Engaging students: Creating class-rooms that improve learning*. Grattan Institute.

Greene, M. (1992). The passions of pluralism: Multiculturalism and the expanding community. *The Journal of Negro Education, 22*(1), 250–261.

Howard, T. C., & Rodriguez-Scheel, A. (2016). Difficult dialogues about race and poverty in teacher preparation. In J. Lampert & B. Burnett (Eds.), *Teacher education for high poverty schools* (pp. 53–72). Springer.

Lampert, J., Ball, A., Garcia-Carrion, R., & Burnett, B. (2019). Poverty and schooling: Three cases from Australia, the United States, and Spain. *Asia-Pacific Journal of Teacher Education: Schooling and Poverty: Re-Thinking Impact, Research and Social Justice, 48*(1), 60–78.

Lampert, J., & Burnett, B. (Eds.). (2016). *Teacher education for high poverty schools*. Springer.

Lee, R. E. (2018). Breaking down barriers and building bridges: Transformative practices in community- and school-based urban teacher preparation. *Journal of Teacher Education, 69*(2), 118–126.

Lee, R., Showalter, B., & Eckrich, L. (2013). Beyond the ivory tower: The role of contextually based course redesign in a community-embedded urban teacher preparation model. In J. Noel (Ed.), *Moving teacher education into urban schools and communities* (pp. 56–72). Routledge.

Lees, A. (2016). Roles of urban Indigenous community members in collaborative field-based teacher preparation. *Journal of Teacher Education, 67*(5), 363–378.

McLachlan, R., Gilfillan, G., & Gordon, J. (2013). *Deep and persistent disadvantage in Australia*(Productivity Commission Staff Working Paper). Productivity Commission. https://www.pc.gov.au/research/supporting/deep-persistent-disadvantage/deep-persistent-disadvantage.pdf

Mitchell Institute. (2016). *Socio-economic disadvantage and educational opportunity persistently linked*. http://www.mitchellinstitute.org.au/fact-sheets/socio-economic-disadvantage-and-educational-opportunity-persistently-linked

Moll, L. (2015). Tapping into the "hidden" home and community resources of students. *Kappa Delta Pi Record, 51*(3), 114–117.

Moll, L., Amanti, C., Neff, D., & González, N. (1992). Funds of knowledge for teaching: Using a qualitative approach to connect homes and classrooms. *Theory into Practice, 31*(2), 132–141.

Murrell, P. C., Jr. (2007). *Race, culture, and schooling: Identities of achievement in multi- cultural urban schools*. Routledge.

Oberle, E., & Schonert-Reichl, K. (2016). Stress contagion in the classroom? The link between classroom teacher burnout and morning cortisol in elementary school students. *Social Science and Medicine, 159*, 30.

Organisation for Economic Co-operation and Development (OECD). (2008). *Growing unequal? Income distribution and poverty in OECD countries*. https://www.oecd.org

Organisation for Economic Co-operation and Development (OECD). (2017). *Promising practices in supporting success for indigenous students*. OECD Publishing.

Shim, J. M. (2012). Pierre Bourdieu and intercultural education: It is not just about lack of knowledge about others. *Intercultural Education*, 23(3), 209–220.

Sleeter, C. (2017). Critical race theory and the whiteness of teacher education. *Urban Education*, 52(2), 155–169.

Smyth, J., McInerney, P., & Fish, T. (2013). Blurring the boundaries: From relational learning towards a critical pedagogy of engagement for disengaged disadvantaged young people. *Pedagogy, Culture & Society*, 21(2), 299–320.

Strahley, L., & D'Arpino, T. (2016). Reframing teacher education for democratic engagement. *New Directions for Community Colleges*, 173, 77–82.

Victoria Department of Education and Training. (2020). *Framework for improving student outcomes*. https://www.education.vic.gov.au/school/teachers/management/improvement/Pages/FISO.aspx

Yosso, T. J. (2005). Whose culture has capital? A critical race theory discussion of community cultural wealth. *Race Ethnicity and Education*, 8(1), 69–91.

Zeichner, K., Bowman, M., Guillen, L., & Napolitan, K. (2016). Engaging and working in solidarity with local communities in preparing the teachers of their children *Journal of Teacher Education*, 67(4), 277–290.

Zeichner, K., Payne, K. A., & Brayko, K. (2015). Democratizing teacher education. *Journal of Teacher Education*, 66(2), 122–135.

Zygmunt, E., & Clark, P. (2016). *Transforming teacher education for social justice*. Teachers College Press.

Zyngier, D. (2017). How experiential learning in an informal setting promotes class equity and social and economic justice for children from "communities at promise": An Australian perspective. *International Review of Education*, 63(1), 9–28.

CHAPTER 6

The Community as Textbook

Preparing Community-Engaged Teachers

Heather K. Olson Beal, Lauren E. Burrow,
Linda Autrey, Crystal Hicks, and Amber Teal[1]

In 2015, Ken Zeichner called for the examination of an unconventional, alternative form of teacher preparation that would highlight the "potential of community-based learning in educating teachers" (p. 119). Zeichner's challenge echoes the concept of "funds of knowledge" (Moll et al., 1992), which urges teachers to seek out and value families as "first teachers" who have significant home-based contributions to their children's early and ongoing learning experiences. Co-envisioned, co-designed, and co-taught by the chapter's authors, the Community Responsiveness and Engaged Advocacy in Teacher Education (CREATE) teacher preparation program track endeavors to put into practice the calls to action of Zeichner and Moll and colleagues through conversations about critical content in courses, family mentorships, sustained engagement at community events, and service-learning work with local organizations in order to CREATE teachers who have the knowledge, skills, and dispositions needed to be the types of culturally responsive educators that students of color and other underrepresented student populations deserve.

Though the program is in only its 2nd year, we can already see that it provides the time, space, motivation, and foundation necessary for teacher candidates to pursue community-engaged opportunities that can lead to transformative thinking, which in turn can give confidence for better practices. In this chapter, we provide the contextual information necessary to understand our setting, briefly describe the components of the program, and then focus on the program's curriculum or, as we like to say, the ways in which our program uses the community as our textbook.

---

1. The research work described in this chapter was made possible, in part, with funding from the Margaret Hoover Perkins Research grant at Stephen F. Austin State University.

LOCAL CONTEXT

CREATE is one track in a traditional teacher preparation program in the Perkins College of Education at Stephen F. Austin State University (SFASU), a large comprehensive university in a rural county in East Texas. The county has a population of approximately 65,000 that covers almost 1,000 square miles. The city is considered a rural area based on its population (approximately 34,000) and due to its isolation from major metropolitan areas. Within the county, there are nine independent school districts with student enrollments ranging from 150 students to 6,200 students. CREATE partners with the Nacogdoches Independent School District (NISD), the largest school district in the county and the one in closest proximity to the university.

NISD has an increasingly diverse student population that mirrors demographic trends across the state of Texas: 48% Hispanic, 30% African American, 19% White. NISD has a significantly higher economically disadvantaged student population than the state (48%), with 80% of the overall student population considered economically disadvantaged. NISD also has an English language learner population (28.5%) that is significantly higher than the state average (17.2%) and the national average (9.6%).

NISD continues to struggle with administrative turnover and low state accountability ratings. Teacher turnover in the district, due to resignations, retirements, and terminations, hovers at approximately 25%. NISD has had four superintendents in the last 11 years and is currently undergoing a search for a fifth. The district's overall rating is a C. The elementary campus and the middle school campus with which we have partnered for CREATE received ratings of C and B, respectively. Three of the six elementary school campuses have spent the last few years mired in what is known as "IR Status" (Improvement Required), which adds to low morale, teacher turnover, and flight from the district.

We share relevant district- and campus-level data with our CREATE candidates because we believe it is important that they are knowledgeable in terms of the community context in which they are teaching. We also critically examine the structures and conditions that produce those statistics, always taking care to also highlight the assets and accomplishments of the students and educators in NISD.

PROGRAM COMPONENTS

CREATE is a unique program track, undertaken by self-selected, preservice, clinical teacher candidates in their senior year that complements and deepens the existing teacher preparation experiences. After the pilot year of the program track, we have continued to push the start of the program earlier into candidates' degree plans. For example, cohort III will begin coursework in the program starting their junior year, while cohort II began in the senior year. It is our intent to build capacity for the program to encompass all four semesters of a student's teacher preparation experience.

The void of culturally responsive teaching that CREATE was designed to address was in direct response to both an anecdotal and formally documented lack of knowledge and skills in our university's preservice teachers in the areas of family-school partnerships and diversity,[2] a deficit that can prevent them from ensuring students' access to an equitable education. To that end, a brief description of the program components is in order.

First, in addition to traditional clinical experiences in local public schools, CREATE candidates engage in several other types of community-engaged clinical practice. CREATE candidates participate in sustained and intentional service-learning work with two local organizations: the Judy B. McDonald Public Library, the sole servicer for the entire county, and C & R Kutt Bottle, a nonprofit corporation founded by an environmentally conscious, local church congregation that recycles glass for the city and creates upcycled art that they sell at local markets to fund the municipal recycling. CREATE candidates also meet bimonthly with mentor families (i.e., local families with one or more school-aged children) who help connect them to local events and organizations, familiarize them with the realities of home-school partnerships and communications, and act as additional teachers and experts. In addition, CREATE candidates routinely attend local community events and meetings in order to learn about the community in which they are teaching. This includes events such as holiday festivities, after-school programs, parent engagement and educational workshops, and school board meetings.

A second unique aspect of the CREATE program is that Early Childhood–Grade 6, Early Childhood–Grade 12, and Grade 7–12 certification candidates are co-enrolled in two courses (i.e., 6 credit hours) with content overlap from a total of four courses (two from the secondary certificate-seeking degree plan and two from the elementary certificate-seeking degree plan). The courses are co-taught by the first two

---

2. Evidence for the need to improve SFASU preservice teachers' understanding of student diversity and knowledge about how to plan learning experiences and design assessments that are responsive to differences among students and that promote all students' learning comes, in part, from our candidates' scores during the past 4 years on the TExES Pedagogy and Professional Responsibilities (PPR) test, one of the statewide exams used to certify public school teachers in Texas.

authors of this chapter. Lauren is an associate professor of elementary education, and Heather is a professor of secondary education. In the traditional educator preparation programs at our university and throughout Texas, elementary and secondary education candidates infrequently take courses together. One of our courses meets during the day, which facilitates traditional school-based interactions, and one of the courses meets in the evening, which facilitates community- and family-engaged interactions. We also sometimes hold class sessions in community spaces, such as a local bookstore, the municipal public library, and locally owned ethnic restaurants.

Third, the CREATE curriculum is possibly the most unique part of the program. Whereas traditional teacher preparation courses might be organized around a textbook-based curriculum or even around articles and learning activities selected by the course professor, we strive to make the CREATE curriculum responsive to our particular local context, to invite community leaders into our learning spaces as additional teachers, and—perhaps most importantly—to take ourselves and our candidates out into the community. To that end, CREATE candidates read a creative writing anthology featuring local youth who have participated in Barrio Writers, a free writing program that we facilitate every summer for youth from underrepresented populations. CREATE candidates also participate in professional development opportunities offered by local nonprofit organizations and NISD and in a wide range of events and activities offered by the public library. Last, the CREATE community relies on local residents acting as "third teachers" with authentic knowledge of our local context. These third teachers include school district social workers, principals, teachers, and parent–community liaisons; mentor family parents and children; school board members; and local attorneys, law enforcement officers, librarians, and pastors. The remainder of the chapter focuses on the unique way these third teachers from our community become the program's most authentic and effective "living" textbook. We will begin with the public library, whose reciprocal partnership is the backbone of the program.

EMBARKING ON A RADICAL COLLABORATION WITH THE LOCAL PUBLIC LIBRARY

We began the first semester of the program having done a lot of thinking and a lot of planning, but admittedly mostly relied on mutual trust in one another as colleagues and a heavy dose of tolerance for ambiguity and flexibility. We asked our candidates and community partners to similarly trust us as we all endeavored to go on this new journey together. In one of our first evening courses, we invited our local librarian to come to our class to talk about opportunities for our candidates to volunteer at library events and to share the kinds of activities the library offers to community members. Although we gave Crystal Hicks, assistant director of the library, an approximate amount of time to spend talking with our candidates, we did not give her much more information than that. We had worked with Crystal previously and valued her professional expertise enough to invite her and trust her to decide what to share with our candidates. In addition, we were admittedly swamped with the logistics of starting the new program and were content to leave it in Crystal's capable hands. Crystal opened her presentation with a slideshow titled "Radical Collaboration," which taught our candidates about her philosophy as a community librarian. In that moment, we looked at each other in dumbfounded amazement that what she was sharing was so closely aligned with the goals of our just-beginning program—we knew we were on the right track with this emerging partnership.

The reciprocity of learning that flowed back and forth between our program track and the library was most readily evident throughout the elementary education candidates' many writing methods course assignments that were directly connected to the library's month-long "NEA Big Read Nacogdoches," a community-wide reading program made possible by their NEA Big Read grant award in 2018. The focus was on *Station Eleven* by Emily St. John Mandel (2014), with free copies of the book made available at the library and a wide variety of activities connected to the book's plot, themes, and settings. CREATE candidates each received a copy of the book during one of their first visits to the library and were expected to complete their reading of the text in time to complete both required course assignments and to participate in a choice of book-based activities sponsored throughout the city. The shared common reading and multitude of corresponding activities offered as part of the Big Read made the job of teaching writing methods to the CREATE elementary education candidates a much easier, more enjoyable, more effective task, as candidates were able to take their learning "off the page" as they freely jumped back and forth between community activities and course assignments.

The candidates were expected to develop their skills as future writing teachers by practicing the skills of writers themselves. They completed both traditional writing assignments, such as an analytical essay responding to the themes of the common reading, and a less traditional mixed-media literacy assignment known as a "novel response" in which they shared their understanding of and personal connections to *Station*

Eleven through creative expression. Each student was required to submit their "novel response" for consideration in the citywide competition hosted at a local art museum.

Attendance at the museum-based reception for the "novel responses" was one of many Big Read events the CREATE candidates enjoyed attending. Other events included conventional book discussions, demonstrations, a cooking class, film screenings, and parties. All candidates enrolled in the CREATE program were invited to participate in a book-themed escape room on a Friday night at the library; this outing served as the first of many casual get-togethers included to build a cohort of candidates, professors, and community members who could simultaneously be learners-teachers-colleagues and compatriots during this critical time of discovery and growth within the program.

A desired outcome of placing candidates in these community spaces as both volunteers and participants was that they would bear witness to the time, energy, and partnership needed to serve families at community-engaged learning events while also accepting that there are experts within our local community who hold knowledge and skills outside the traditional university campus classrooms. Seeing the fluidity with which community members could become teachers at a "How-To" festival one week and then take on the role of learner at a cooking demonstration the next week helped our candidates redefine the value of multiple forms of knowledge. Many of the CREATE candidates were often disappointed by the low attendance at these marvelously crafted, well-planned activities: "If we hadn't shown up, there wouldn't have been anyone there at all," one student remarked after a particularly fun evening activity. Referring back to critical discussions in class around "reasonable expectations" and "realities" when inviting parents/guardians to attend after-school events, we were proud of the candidates for realizing there was no "blame" to assign to tired parents who just could not rally to attend the activity that had been crafted with them in mind; nor was there "fault" in the library staff, who had done their due diligence marketing the event and maintaining a reputation for solid, delightful programming. Instead, many of the candidates recognized that true home-school-community relationships take time, will ebb and flow like "seasons," but must be consistently pursued with passion and patience. They learned to thank the families who could come, when they came, and to bear no ill will toward those who chose not to come or could not attend, but to continue to reach out and co-construct in response to the preferences and needs of those with whom they were seeking to partner.

In the following section, Crystal Hicks, assistant library director, shares her understandings of "radical collaboration" and her experiences as a CREATE community partner.

Radical Collaboration[3]

Collaboration is an oft-overused term with a variety of meanings and levels of activity or interconnectedness. My definition functions as both a deeper and more profound concept of participation and a narrowing of intention. Essentially, I want to drill down to the most important and impactful aspects of professional collaboration as I see it, in part breaking down the separation between professional and personal. I find the ethical, moral, and political implications of my daily work to be inseparable, in many ways, from my personal beliefs. As a public librarian, my job is to serve both patrons and partners alike. I see my role as a complex one with a simple basis. I connect people with what they need. Sometimes they know what that is, but many times they do not. Sometimes it's easy to help, and other times it is impossible. And the best, the only, way that I can be successful at that is to practice what I see as radical collaboration. It means that I say "yes" first, without always knowing if I will benefit from the interaction and sometimes knowing that I will not. It means valuing openness, without fear of failure or wasting time. It's not a "Pollyanna" belief that everything will come up sunshine and roses, but that there is value in the willingness to try and that so-called failures yield important truths. I aim to ensure representation and access to information and resources for everyone. Rather than a neutral position, that is an increasingly political one inextricably tied to what I think it means to be a person in the world.

I define radical collaboration as seeking out and embracing ideas, input, and creative energy from others, regardless of their field, while offering the same in return with no expectations. I believe that this lack of expectation is what elevates our daily work to the radical. When I began practicing this notion and reaching outside my comfort zone, success was not immediate, and the success I had was not grand. However, the feedback I heard from the few gave me hope for how to reach the many. The CREATE program has been an inspiring and encouraging example of how this practice can be shared and amplified.

In the 3 years of our Big Read program, our attendance has doubled, and our year-round programs routinely fill up and overflow into waiting lists. I believe that is not because we are offering perfect experiences, but because people feel heard and seen and appreciated. They see library staff at events all over town of all shapes and sizes, testimony to the notion that we must reach our patrons where they are. Radical collaboration is about

---

3. Crystal's definition of radical collaboration was inspired by the concept articulated by Tamm & Luyet (2010) in *Radical Collaboration: Five Essential Skills to Overcome Defensiveness and Build Successful Relationships*.

warm appreciation, curious inquiry, genuine interest, and an earnest desire to connect or contribute in whatever small way we can, because we know it has meaning and value, whether those who benefit can or will articulate that. We know it because it is the right thing, and we serve our community by getting to know them. We best help our partners when we understand their motivations and concerns, and we do that by not placing limitations on what we can or cannot do.

I know the caveats to this mindset very well. I hope it goes without saying that I am not proposing a self-effacing, impossible approach. I am not calling for martyrdom to the cause. In the simplest of terms, I'm saying "no" to shallow networking and partnering by merely showing up and exchanging favors. I propose to seek deeper connections that can come about only if we don't have preconceived ideas about what we will encounter or receive in return.

CREATE students participated in nearly every event of our Big Read, both as volunteers and as attendees. We can attribute a considerable element of our growth to not only their participation, but their enthusiastic promotion of our programs to their peers and families. Students are often marooned on campus, and many rarely venture out into the surrounding community in a meaningful way. While it may be merely anecdotal, our program attendance in the college age bracket has increased significantly, in part because our close interaction with the CREATE teacher candidates helped us better understand and connect to their demographic.

Libraries are *third spaces*[4] outside of home and work or school, and such places are at once extremely important and increasingly diminishing. These are the spaces where we meet new people, stretch, learn, challenge old notions, and generally enrich our lives. This is accomplished when the third space is a safe space in which we can build confidence and knowledge through collective input, whether directly or indirectly. It is not uncommon for me to discover that patrons with whom I've never interacted are some of the most avid supporters and vocal advocates for the library. I attribute this to the unique status a library may enjoy, that it can (and should) be many things for anyone. It can be used in an infinite number of ways, but most successfully only if the needs of the community are considered and actively addressed.

For us, the library partnership is an invaluable teaching and learning space that highlights community expertise and consistently provides a

---

4. Crystal's characterization of the library as a "third space" is born from an idea from Oldenburg (1989), which asserts that a person needs three different and important places: home, work, and a third undefined place.

wide range of informal and formal opportunities to get candidates off campus and into the community for fun, fellowship, and funds of knowledge-in-action. The library is also a community space in which teaching, learning, and community interaction take place *outside* of school settings, which is an important component of the CREATE program track, and which we believe is essential for our candidates to experience as part of their growing appreciation for the role of teachers in the community and the potential for community in the classrooms. Teacher education programs can and do tell our candidates that community and family engagement are important; our library partnership enables them to actually participate and even facilitate community and family engagement outside of school settings.

CREATE MENTOR FAMILIES

One of the most valuable and unique components of the CREATE program is our committed mentor families who serve as second teachers in community spaces. CREATE candidates are paired together (typically one elementary-level and one secondary-level certification student) with a local family with one or more children who attend NISD. We originally started out by asking the principals of our two partner campuses to recommend families they thought might be interested in volunteering as mentor families. When that effort resulted in no recommendations, we began asking personal contacts and friends of friends. Through the initial mentor family selection process, it became clear to us that what we were asking of would-be strangers was a really big request—especially considering that we (Heather and Lauren) were two White women making the request of historically marginalized and underrepresented populations, who, rightfully, might be reluctant to jump into such an unknown space.

However, we managed to find eight willing families the 1st year to embark on this experiment with us and with our candidates. Among the eight mentor families the 1st year were four White families, one Latinx family, two African American families, and one Asian American family. By default, the mothers were our primary point of contact; they were the ones who volunteered or whom we knew, more than the fathers. Between the eight families, there were a total of 19 children.

So, what were our selection criteria when selecting mentor families? First, they had to be families with early childhood–grade 12 children who attended a school campus at our partner school district. Second, we strove to find families representative of racialized, ethnic, and linguistic identities counter to our primarily White, non-Hispanic, monolingual

English-speaking students. Additionally, we sought families who could provide perspectives and experiences different from the teacher candidates' primary instructors. Both of us are White, upper middle class, raised in Christian families, with male spouses and terminal degrees in education. Lastly, we needed families willing to let two or three university teacher candidates into their family's life.

We asked families and candidates to meet twice a month in a mutually agreed-on space in the community. We emphasized to families that they need not do anything special with or for the candidates—they should simply go about their lives while inviting the candidates along. For safety reasons and to model best practices should candidates want to do home visits once they become full-fledged teachers, we required both of our candidates to be present at any gathering. The following is a list of some of the activities in which the mentor families and our candidates have participated together: church services, a quinceañera and family birthday parties, grocery shopping, going out for pizza, dinner at the family's home, playing board games with the family, library events, therapy appointments (in the case of the family with sons with autism), Cub Scout and Girl Scout meetings, watching the mentor family's kids' soccer and volleyball games, and taking walks in community parks.

After the 1st year, we asked the mentor families to decide whether they wanted to sign up for a second cohort of candidates. The 2nd year, we had seven mentor families—six of whom were 1st-year families signing on for another semester. The one new participant was a single African American mother of two children. When asked, in open-ended survey questions, why they wanted to be a mentor family, the following were some of their responses about the mentor family experience:

> "I love to have, and give, the opportunity to learn more about other people and their lifestyles/cultures."

> "I'm excited to give someone the opportunity to learn about me and my family, my parenting techniques, and the challenges my kids face at school and how that affects home life."

> "I thought it was a good opportunity to connect to SFA as a community member and felt that the program can help create better teachers for NISD and other communities."

> "I was asked to help, and we are very involved with the community"

> "I want to help!!!"

"It was such a great experience last year. I couldn't imagine not doing it this year."

"Made a lifetime friend doing it."

"I loved the connection to teachers in training whether it was sharing our lives or answering their questions."

When we asked them what they hoped to gain from serving as a mentor family, one mother said, "An understanding of other people's lifestyles as well as to share some insight about my community and parenting and lifestyle."

From our standpoint as teacher educators preparing our candidates for future classrooms of their own, it has been invaluable to have additional teachers both to echo perspectives we share in class *and* to question or add an alternate viewpoint. One day in a lesson on classroom management, we had a conversation about good (and poor) strategies to promote positive student behavior. The conversation was mostly theoretical, with some anecdotes from us regarding experiences we have had with our own children and their school experiences. That night, one pair of candidates met with their mentor family. They were able to witness what happened when the young daughter opened her backpack and took out a behavior chart and showed it to her mother. The candidates were able to participate in the ensuing conversation. It was a very authentic and immediate conversation made possible only by the relationship with the mentor family. Candidates have also returned to class after meet-ups with their mentor family to talk to us about how a family experienced an assessment practice we had talked about in class.

Other times, the lessons from our mentor families have been more intentional and made available to our entire cohort for the explicit purpose of gaining access to parent perspectives on the typical teacher preparation topics we cover in their degree program. For example, we have formally convened panels of mentor family groups (parents and their children) to share their thoughts on homework, home visits, and best practices in school–home communications. These panels give our CREATE candidates unprecedented access to ask for guidance and clarification regarding the practices and policies they are being taught and witnessing in their school-based field experiences. Learning to seek parent/guardian input on classroom policies is one way we encourage a power shift from teacher "knowing all" to teacher seeking families' expertise.

Some of our mentor families are able to provide an authority and authenticity that we, as White professors, lack. When we tackle the social injustice topics about which we care deeply, but from which we are mostly protected due to our White privilege, we appreciate how our community partners can step in as experts to share their firsthand experiences, thereby enriching our conversations. For example, when discussing the reality that White teachers, for the safety and success of their Black and Brown students, urgently need to critically examine and address the biases they bring into the classroom, the feelings of "guilt" and "protest" among our majority-White candidates were quickly subdued when we shared a poem written by Amber Teal, one of the Black mothers in our mentor family cohort:

Talk with My Son

Good morning and welcome to our talk son
'Cause In this country the fate of your life was determined before it begun.
No son, you can't play outside with fake guns
'Cause Police are out here shooting Black women's sons
No son, you can't walk around with your hood on
'Cause I don't need you lying bleeding on someone else's lawn
No son, you can't buy Skittles and Arizona Tea
'Cause every night you need to make it home safely to me
No son, you can't sell CDs
'Cause I don't wanna see a video of you yelling #icantbreathe
No son, you can't sell cigarettes
'Cause some random person may feel that you're a threat
No son, you can't sit at Starbucks waiting for friends
'Cause you'll end up in handcuffs before your visit ends
No son, you can't hold a phone in grandma's yard
'Cause the police may get a call that a Black man is breaking into cars
No son, you can't have a gun and permit to carry
'Cause you could get shot beside the person you're wishing to marry
No son, you can't question the rules they demand we abide
'Cause then you'll end up dead in jail and they'll say it was suicide.
No son, you can't ask for directions after missing the bus
'Cause you're "one of those people" and to some that's enough
No son, you can't fight at school
'Cause that write-up will put you in the prison pool
Yes son, your pants will not sag
'Cause if you do you'll be labeled a thug and become a hashtag
Yes son, you will say yes sir and yes ma'am
'Cause I don't want to see an altercation through a body cam
Yes son, you will always walk with your hands out of your pockets

'Cause I will not see your name on the county court dockets
Yes son, you will work hard and always do your best
'Cause where you grew up doesn't matter, the east or the west
Yes son, of you I have high expectations
'Cause you were born with odds against you 'cause you're not Caucasian
Yes son, you will love who you are
'Cause I'm teaching you to strive and in life you will go far
Yes son, I agree 100% that life isn't fair
'Cause of your melanin and the texture of your brown hair
Yes son, to you I will do all I can to protect
'Cause being born a Black boy you were born a suspect
Yes son, I will hug you and teach you right
'Cause all I want is to be able to tuck you in every night.
My son, don't let being Black be your excuse to not succeed
'Cause I want you to prove the statistics wrong and always sow good
seeds.
My son, know I'll have your back 'til your last breath son
'Cause you're my only Black son and I love you to death son.

Though the experiences and the depth and quality of the relationships vary as much as the families and the preservice teachers involved in these experiences, the impact of our candidates' interactions with their mentor families is undeniable. With their mentor families as guides, our preservice teachers get to see, in an authentic way, what their mentor family's life is like outside of school—something they would not get to experience in a traditional teacher preparation program. They get to practice communicating with actual families. They get to experience—before becoming a teacher—what it feels like to have plans fall through and to have to recalibrate the reasons why families engage (or cannot / choose not to engage) in school events and activities both during and after the traditional school day. They get to know the community—the places, spaces, neighborhoods, stores, restaurants, organizations, and social events—in which they are completing traditional school-based clinical experiences *with* real people who actually live in the community. The mentor family experience is critical to their preparation as teachers and is one without which—having now done it with two student cohorts—we cannot imagine sending them into the teaching field.

EXCERPTS FROM OUR "LIVING TEXTBOOKS"

To continue to work toward shifting the traditional power structure of who is considered authoritative, even in this chapter, we share narratives written by two of our mentor family mothers. The first, Amber Teal, is a Black single mother of two children who attend our local public schools. Amber is a first-time mentor family partner. The second is Linda Autrey, a Korean American mother of two, who also works in our partner school district and is a returning mentor family partner. Linda's husband is the principal of one of our partner school campuses. Our lived experience with the candidates and with the mentor families, along with qualitative data we have collected from our candidates, suggests that the mentor family component of the program is fulfilling its desired objective, which is to call our candidates' attention to and acceptance of the validity of the funds of knowledge that live, work, and parent in our local town.

Being a CREATE mentor family (Amber)

I chose to be a CREATE mentor family because I am heavily involved in my children's education and am fully aware of the injustices within the educational system. This was a way for me to help "CREATE" more aware and diversely educated teachers. I am a single mother of two children: Xavior is 11, and Iyana 7.

Growing up, the only Black teachers I had were at Head Start in the 6th grade, so for the most part my teachers could not relate to a lot of my daily struggles as a Black student. This experience has allowed me to shed light on some hot topics for my family, such as retention, the fight for services (504 and Special Education), conduct versus normal human behavior, appropriate punishments, and systemic racism within the schools.

My family, myself and my two children, were able to extend our family +3. My daughter and son refer to our CREATE candidates as "the ladies." Iyana refers to one of them as her "twin." This came about after one of our first family meet-ups at CiCi's, where Iyana and her "twin" realized they wear the same shoe size. This happened as they raced barefoot and turned cartwheels outside the restaurant. *facepalm*

This experience has allowed me to share my family experiences, struggles, and love with not only my new three "daughters," but the entire cohort. We will forever keep in touch with our CREATE candidates, and have an ornament that they made to hang on our Christmas tree in remembrance of the fun times we had together: CiCi's (where we played the Cups song with our cups and discussed microaggressions), bowling (where we all sang every song that came on), painting at Xavior's and Iyana's birthday party (where they met our extended family and friends), SFASU basketball games (where Iyana and her twin danced to get featured on the Jumbotron), and

Iyana's softball practice (where we learned who was athletic and who had no idea how to put a glove on). I have truly enjoyed this opportunity and would do it again and again and again. Hopefully, the candidates take what they learned and go out and impact the educational system, wherever they choose to go, in a major way.

Being a CREATE mentor family (Linda)

I spoke with my family about volunteering for this when we heard mentor families were needed. They all wanted to do it. My children are pretty sociable, so this was something new and exciting for them. My husband and I are both long-time educators in public schools and wanted to volunteer because we work with many new teachers in our school district. We hear over and over about the many things they wished they'd learned prior to entering their own classrooms full time. I thought that, as a family in our community and as public school educators, we had a unique perspective to offer the teacher candidates we would mentor. We have one child in our local public school and one in pre-K. The 1st year we volunteered, our daughter was in elementary school. This is our 2nd year, and our CREATE preservice teachers have gotten to see her through her transition to middle school.

I've found our CREATE candidates to be particularly inquisitive about so many things, and our relationship begins revolving around our family activities. They've gotten to meet us out for dinner and rush to after-school activities like Girl Scouts or martial arts classes. The four we've had have all remarked on how hectic it seems to be to work all day and then run kids to activities. It's helpful for them to see how little weekday evening time most children have and think about the impact that extensive projects and homework have on a child's home life.

Eventually, our relationships have evolved to mentoring our CREATE candidates professionally and discussing their philosophies of education and how they see themselves as educators. We've spoken with ours about everything from how to interview, what education trends mean, what teacher advocacy looks like in politics, to planning for retirement. This runs parallel with our personal relationships with our CREATE candidates. This year, they've really become a part of the family. They come over for dinner and participated in birthday parties for our children. Our children have become attached to them and really look forward to seeing them more regularly. The flip side of it all is that my children see a side of teachers that they may not have seen before, even though they've grown up in this industry. In working with this second group of candidates, we have learned to become even more comfortable sharing our lives and perspectives with them so that the relationships we've developed with [our candidates] have extended beyond the semester of their CREATE class.

The potential impact of this class is limitless. It helps build better, more empathetic, more well-prepared and well-rounded 1st-year teachers by allowing them to extend their initial practice beyond the four walls of a classroom and get a glimpse into the lives of the families in their communities. For a small, rural district like ours that is remote from major metropolitan areas, I think it helps with recruitment and perhaps even retention. Candidates begin their careers as teachers having developed important relationships within the community that surpass the limitations of education theory and the more traditional or "canned" experiences they might get as a preservice teacher. We have learned just as much from our CREATE candidates as I hope they have learned from us. This really is one of my favorite things I've gotten involved with since moving here nearly 3 years ago.

CIVIC ENGAGEMENT

A final way in which we try to use the community as our textbook is by creating a course structure that is open and flexible enough to both antic-ipate and react to community events and issues. For instance, our first co-hort of candidates started the program in fall 2018, when the country was gearing up for midterm elections. Though we did not plan for this, it be-came clear early on that voting needed to be foregrounded in our course. So many of our candidates were woefully unaware of the importance of, power in, and even logistics surrounding voting. Our candidates had ei-ther never engaged in this civic activity and/or did not understand their re-sponsibility to commit to voting as a means of advocating for themselves, their students, their profession, and their communities.

During our first cohort semester, Texas was awash in Beto (O'Rourke)-mania as he cruised around Texas, live-streaming campaign stops, hair-cuts, and even stops at the laundromat to wash laundry. Our curriculum had to be flexible enough to respond to the candidates' written request (because many of them were in a writing class and were seizing an au-thentic opportunity to demonstrate that they could effectively utilize per-suasive writing) that we go on a class field trip to attend a Beto O'Rourke rally in an adjacent town. Candidates were given the choice to join the class at the rally or to attend a local event held for incumbent Senator Ted

Cruz (O'Rourke's opponent). None of the candidates had ever attended a campaign event or town hall meeting with a legislator or a candidate. All the candidates but three attended the rally together as a class, which was a valuable collaborative learning experience. At the end of the event, the candidates waited in line to meet Beto and were thrilled when a picture of our class showed up on his social media account, with our university tagged and the caption, "Great group of future educators!" Some of the candidates even made it into some footage of the *Running with Beto* documentary that came out in 2019. Many of our candidates were charmed by Beto's charisma and his social media presence, but most were still either uninformed, disinterested, and either not registered or not planning to vote.

Their piqued political interest turned to understanding and action, however, when we turned the course discussions to a local issue with potential to directly impact our local schools. Our partner school district had proposed a bond that was on the November ballot—their third proposed bond after two previous and recent failures. To prepare our candidates to be able to make educated decisions in the ballot box, we began by informing them of registering processes. We taught them about how the bond money would be used. We encouraged them to attend community meetings sponsored by the school district wherein school board members and the superintendent likewise described how the bond money would be used and took questions from community members. We read local newspaper articles and letters to the editor both for and against the bond proposal. Several candidates attended meetings hosted by a local PAC (political action committee) formed to support the bond. As part of their efforts, the PAC solicited statements from community members in support of the bond and shared them on social media. One of our candidates was so convinced—after our conversations and after spending two semesters doing clinical teaching in our local schools—that we needed to pass the bond that she wrote a letter to the editor of the local paper explaining why the community should pass the bond. The local paper declined to print it because it was submitted after early voting had begun, so she sent it to the PAC, and they shared it on social media. She came to class just thrilled that her letter had been published. Several of our candidates registered to vote in our county just so they could vote in favor of the local school bond (side note: it passed).

A willingness to allow our syllabus to ebb and flow, as guided by our "living textbook," can cause some frustration in our candidates who are used to more traditional, teacher-directed/-decided curriculum. However, despite some pushback, in the end they appreciate the value of a more authentic teacher preparation experience, and most can articulate how our intentional replication of the reality of teaching (i.e., flexibility) provides them an authentic model for the type of culturally responsive teaching we expect them to embrace and enact in their own classrooms.

CONCLUSION

In 2018, the American Association of Colleges for Teacher Education's (AACTE) Community-Engaged Teacher Preparation Topical Action Group (TAG) was created to support those teacher preparation programs committed to "preparing socially just, equity-focused, community teachers with the capacity to enact pedagogies that are culturally relevant, responsive, and sustaining." This TAG echoes AACTE's continued call for teacher education programs to focus on preparing teacher candidates with creative, innovative, and culturally relevant pedagogy so as to provide schools with candidates who are competent and committed to addressing the needs of all students. If candidates are to be prepared for innovative teaching, their teacher preparation programs must be willing to prepare them—innovatively. If candidates are to be ready to effectively and respectfully teach a community of diverse learners, they must get to know those learners within the variety of communities they inhabit—early, often, and with authenticity. Community-engaged teacher preparation programs like CREATE, which partner with their local communities to share in the responsibility of preparing teacher candidates, can provide the authentic environment of knowledge acquisition and community familiarity necessary to transform candidates into engaged and active learners within the communities in which they intend to teach.

The impetus for the design and initial implementation of CREATE was prompted by inspiring examples shared with us during Ball State University's Summer Institute on Community-Engaged Teacher Preparation in 2017. From there, we leaned into our previous knowledge with principles such as Urie Bronfenbrenner's (1979) Ecological Systems Theory to build a program track that prioritized an awareness of *where* our candidates were teaching as a means of guiding *what* and *how* our candidates should be teaching. But what keeps us committed to the continued development and improvement of this program are the lessons we have learned from our "living textbook"—there is an urgent need and responsibility to ensure that our candidates are more aware and accepting of *who* they teach. As education professors, we are critically aware and enthusiastically accept that often the best educators to transmit these urgent educational experiences to our candidates are going to be the spaces, places, and people that make up our local school district and its surrounding communities. CREATE continues forward as a grand experiment that seeks to complement and deepen traditional teacher preparation experiences by asking candidates who seek to teach within our local communities to first be willing to learn within and from those same communities.

REFERENCES

American Association of Colleges for Teacher Education. (2018). *Community-engaged teacher preparation*. Topical action groups. https://aacte.org/professional-development-events/topical-action-groups/community-engaged-teacher-preparation

Bronfenbrenner, U. (1979). *The ecology of human development*. Harvard University Press.

Mandel, E. (2014). *Station eleven*. Harper Avenue.

Moll, L. C., Amanti, C., Neff, D., & González, N. (1992). Funds of knowledge for teaching: Using a qualitative approach to connect homes and classrooms. *Theory into Practice (31)*2, 132–141.

Oldenburg, R. (1989). *The great good place*. Paragon House.

Tamm, J. W., & Luyet, R. J. (2010). *Radical collaboration: Five essential skills to overcome defensiveness and build successful relationships*. Harper Collins.

Zeichner, K. (2015). Engaging local communities in the preparation of teachers. *Kappa Delta Pi Record, 51*(3), 118–120.

Part II Reflection

Reverend Halford E. Luccock was quoted as saying, "No one can whistle a symphony; it takes an orchestra to play it." This quote reminds us that the synergy of strings, woodwinds, brass, and percussion is a function of planning, practice, tuning, and temporal synchrony—an alignment of rich and reverent resonance—in the words of Kassem (2011), "a divine design." And so these chapters tell such a story: one of collaboration and mutuality dependent upon shared aspiration, a recognition of the limitation of solitary endeavor, and the imperative of interdependence to achieve a heretofore imagined, yet unrealized, vision.

Wenger (1998) defined "communities of practice" as the interaction of individuals and groups with a mutual concern and united passion about a problem or topic, and whose ongoing interface deepens their knowledge and expertise. In such a community, the members bring unique perceptions and perspectives, strengthening the collective's capacity to envision possibilities and execute solutions. According to Wenger and colleagues (2002), cultivating such communities requires a concerted commitment. And with "cultivation" as an analogy, the authors suggest,

> A plant does its growing, whether its seed was carefully planted or blown into place by the wind. You cannot pull the stem, leaves, or petals to make a plant grow faster or taller. However, you can do much to encourage healthy plants: till the soil, ensure they have enough nutrients, supply water, secure the right amount of sun exposure, and protect them from pests and weeds. There are also a few things we know not to do, like pulling up a plant to check if it has good roots. (pp. 12–13)

These three chapters have exemplified the techniques of "good gardening," including planning, persistence, and patience in realizing a communal vision. These partnerships have been forged with authentic care and concern, grounded in a critical hope (Duncan-Andrade, 2009) for the development of teachers who are prepared to *reach*, and therefore *teach*, students whose lived experience has been traditionally marginalized. This critical hope is characterized by Duncan-Andrade as embodying *material hope*, which communicates to our future teachers that a rigorous program of educator preparation must not be divorced from one imbued with an explicit ethic of social justice; a *Socratic hope*, which compels us to "examine our lives and actions within an unjust society" (pp. 187–188); and an *audacious hope*, which "stands in solidarity with urban communities, sharing the burden of their undeserved suffering as a manifestation of a humanizing hope in our collective capacity for healing" (p. 190).

In these chapters, we have seen individuals who inhabit disparate contexts—often with competing priorities—align in steadfast determination, animating the mantra "the whole is greater than the sum of its parts." This coming-together is not an easy road but demands a courageous and concerted reflection upon the limits of individual capacity, regardless of aspiration, and a recognition of the interconnectedness of our humanity.

In Ecclesiastes 4:9–12, it is written, "a cord of three strands is not easily broken." While universities and schools have held longstanding relationships that privilege practicum and professional development, this "two-legged stool" has neglected the voice of community and failed to recognize and honor the wisdom, expertise, and cultural wealth (Yosso, 2005) that inform students' lived experience, and which serve as an important bridge to ensure a relevant, engaging, and culturally responsive and sustaining education. The imperative of braiding the community voice into the establishment of a mutually agreed-on vision for students' success cannot be sufficiently underscored and responds to Zeichner and colleagues' question, "Whose knowledge counts in the education of teachers?" (2017, p. 172).

As a cautionary note, the dynamics of power in uncharted alliances can venture into the terrain of tokenism, offering a seat at the table, absent an equitable esteem for the funds of knowledge (Moll et al., 1992) of communities and their critical contribution to the larger project of teacher preparation. The chapters in this section illustrate, instead, how these unique and varied communities of practice intentionally honor the individual contributions of their constituent members and strive to elevate all voices equally toward the achievement of their vision for the future.

REFERENCES

Duncan-Andrade, J. (2009). Note to educators: Hope required when growing roses in concrete. *Harvard Educational Review*, 79(2), 181–194.
Kassem, S. (2011). *Rise up and salute the sun: The writings of Suzy Kassem*. Awakened Press.

Moll, L. C., Amanti, C., Neff, D., & González, N. (1992). Funds of knowledge for teaching: Using a qualitative approach to connect homes and classrooms. *Theory into Practice, 31*(2), 132–141.

Wenger, E. (1998). *Communities of practice: Learning, meaning, and identity.* Cambridge University Press.

Wenger, E., McDermott, R., & Snyder, W. (2002). *Cultivating communities of practice.* Harvard University Press.

Yosso, T. (2005). Whose culture has capital? A critical race theory discussion of community cultural wealth. *Race, Ethnicity, and Education, 8*(1), 69–91.

Zeicher, K., Payne, K. A., & Brayko, K. (2017). Democratizing teacher education. In K. Zeichner (Ed.) *The struggle for the soul of teacher education* (pp. 171–196). Routledge.

BECOMING COMMUNITY TEACHERS

TEACHING FOR EQUITY AND SOCIAL JUSTICE

Integral to a philosophy of community-engaged teacher preparation is the belief that much of the knowledge required to improve schools and subsequent outcomes for children lies outside the expert sources toward which we typically turn. As such, community-engaged teacher preparation is predicated upon the development of community teachers, who work to understand the cultural knowledge traditions of children, families, and the community being served, and use these traditions to make meaningful connections for and with children and families. This work is achieved through authentic and caring relationships in which candidates and members of the community work alongside each other to further community priorities, practicing both advocacy and activism, and building the resiliency necessary to advance social justice and equity. The outcome of these efforts is operationalized in a more culturally relevant, responsive, and sustaining education for children.

Community-engaged teacher preparation privileges both content and pedagogy to which children can connect based on their lived experience. This paradigm affirms the cultures from which students come as a strength upon which to build, rather than a deficit in need of remediation so as to conform to societal norms. In support of this approach, the literature on culturally responsive, relevant, and sustaining teaching shows promise for increased academic outcomes for students (see Krasnoff, 2016). Educational experiences that are culturally relevant, responsive, and sustaining not only connect content to students' experience, but further their academic success by holding them to high academic standards while encouraging their critical consciousness about the world. When engaged in culturally relevant and sustaining pedagogies, students emerge as more critical consumers of information in the world and are subsequently more empowered to reenvision a new tomorrow that includes the richness of truth constructed by a diversity of cultures throughout time. Students learn to challenge traditional narratives about marginalized populations and the single stories (Adiche, 2009) that glorify voices of power at the expense of those who have been traditionally alienated from positions of privilege.

Community-engaged teacher preparation is intentionally grounded in the development of community teachers who understand systems of power and privilege and are compelled to work collaboratively toward a socially just society in order to rectify conditions that disadvantage populations of children. A community teacher aspires to contribute to and participate in a collective will to make educational equity a reality. This activist approach recognizes the social, cultural, historical, and political forces that must be addressed, and the commitment required—both in and out of the classroom—to work collaboratively and creatively to move the needle in the direction of social justice. In other words, it is imperative that they practice what they teach (Picower, 2011). This transpires only through a concerted conviction, cultivated through caring relationships that inform one's perception of the world and one's position as an agent of change. A program of community-engaged teacher preparation positions candidates at the launch of this journey. Through caring relationships with faculty, peers, teachers and administrators in local schools, and members of communities, candidates come to both conceptualize and practice how they can act on their convictions and advance a social and moral agenda that recognizes the promise, potential, and inherent worth of all individuals.

Opportunities to intentionally and critically reflect on one's cultural lens, personal bias, assumptions, values, and beliefs, in concert with an examination of societal oppression and the mechanisms that maintain and perpetuate injustice, are essential elements in the equation of community-engaged teacher preparation. Additional recognition of and reflection on one's positionality and its consequences are crucial. Not accomplished in isolation, careful mediation of these reflections by faculty can further engage candidates in the complex process of negotiating cognitive disequilibrium, deconstruction of prior schema, and rebuilding of a new lens through which to approach teaching and learning. Pedagogies such as dialogue journaling, courageous conversations (Singleton & Linton, 2006), mind-mapping, and digital storytelling, in combination, can be facilitative of opportunities to reflect. Engaging candidates' multiple languages in the expression of their emerging schema has been shown to be a productive means through which to encourage the metacognitive growth critical to becoming a community teacher (Zygmunt & Clark, 2016).

Community teachers understand that their students should be equipped and empowered to effectively participate in the work of social justice. Understanding that young people have a nuanced understanding of what is "fair," community teachers engage in pedagogies that develop their students' critical stance, encouraging their action to remedy injustice and supporting their emerging agency. It is through these experiences that students discover their personal power in addressing societal injustice, and their capacity for courageous engagement in work that advances equity.*

REFERENCES

Adiche, C. (2007). *The danger of a single story* [Video file]. https://www.ted.com/talks/chimamanda_adichie_the_danger_of_a_single_story

Krasnoff, B. (2016). *Culturally responsive teaching: A guide to evidence-based practices for teaching all students equitably.* Equity Assistance Center at Education Northwest.

Picower, B. (2011). Resisting compliance: Learning to teach for social justice in a neoliberal context. *Teachers College Record, 113*(5).

Singleton, G. E., & Linton, C. (2006). *Courageous conversations about race: A field guide for achieving equity in schools.* Corwin Press.

Zygmunt, E., Cipollone, K., Tancock, S., & Clark, P. (2018). Community-engaged teacher preparation. In J. Lampert (Ed.), *Oxford encyclopedia of global per-*

---

spectives on teacher education. Oxford University Press. https://doi.org/10.1093
/acrefore/9780190264093.013.476

Zygmunt, E., & Clark, P. (2016). *Transforming teacher education for social justice.* Teachers College Press.

CHAPTER 7

"We Still Have Work to Do"

Community-Engaged Experiences and Impact in an Urban Social Justice Program

Tasha Austin, Kisha Porcher, Mary Curran,
Jaime DePaola, Jessica Pelaez-Merino, and Lauren Raffaelli

When our Urban Social Justice Teacher Preparation program was established in September 2017, our primary aim was "fostering a deep understanding of students from historically marginalized linguistic, economic, and cultural backgrounds and communities" (Shamsi, 2017). The program founders, the professors who lead the courses and supervise fieldwork, the teachers and future teachers who enroll in our program, our community partners, and everyone involved in supporting the program are fiercely committed to that aim. What we've learned in the past 3 years, though, is that accomplishing our aim is hard—and there's still so much for us to do. In this chapter we share the work we've done, the work we're doing, and the work we have yet to do.

Our work started when we realized most teacher preparation programs see surrounding community school districts solely as a means of securing clinical placements for teacher candidates. The relationship between the two organizations is typically unidirectional, yielding learning opportunities for students with some incidental opportunities for them to participate more fully in the districts. Over the past 2 decades, higher education institutions have come to acknowledge the value of community engagement partnerships and have moved toward mutually beneficial relationships that connect the university with the surrounding communities (Porcher et al., 2020). Engaging in true partnership and collaborations requires a shift in the nexus of knowledge creation from the university to a more democratic model that situates community voices as equal contributors (Porcher et al., 2020; Zeichner et al., 2016). According to Zygmunt and Clark (2016), the missing piece in the model is "the intentional engagement of community wisdom and expertise in the training of teachers"

(p. 6). This democratic model requires collaboration to design and engage in activities that are beneficial for the university and its students, the district and its students, and the local community.

The academic year 2020 marked the perfect opportunity for us to get a more formal understanding of the impact of our Urban Social Justice Teacher Education program. We wanted to better understand how community-engaged coursework prepared our students to understand and collaborate with the communities in which they teach. It was our hunch that by redesigning the program we were better able to fulfill our department's tagline and impact beliefs of graduates and faculty. Further, we wanted to better understand the practical experiences of our graduates in their 1st year of teaching after leaving this program. The information we discovered enables us to commit to next steps for the continued development of the Urban Social Justice Teacher Preparation program.

Our graduate program for initial teacher licensure is housed in Rutgers, the State University of New Jersey's Graduate School of Education (GSE), located in New Brunswick, New Jersey. Our department adopted the tagline *Advancing Excellence & Equity in Education*, and faculty members recognized that in order to make manifest the ideals of the tagline, we would have to revamp our teacher education program with an explicit focus on the most vulnerable populations. Trying to do that, however, while maintaining a focus on what we needed for our students and ignoring the needs of the surrounding community would not move us into an essential "third space" (Whitchurch, 2012). Some of the early work involved getting a clear understanding of the realities of community-university interactions.

For a relationship to be truly beneficial for all involved, the students in the teacher preparation program's clinical experiences need to adopt an asset-based perspective of the community and develop authentic, reciprocal relationships with the communities and districts. To do this, their program, the participants, and professors must occupy a "third space" (Whitchurch, 2012) that combines academic, student affairs, and community-engaged work over the long term. In this "third space," emphasis is placed on sharing university resources in the form of social and intellectual capital and in alignment with community and district-led efforts (Porcher et al., 2020).

Communities have a lengthy experience with universities that do research "on" them as opposed to "with" them. They've often been on the receiving end of well-meaning students sent to "serve," knowing those students and their professors are likely to be ignorant of, or dismiss, community-led problem-solving efforts. Changing that required everyone involved, especially those of us associated with the GSE, to alter our thinking from viewing the work as a transactional relationship, to one that builds trust between all participants in the partnership (Porcher et al., 2020) and meant describing and understanding the positionality of our students and the communities with whom they would engage. Our efforts were built on the acknowledgment that "student teachers in urban placements, particularly privileged White female teachers teaching youth of color [. . .] lack [. . .] knowledge of the children they are teaching, along with their families and communities, [which] may further perpetuate deficit views" (Cross, 2016, p. 121).

To bridge the gap between the experiences of the mostly White, monolingual teacher candidates in our program and the racially and linguistically diverse students in their classrooms, we needed to help future teachers understand and connect with communities (Howard, 1999). They would have to recognize and appreciate students' and communities' assets and conditions (Love, 2019). The GSE would have to put at the center the voices, experiences, and needs of the districts and communities of color with whom we worked. We couldn't do that if our relationship with schools benefited only us. We dismantled our unidimensional relationship with the local communities and began to build new urban community–university partnerships, known as the Graduate School of Education Community School Partnership Network, based on the goals of our Urban Social Justice Teacher Preparation program and the local community's needs and objectives.

COMMUNITY-ENGAGED TEACHER PREPARATION: OUR PROGRAM

Rutgers is the leading public university in New Jersey and one of the top comprehensive research institutions in the nation. Serving more than 50,000 students, Rutgers conspicuously highlights information about its diverse student population on its website (https://newbrunswick.rutgers.edu/about/we-are-diverse). In 2019, the Rutgers New Brunswick undergraduate student body was 50% men and 50% women, which included students from 63 countries. Of those students, 36% were White, 29% Asian, 13% Hispanic/Latino, 6% African American, 4% two or more races, 2% race/ethnicity unknown, and 10% non-resident alien.

The Graduate School of Education (GSE)'s 5-year and postbaccalaureate teacher education certification programs enrolled 196 students, 80% of whom were women. The majority, 64%, were White; 13% were Asian; 9% were Hispanic, non–Puerto Rican; 4% were Black non-Hispanic; 4% were Puerto Rican; 2% identified as two or more races; and 8 students provided no racial demographic information. Our enrollment matches the national trends as seen in the National Center for Education Statistics (2020) data of a predominantly White, female teaching force.

Our GSE partnered with eight public school districts, creating the Graduate School of Education Community School Partnership Network (GSE-CSPN). Our teacher candidates are placed in schools with large numbers of students from historically marginalized linguistic, economic, or cultural backgrounds and those living in poverty. The schools are located in neighborhoods with high population density combined with inequality. Through the GSE-CSPN, we could build reciprocal and collaborative relationships with our partner schools. This approach is aligned with Zygmunt and Clark's (2016) framework, as we emphasize the intentional cultivation of collaborative relationships among universities, communities, and schools. We also worked to elevate the funds of knowledge and community cultural wealth (Moll et al., 1991), which allowed our students to participate in an in-depth analysis of social inequality, positionality, and the intersections between the two. In our program, we viewed the linguistic and cultural diversity of the students and families in our communities as an asset and put issues of equity at the core of education (Love, 2019).

It is our belief that unless our mostly White women teachers are grounded in a deep understanding and respect for their students' linguistic and cultural repertoires, they cannot fully engage in pedagogy that will support full engagement and participation in the many communities of practice (Lave & Wenger, 1991) they will encounter over their lifetimes. This meant that we had to immerse our candidates in the strengths and challenges present in urban settings and the rich linguistic and cultural diversity and resources of our communities (García, 2008). We needed to provide them with the skills to provide culturally responsive and sustaining pedagogies (Ladson-Billings, 1995; Paris & Alim, 2017), and they had to understand community-engaged education (Zeichner et al., 2016; Zygmunt & Clark, 2016). To accomplish these key objectives, we had to challenge their understanding of the status quo.

When creating pedagogical spaces based on critical pedagogy where the status quo is questioned (Flores & Rosa, 2015; Freire, 2000; Giroux, 1983; hooks 1994; Love, 2019; Macedo & Bartolomé, 2006; Paris & Alim, 2017), the voices, languages, and cultures of the marginalized and oppressed members of our communities must be at the center. When we do this, we mobilize educational efforts and resources for the emancipation of *all* students. We urgently need teachers prepared to affirm, sustain, and nourish their students' linguistic and cultural repertoires, but knowing how to do this is not an innate skill. School–university partnerships for teacher education, when intentionally designed, have the potential to provide mutually beneficial, transformative spaces for candidates, students, and teachers (Burroughs et al., 2019); however, it is important to move beyond traditional clinical placements in schools to also provide opportunities of engagement in out-of-school settings where preservice teachers connect with parents, community members, and community organizations (Campano et al., 2016; Zygmunt & Clark, 2016).

It is through guided reflections on these community-engaged interactions that we can enact the concept of *radical hospitality* from the St. Thomas Aquinas parish community, as described in the work of Campano and colleagues (2016). Radical hospitality urges us to consider the imperative ethical questions of how we are implicated in each other's lives, and what obligations we have to each other. A radical hospitality "does not merely reproduce insider-outsider dichotomies but instead conceives of community more expansively, beyond political borders and social boundaries" (p. 8), and this inclusive, broader, welcoming reconception of community necessitates that we also center the desire for *all* youth to flourish academically (Campano et al., 2016). This also requires that, through our community engagement, we are changed and begin to enact new ways of living and being with each other, working to create a community of solidarity.

We knew where we wanted to go when we started the program and how we thought and hoped the changes we made when redesigning the program would move us closer. We didn't know, however, if we were successful.

EXAMINING OUR URBAN SOCIAL JUSTICE PROGRAM

As previously noted, the GSE had recently shifted its approach to teacher education to be an Urban Social Justice Teacher Preparation program. This shift was undergirded by two major organizational and instructional enhancements. The first was the addition of partner leaders who serve as context teacher education experts linking the GSE and partnership districts. The partner leaders supervise and support candidates during their 2 years in the program, as they are placed in schools where they will eventually student-teach full-time. They serve as faculty experts, supporting candidates in schools with large populations of historically marginalized students, communities, and families.

The second innovation was the development of three required cross-cutting courses that aim to provide dispositional scaffolding and instructional expertise for teacher candidates of all disciplines, working in urban settings. The courses are:

1. Introduction to Urban Education I and II
2. Teaching Emerging Bilinguals I and II
3. Students, Communities, and Social Justice

OUR URBAN SOCIAL JUSTICE COMMUNITY-ENGAGED COURSES

The three courses provide the opportunity for our students to engage with the community. The sections of Introduction to Urban Education I and II and Teaching Emerging Bilinguals I and II are scheduled for the students' 1st year of the 2-year program (a one credit module of each is taken in the fall and the spring semesters). In the fall of their 2nd year, teacher candidates engage in a full-time student-teaching placement. In the fourth and final semester of the program, teacher candidates enroll in one of our Students, Communities, and Social Justice course sections. While they can choose a course section to fulfill the requirement, all sections of the course are designed to immerse students more deeply in the communities in which they have been learning and working. In differing ways, the Students, Communities, and Social Justice course sections support teacher candidates in appreciating the assets and conditions of diverse local communities as they prepare to enter the profession full-time.

Introduction to Urban Education I and II

In the two sections of Introduction to Urban Education, teacher educators guide preservice teachers to examine urban education from multiple perspectives in order to develop their understanding of the social, political, historical, and structural foundations of inequality in U.S. society and their implications for educational settings. Students engage with the following key questions:

- What defines urban? What constitutes an urban community?
- How do urban contexts shape schools and schooling?
- What are the historical, political, social, and economic contexts in which urban schools are situated? How might understanding urban schooling within these larger frameworks help educators?
- What is the role of schooling in urban settings? How might schools reproduce or reduce economic inequality?
- How do youth develop as learners in urban settings? What practices push this development in a positive direction?

The course goal is for students to be able to articulate and implement a capacity-based approach to teaching in urban communities. Course assignments in the Introduction to Urban Education I and II courses include a mapping project of an urban community and its schools, an autoethnography, and educator and community member inquiry projects. Through these assignments, teacher candidates learn from theory–community–practice connections.

Teaching Emerging Bilinguals I and II

The two-part Teaching Emerging Bilinguals courses have two goals:

- Support preservice teachers as they develop an understanding of the strengths and challenges of emerging bilinguals and their families
- Develop a foundation on which preservice teachers can build a set of general and content-specific pedagogical practices

In Teaching Emerging Bilinguals I, instructors focus on articulating and developing dispositions with asset-based perspectives toward their future emerging bilingual students that includes an understanding of the relationship between language and power and the sociopolitical context of learning English and other languages in U.S. public school settings. Course content includes language rights as protected in education policy, the key court cases protecting language rights, and the New Jersey state code regarding languages and education. Teacher candidates consider the impact of deficit labeling and thinking (García, 2008; Moll et al., 1992).

In Teaching Emerging Bilinguals I, key assignments include an immersion simulation experience, watching the video *Immersion* (Media That Matters, 2009), guided reading and discussion reflections, and conducting a linguistic landscape inquiry (Curran, 2018) in a partnership district. In Teaching Emerging Bilinguals II, the focus is on building a toolkit of strategies and practices that support language development and affirm heritage languages while practicing culturally sustaining pedagogies (Paris & Alim, 2017). In the second module of the course, key assignments include lesson plan adaptations grounded in community-theory-practice connections. These community-theory-practice connections grow from their ethnographic inquiry into the ways community languages are or are not visible in the local landscape, their experiences at their clinical setting, and the guided reflections facilitated by course instructions.

Students, Communities, and Social Justice

This course is taken during the final semester of the Urban Social Justice Teacher Preparation program. This course assumes the following three key elements:

- Student learning is situated within and actively connected to the school and the broader community. As such, teachers must seek opportunities to learn from and with community members outside of school.

- Public education has the potential to be a site for social change and equity. It is the only institution in the United States universally available to all students from diverse cultural, linguistic, and economic backgrounds. As such, teachers must see themselves as embedded in a larger community. As members of—perhaps multiple—broader communities, teachers must be able to notice and question their own assumptions and prejudices in order to be able to recognize the potential impact of those assumptions and prejudices on students, communities, and professional practice.
- Teachers have a responsibility to work alongside students, families, and communities to actively participate in creating and perpetuating a just, humane, and democratic society. As such, teachers must understand how who we are impacts how we teach and how we make alliances with community stakeholders inside and outside of the school building.

The course learning objectives are that students will

- work alongside community members to jointly develop a program of engagement,
- engage in meaningful interactions with members of a community other than school personnel, and
- interact with students, community members, and family members both with the presence of a GSE instructor and independently without GSE instructor mediation.

Each professor interested in teaching the Students, Communities, and Social Justice course is given the flexibility to design the course in the way they choose, as long as they adhere to the course objectives. This course and the firsthand experiences that are mandatory within it form part of the broader GSE Urban Social Justice Teacher Preparation program by

- fostering preservice teachers' critical analysis of urban, rural, and suburban schooling;
- providing preservice teachers with new experiences learning from and teaching within the economically, racially, ethnically, and linguistically diverse communities and schools in New Jersey; and
- scaffolding preservice teachers' community-based fieldwork placements in partner districts.

OUR APPROACH TO SELF-STUDY

Reflecting on our program redesign, the first graduating class marked a great opportunity to examine the success and impact of our Urban Social Justice Teacher Preparation program. After considering a number of frameworks for reflection, we elected to use a collaborative Self-Study in Teacher Education Practices (S-STEP), a type of practitioner inquiry undertaken by teacher educators with the dual purpose of improving our practice while also acknowledging our role in teacher learning in the larger project of preparing high-quality teachers to teach in urban schools (Sharkey, 2018). S-STEP is rooted in action research and reflective practice, particularly from a critical social justice perspective (Sharkey, 2018; Vanassche & Kelchtermans, 2015). The model has helped various teacher educators reflect on their practices and has contributed to the scholarship of teacher education pedagogies and practices (Loughran, 2014; Sharkey, 2018; Zeichner, 2007). S-STEP offered a structure for us to not only reflect as teacher educators, but to elevate the voices of our former teacher candidates who experienced our teacher education program. In teacher education, self-study is powerful because of its potential to influence prospective teachers, as well as impact one's own learning and practice as a teacher educator.

Our Self-Study Team

To start our work of assessing the impact of the newly designed program, the three faculty members met to determine a productive forum for this self-study. As our first cohort under the redesign had just graduated, we felt this was an opportune time to (1) examine the extent to which the program is meeting its goals, (2) identify areas for growth, and (3) better understand the ways in which we engage with the community. We identified three members of the first graduating class who were actively engaged candidates in our courses and invited them to join the self-study project.

This resulted in a self-study team of three faculty members and three recent graduates, currently teaching in New Jersey schools. Two of the graduates are now teachers in one of the GSE-CSPN districts, where the majority of our teacher candidates complete their clinical practice. Each faculty member teaches at least one of our community-engaged courses. The students had preexisting relationships with at least one faculty member, as they had all taken at least two of the community-engaged courses.

All six of us on the self-study team identify as women. Half of us identify as people of color, and half of us identify as White. The demographic data are displayed in Table 7.1.

Table 7.1. Participant Demographic Information

Name	Self-Identified Racial & Ethnic Identity	Position & Role	Courses Taken/Taught
Tasha Austin	Black	Lecturer in Language Education	Teaching Emerging Bilinguals I and II Intro to Urban Education I and II
Mary Curran	White, European American	Professor of Professional Practice Coordinator for Language Education Program	Teaching Emerging Bilinguals I and II Students, Communities, & Social Justice
Jaime DePaola	White, Italian American	ESL High School Teacher (program graduate)	Teaching Emerging Bilinguals I and II Intro to Urban Education I and II Students, Communities, & Social Justice
Jessica Pelaez-Merino	Hispanic, Mexican American	Elementary Teacher (program graduate)	Teaching Emerging Bilinguals I and II Intro to Urban Education I and II Students, Communities, & Social Justice
Kisha Porcher	Black	Assistant Professor of Professional Practice; Partner Leader: New Brunswick	Students, Communities, & Social Justice
Lauren Raffaelli	White	Dance Teacher (program graduate)	Teaching Emerging Bilinguals I and II Intro to Urban Education I and II

Self-Study: Faculty and Graduate Collaboration

The faculty contributors developed three questions for the self-study, based on our understanding of the developing social justice teacher preparation program, the research base, and conversations we had with candidates, graduates, and community members. These questions served as a lens through which the self-study was guided from beginning to end. With a clear goal orientation, "analysis then is not the last phase of the research process" (Lee & Fielding, 1996, p. 6); the cyclical nature of description, analysis, and interpretation was paramount for the duration of the self-study. Our questions included the following:

1. How does an urban social justice teacher preparation program impact faculty and teacher candidate beliefs surrounding teaching and learning?
2. In what ways do the courses in the Urban Social Justice Teacher Preparation program prepare teacher candidates to become community-engaged 1st-year teachers?
3. How does an analysis of the community-engaged experience inform us regarding program development?

In keeping with the goals of the S-STEP approach, we solicited not only valuable, but critical, insights of the novice teachers who experienced our revamped program as teacher candidates. Integral to our ability to see our work and its impact clearly are the reflections of those who entered the program as novice teachers, and who are now applying their preparation in K–12 spaces.

The questions, along with supporting guiding questions, were sent via email to all participants, and the responses, when returned, were housed electronically. In Table 7.2 we present the guiding questions, their alignment with the self-study questions, and the participants who answered each guiding question.

Recognizing the heavy workload of the new teachers on the team, the faculty members conducted a discourse analysis of the submissions. This analysis was then shared with all participants for their feedback and suggestions.

What We Found

Each submission was read and coded as subcategories of emergent themes that appeared frequently across all submissions. If a new code arose that was not previously recognized, the prior submissions were read again to

Table 7.2. Self-Study Question Response Alignment

Self-Study Questions	Guiding Questions	Respondents
1. How does an urban social justice teacher preparation program impact faculty and teacher candidate beliefs surrounding teaching and learning?	Describe who you are and the community in which you grew up.	All
	Before experiencing the Urban Social Justice Teacher Preparation program, what were your beliefs about teaching and learning? In urban schools?	All
	Describe the school and community where you are teaching.	All
2. In what ways do the courses in the Urban Social Justice Teacher Preparation program prepare teacher candidates to become community-engaged, 1st-year teachers?	How did the community-engaged courses prepare you to understand the communities you engaged in during your clinical practice?	All
	How did your community-engaged courses prepare you to understand the communities where you will teach?	Graduates
3. How does an analysis of the community-engaged experience inform us regarding program development?	After experiencing the Urban Social Justice Teacher Preparation program, what were your beliefs about teaching and learning? In urban schools?	All
	What suggestions do you have to improve the community-engaged experiences in the GSE courses and programs?	All

provide opportunities for that new code to reveal itself. There were 346 instances of these codes across the six participants' contributions, inclusive of phrases that were double- and sometimes triple-coded. This process resulted in the identification of 12 codes, which fell into three categories aligned with the study questions: (1) grounded beliefs versus raised awareness, (2) strengthen and deepen our community-engaged practices, and (3) continuation of the work.

Grounded Belief Versus Raised Awareness. Participants' answers to the first self-study question—"How does an urban social justice teacher preparation program impact faculty/preservice teacher beliefs surrounding teaching and learning?"—reveal striking differences between participants of color and White participants. When reviewing the coding, we found that faculty and graduates of color had prior grounded beliefs and understandings of the conditions and assets of students in urban schools and communities. For example, in responding about beliefs held before experiencing the newly revamped program, one faculty participant of color stated, "I held and maintain deeply rooted beliefs in the power of access and opportunity. I had come to believe just a minimal amount of equity could go such a long way to provide students from marginalized communities a glimpse of what could be." Utilizing the words *held* and *maintain* demonstrates that the faculty participant of color entered the program with positive and asset perspectives of teaching and learning for communities of color. For the same question, another faculty of color participant also highlighted asset and positive perceptions about teaching and learning for communities of color: "I also believed that all students have funds of knowledge and are geniuses; it is the role of the teacher to elevate their genius." This response demonstrates that the faculty of color believed that students of color *enter* the classrooms with assets, and that teachers have the power to cultivate their geniuses. Finally, the graduate of color agreed with the faculty of color for the same question in sharing, "I also believed that all students were capable of learning and doing great things, but I knew that things would be harder for my peers and I because of the financial and immigration issues our families were in." This response shows that before the graduate entered the program, she believed all students were capable of learning, but as for herself and her peers as people of color, she anticipated challenges.

These statements were in stark contrast to the White faculty member and graduates responding to the same question, whose contributions were coded more often as a *raised awareness* due to their engagement with the urban social teacher education program. For example, the faculty member indicated, "This new program has required me to up my game in several ways—I have been pushed to articulate what I've been doing and share this with my colleagues." This response demonstrates that it was a learning process for her. One of the White graduates highlighted how the program raised her awareness: "I was completely sheltered from the racial, linguistic, and socio-economic diversity [. . .] I had fallen under the impression that 'diverse' and 'urban' schools were primarily schools for students of color." It was clear that the Urban Social Justice Teacher Preparation program raised awareness about the misconceptions concerning teaching and learning for students of color. Further, another White graduate shared, "My beliefs about urban education have evolved to understand that no matter the environment, all children deserve a bountiful education." The program raised her awareness of teaching and learning for all students. Our data suggest that the program increased awareness for mostly White participants, whereas participants of color entered the program with asset-based and positive orientations concerning teaching and learning grounded in social justice, and the program affirmed those orientations.

Strengthen and Deepen Our Community-Engaged Practices. Our second self-study question was, "In what ways do the courses in the Urban Social Justice Teacher Preparation program prepare preservice teachers to become community-engaged 1st-year teachers?" In terms of how the program prepared graduates, all faculty and graduate participants reported that the Urban Social Justice Teacher Preparation program, while valuable, needs to continue its efforts to *strengthen* its reciprocal impact and *deepen* the understanding of urban and community immersion elements of the program. For example, one graduate argued that "Maintaining relationships with people that our families value and trust will allow us [teachers] to help our students succeed." This shows the importance of not just introducing students to the importance of relationships, but how maintaining them with families and community members can strengthen our relationships with students and positively impact their achievement. A faculty member agreed with the student in her response, sharing, "These relationships need to be sustained (can't be limited to one class, which may or may not run each year or semester.)" This illustrates that our program must be intentional in sustaining relationships beyond our courses.

In the relationships developed and maintained with community members, both the faculty and graduates suggest that our understanding of teaching and learning should be co-constructed with community members and our engagement should be reciprocal. One faculty member urged, "The community course should be co-created with community members, based on their needs." We knew when we started that community members should influence our Urban Social Justice Teacher Preparation program, but we clearly hadn't made that happen. One graduate provided an expanded holistic view of teaching and learning: "I want students to know their education will come from a variety of sources aside from their teacher." This illustrates the shift from teachers as centered experts in community-engaged teacher education, to community members bringing equal value to the strength of the program.

Both graduates and faculty also argue that we need to deepen our understanding of community-engaged teacher education by expanding our knowledge of urban social justice and elevating the voices of faculty who have expertise in this area. For example, prior to the program redesign, existing relationships between districts and the GSE were not necessarily urban. With the new design, students found that their clinical placement experiences were disparate per our understanding and definition of "urban" districts. One graduate commented:

> I would suggest for the GSE to eventually give each teacher
> candidate the opportunity to teach in an urban setting in some
> capacity [this graduate highlighted that some partnership districts
> are not truly *urban* but *urban-adjacent*] to prepare our teacher
> candidates for the realities of urban schools.

This shows that the convenience of maintaining relationships with former districts did not align with our goal to place all students in urban districts. The disconnect is further highlighted by experiential expertise of faculty members of color. A faculty member argues for elevating the voices of those who have both experience in urban schools and an understanding of urban social justice, which can serve to rectify this misrepresentation. For example, the faculty member shared, "Colleagues do not take advantage of the command of these complex topics that we have in-house and responsibilities regarding advancing our mission is compartmentalized." We need to draw upon our in-house expertise in urban social justice education, changing the hierarchy in higher education where what is privileged (traditional research and scholarship) is not what is needed when preparing teacher candidates for today's students and schools. With the hiring of partner leaders who are at the forefront of our university-district-community initiatives, we need to find ways in which the expertise of these newer faculty members is heard, valued, and allowed to impact and change our usual ways of conducting teacher education. Often program expertise is siloed, and we need to make sure experiential expertise is at the core of the program and led by faculty of color.

Faculty and graduates made similar suggestions that to prepare our teacher candidates, we need to prioritize and strengthen relationships in the community, programmatic coherence, consistency and the co-construction of knowledge in our pedagogy, and curriculum design and implementation. It was clearly expressed that the GSE should continue to build and deepen relationships, highlight asset-based approaches that draw on community knowledge, and provide realistic apprenticeships with scaffolding and support.

We Still Have Work to Do. In looking at responses to self-study question three—"How does an analysis of the community-engaged experience inform us regarding program development?"—there was clearly an overall positive response in both faculty's and graduates' valuation of community engagement as a deep and meaningful part of their preparation. However, both groups offered critiques and suggestions for this developing program consistent with those reported by Zygmunt and Clark's call for a "seamless experience" as opposed to "discrete courses" (2016, p. 13). Engaging in truly collective planning and reflection by all—faculty, district teachers and administrators, teacher candidates and graduates, students, parents, and community members—will improve the integrity and consistency in understanding the context, resources, urgencies, and suggestions for the evolution of the program in years to come. For example, the self-study responses revealed several ways to act, such as striving for more reciprocal impact and co-creating community-engaged courses with community input. We see that we need better-sustained and deeper community connections. This is evident in a graduate's feedback: "I don't think people truly understand the issues a community faces until they see for themselves. Students [preservice teacher candidates] should go out to the communities they student-teach in and learn about the issues that the community faces." The graduate refers to the one or two opportunities provided in the Urban Social Justice Teacher Preparation program to engage with the community. These opportunities occur only in the last semester of the program.

A significant finding from this self-study is the differing orientation between participants of color and White participants concerning grounded beliefs and understandings prior to participation in the program versus a raised awareness of the conditions and assets of students in urban schools and communities as a result of involvement in the program. In our self-study, we found that faculty, as well as graduates of color, hold clear, weighty, and distinct understandings of social justice as the responsibility of educators; this was key in their evaluation of both the institutional and community-based impact of the program for people of color. White participants, on the other hand, express their growing awareness of issues of equity, which is, we hope, beginning to influence their beliefs and dispositions. This is clear in the following faculty member's statement: "Engaging with the community also requires that I confront my own racist or deficit perspectives. This is painful, but a lifelong journey—which cannot be done in isolation, nor as a purely intellectual activity."

While evaluating their own program at Ball State University, a similar theme of values and beliefs has been corroborated by Zygmunt and Clark (2016), in that reflections on engagement with racialized communities reveal an underlying commitment to "culture and faith" (p. 64) from which one might construct a culturally responsive set of approaches. In addition, in practice, novice educators noted a need to ensure that the "morals and values" being centered were representative of the students and community rather than their own (p. 65).

As we considered implications for our program, we identified that we have to elevate the expertise among our faculty, teacher candidates, and graduates of color who have experiential knowledge and come with a familiarity of the prevailing themes of inequitable practices in schools.

Acknowledging these funds of knowledge would orient program administrators to value and design programmatic structures to increase respect for this expertise, while providing growth and impact opportunities for those involved. At the same time that we increase how this experience and knowledge are valued, we need to be respectful and cognizant that we not ask our faculty and students of color to do all the work of educating others or bearing the full burden of the urban social justice program (Tuitt et al., 2009).

In acknowledging the expanded awareness of urban social justice for White students, our findings indirectly suggest that our instructional approaches center Whiteness, as teacher candidates of color enter the program already with experiential knowledge of these concepts. This shows that the program focuses on teaching White teachers how to teach in urban schools, without direct instruction or experiences that advance the funds of knowledge with which graduates of color enter the program. Furthermore, for faculty of color who primarily serve in partner leader roles, professional knowledge is not elevated as expertise to improve our program. For example, one faculty member of color stated that "The bulk of my work is feedback for students during their clinical experience. With my lived, community, and clinical experience, wouldn't I have feedback concerning the changes that should be made to improve our program and community relationships?" These findings demonstrate that in some instances our program perpetuates, reproduces, and strengthens racial inequality and the status quo. This is documented in the scholarship of critical race theory (Bell, 1995; Delgado & Stefancic, 1993), which unveils the normative centering of Whiteness and argues for resources of historically marginalized communities of color at the center of teacher education.

To achieve our tagline of *excellence and equity* and the program goals in our Urban Social Justice Teacher Preparation program, Rutgers GSE White faculty and students must engage in the important work of understanding Whiteness and the way their White identities position themselves and their students, impact how they understand teaching and learning, and privilege and position Whiteness as the standard and norm. We are currently conducting workshops for faculty and staff focused on implicit bias, and a focus on Whiteness for upcoming professional development was suggested to our current administration. However, as urged by a faculty member of color at a recent department meeting (Randall Weeks, 2020), we must move beyond consciousness raising and awareness to taking clear, strategic actions to make substantial changes that decenter Whiteness and center the children and knowledge of marginalized communities as the guiding and driving forces in our program.

CONCLUSION

For years, members of the Rutgers GSE teacher preparation program felt we weren't doing the necessary work to prepare educators to be fully present and fully prepared in the classroom. This self-study and reflection have provided a forum to push each of us as learners and teachers. It reminded us that while we have embarked on an ambitious project of redesigning, implementing, and participating in a teacher education program rooted in social justice in urban settings, we have a long learning curve ahead of us. For example, our ongoing interactions revealed an uneven demonstration of actively promoting teaching for social justice, requiring reciprocal community-engaged coursework, and building university-community relationships alongside clinical experiences (Richmond, 2016), as we hoped. Although we have a program-wide focus on urban social justice, we have found that we have work to do to ensure that it is systemic and not just in pockets of courses or with specific faculty members. It reminds us of the enormous challenges and discomfort inherent in this work, and the obligation for White faculty and teacher candidates to commit to learning through the discomfort as they decenter Whiteness. As a result of this honest, deep reflection on the program, we are able to move closer to repositioning power, and fully operationalizing teacher education as a reciprocal partner alongside the genius of communities of color.

While this study is based on a small sample size of self-reports, it is the participants' positionality in terms of identity and roles that provides depth and nuance. We have found that these different positions, as people of color or White people, as faculty members or graduate students, allowed us to access multiple perspectives on the experience, especially in this initial review in which we are beginning to formally capture the program's impact.

Although we were a small group, this self-study highlighted ways in which we could deepen our understanding of the program's success. We are considering (1) going beyond self-reports on experience to include observations and collection of teacher candidate and teacher artifacts; (2) assessing candidate dispositions during the program and after graduation; (3) following graduates into the classroom and evaluating the impact on their students' learning; (4) charting faculty orientations to the program as the program matures and changes; and (5) linking faculty orientations to the impact on the graduates in their programs. We know we also need to evaluate the impact of our programming on our partner districts, community organizations, and community members. We further believe that to align with our beliefs and frameworks, it is necessary to practice public-facing scholarship and develop inclusive ways to speak together with, from, and to the community with whom we are working.

We hope that our reflection and self-study can inform others who are embarking upon the planning and implementation of an urban social justice community-engaged teacher preparation program. Based on our own challenges and successes, our suggestions would include:

1. Engage in a norming process to define key terms, such as "urban," "social justice," and "community-engaged," so that all partners have a mutual understanding.
2. Develop a shared agreement across the teacher preparation program in which everyone is committed to the goals and expected outcomes of the program, including community partners, faculty, and teacher candidates.
3. Conduct an internal process of assessing the goals and growth of the program, as well as an external programmatic evaluation by the community to provide feedback about the program's perceived growth and impact.

This initial program review involved creating a culture of honest reflection and willingness to change as we work toward fully realizing a democratic urban social justice program. Only by doing this urgent work can we make the necessary changes to our programmatic structures, hiring and promotion practices, curriculum, pedagogies, and relationships among colleagues and communities in order to ensure that our graduates believe in and elevate the wealth of knowledge and genius of every student.

REFERENCES

Bell, D. (1995). Who's afraid of critical race theory? *University of Illinois Review*, *1995*, 893–910.

Burroughs, G., Battey, D., Lewis, A., Curran, M., Hyland, N.E., & Ryan, S. (2019). From mediated fieldwork to co-constructed partnerships: A framework for assessing K–12 school-university partnerships. *Journal of Teacher Education*, *71*(1), 122–134.

Campano, G., Ghiso, M. P., & Welch, B. J. (2016). *Partnering with immigrant communities: Action through literacy.* Teachers College Press.

Cross, S. B. (2016). Reexamining pitfalls of experience in urban teacher preparation. *Journal of Urban Learning, Teaching, and Research*, *12*, 116–123.

Curran, M. E. (2018). *Our linguistic landscape: Preparing teachers to see, hear and affirm the community.* Presentation at the American Educational Research Association Annual Meeting, New York.

Delgado, R., & Stefancic, J. (1993). Critical race theory: An annotated bibliography. *Virginia Law Review*, 79(2), 461–516.

Delgado, R., & Stefancic, J. (2017). *Critical race theory: An introduction*. NYU Press.

Flores, N., & Rosa, J. (2015). Undoing appropriateness: Raciolinguistic ideologies and language diversity in education. *Harvard Educational Review*, 85(2), 149–171.

Freire, P. (2000). *Pedagogy of the oppressed*. Continuum.

García, O. (2008). Multilingual language awareness and teacher education. In J. Cenoz & N. H. Hornberger (Eds.), *Encyclopedia of language and education* (2nd ed., pp. 385–400). Springer.

Giroux, H. (1983). *Theory and resistance in education: A pedagogy for the opposition*. Bergin & Garvey.

Howard, G. R. (1999). *We can't teach what we don't know: White teachers, multiracial schools*. Teachers College Press.

hooks, b. (1994). *Teaching to transgress*. Routledge.

Ladson-Billings, G. (1995). Toward a theory of culturally relevant pedagogy. *American Educational Research Journal*, 32(3), 465–491.

Lave, J., & Wenger, E. (1991). *Situated learning: Legitimate peripheral participation*. Cambridge University Press.

Lee, R. M., & Fielding, N. (1996). Qualitative data analysis: Representations of a technology: A comment on Coffey, Holbrook, and Atkinson. *Sociological Research Online*, 1(4), 15–20.

Loughran, J. (2014). Professionally developing as a teacher educator. *Journal of Teacher Education*, 65(4), 271–283.

Love, B. L. (2019). *We want to do more than survive: Abolitionist teaching and the pursuit of educational freedom*. Beacon Press.

Macedo, D., & Bartolomé, L. I. (1999). *Dancing with bigotry: Beyond the politics of tolerance*. Palgrave.

Media That Matters. (2009). *Immersion* [Video File]. YouTube. https://www.youtube.com/watch?v=I6Y0HAjLKYI

Moll, L., Amanti, C., Neff, D., & González, N. (1992). Funds of knowledge for teaching: Using a qualitative approach to connect homes and classrooms. *Theory Into Practice*, 2, 132–141.

National Center for Education Statistics. (2020). *The condition of education 2020*. https://nces.ed.gov/programs/coe/indicator_clr.asp

Paris, D., & Alim, H. S. (Eds.). (2017). *Culturally sustaining pedagogies: Teaching and learning for justice in a changing world*. Teachers College Press.

Porcher, K., Michael, A., & Mir, C. (2020). Community-engaged teacher education: Redesigning programs to redistribute power and privilege to the community. *PDS Partners: Bridging Research to Practice*, 15(3), 11–15.

Randall Weeks, M. (2020) Personal communication.

Richmond, G. (2016). The power of community partnerships in the preparation of teachers. *Journal of Teacher Education 68*, 6–8.

Shamsi, A. (2017, October 11). *Rutgers GSE Launches The Urban Social Justice Teacher Preparation Program*. [Press release]. https://gse.rutgers.edu/content/rutgers-gse-launches-urban-social-justice-teacher-preparation-program

Sharkey, J. (2018). Who's educating the teacher educators? The role of self-study in teacher education practices (S-STEP) in advancing the research on the professional development of second language teacher educators and their pedagogies. *Íkala, Revista de Lenguaje y Cultura, 23*(1), 15–18. https://doi.org/10.17533/udea.ikala.v23n01a02

Tuitt, F., Hanna, M., Martinez, L. M., Salazar, M., & Griffin, R. (2009). Teaching in the line of fire: Faculty of color in the academy. *Thought & Action, 25*, 65–74.

Vanassche, E., & Kelchtermans, G. (2015). The state of the art in self-study of teacher education practices: A systematic literature review. *Journal of Curriculum Studies, 47*(4) 508–528.

Whitchurch, C. (2012). *Reconstructing identities in higher education: The rise of "third space" professionals*. Routledge.

Zeichner, K. (2007). Accumulating knowledge across self-studies in teacher education. *Journal of Teacher Education, 58*(1), 36–46.

Zeichner, K., Bowman, M., Guillen, L., & Napolitan, K. (2016). Engaging and working in solidarity with local communities in preparing the teachers of their children. *Journal of Teacher Education, 67*(4), 277–290.

Zygmunt, E. & Clark, P. (2016). *Transforming teacher education for social justice*. Teachers College Press.

CHAPTER 8

Successes and Challenges in Becoming Equity Educators
Former Candidate Perspectives

Kristin Cipollone, Kaylie Johnston, Hailey Maupin,
Kylie Kaminski, and Jacob Layton

> Having beliefs or guiding principles is one thing. Figuring out how to put them into practice, I learned, is another matter altogether [. . .] it's easy to lose your footing as a novice teacher, to begin to drift from your anchorage, to be seduced by the convention or expedience or outside demands. The undertow of schooling, you quickly figure out, can be as strong and stealthy as any ocean's—maybe even more so. (Michie, 2010, p. 705)

For far too long—despite the many "good intentions" of educators—education has failed to live up to the vision articulated by Horace Mann: that schools can be the great societal equalizer. In fact, as a long history has shown, schools have done just the opposite, serving to reproduce inequality (Bowles & Gintis, 1976; Labaree, 2010; Spring, 2004), entrench boundaries along class and race lines (Anyon, 1980; Orfield & Lee, 2005), and do real and significant harm to children from marginalized backgrounds (Love, 2019; Paris & Alim, 2017). The opportunity structures to which children have access (Anyon, 1980; Cipollone et al., 2020; Oakes, 1985; Weis et al., 2015), the curriculum (Apple, 1992, 2004), placements in special education (Sciuchetti, 2017; Skiba et al., 2014), and school suspensions and disciplinary referrals (Anyon et al., 2014; Skiba et al., 2014; U.S. Department of Education, Office for Civil Rights, 2014), among other elements, are all influenced by race and class.

It is, of course, unfair to lay the blame for systems of inequality and their resultant impact and outcomes solely at the feet of educators, yet teachers do have an important role to play in mitigating the effects of educational inequality on children. While many, often unintentionally, further the goals and outcomes of the system, educators *can* act as disrupters to make the system more equitable. They can be teachers who honor, affirm, and nurture the growth of all children *in schools* while working simultaneously to reduce injustice *outside of school* (Picower, 2012). In order to do this, we need to develop educators with the *will* and *skill* to reach all children: educators who possess dispositions toward equity and social justice, with the capacity to put these dispositions into practice (Zygmunt & Cipollone, 2019; Zygmunt et al., 2018). Developing these dispositions is a challenge; some, like Martin Haberman (1991), may even question whether it is possible, particularly given that the overwhelming majority of teacher candidates are White, monolingual, middle-class women. At our institution, the majority of candidates additionally come from small, rural or suburban, racially homogenous communities.

And yet, dispositions are not enough. Many candidates profess a commitment to equity and justice while in their teacher education programs, yet fall back into traditional practices upon entering the field. We need educators who can move from thought to action (Aldridge Sanford, 2020), who possess a critical and robust understanding of the larger social structure (Sleeter, 2012), are willing to embrace identities as activists to fight for societal change (Picower, 2012), and have the pedagogical skills to make it happen.

Well into its 2nd decade, Schools Within the Context of Community (SCC), an intensive community-engaged teacher preparation program for first-semester juniors at Ball State University, has shown significant promise in building a new and better educator (see Zygmunt & Clark, 2016, for a complete description of the program). The program is premised on the belief that the only truly effective teaching is community responsive teaching (TFAEvents, 2016). In other words, without deep appreciation for and knowledge of the community(ies) in which one teaches—without an understanding of the history, funds of knowledge (Moll et al., 1992), and cultural wealth (Yosso, 2005)—no amount of content and pedagogical knowledge will allow an educator to connect with, and thus teach, children. SCC is led by a team of faculty and community members/educators who work to embed teacher preparation within the community of Whitely, a historically and presently African American neighborhood near the university. Candidates are removed from campus and complete their coursework (including courses in pedagogy, educational psychology, literacy, social studies, and foundations of education), a practicum placement, and critical service-learning all within the community. Each candidate is placed with a mentor family who helps initiate them into the rhythms of the community, allowing them to participate more authentically in community life. In addition to building candidates' content and community knowledge, all instruction is approached from a lens of equity and social justice. Candidates expend a great deal of time learning about power, oppression, and their own positionality and how all of this relates to teaching in general, and their teaching specifically. It is important to note that the majority of candidates who participate in the program, like the larger teacher preparation program at Ball State, are White.

Studies of the program have demonstrated that candidates adopt orientations that are equity focused and socially just, understand the tenets of community engagement, and have the capacity to plan culturally responsive and socially just instructional experiences (Zygmunt & Cipollone, 2019; Zygmunt & Clark, 2016; Zygmunt et al., 2018). While we have learned a great deal about what happens for candidates while they are in the program, the inevitable question is: What happens once students leave the protected space of the program and venture out to the field? In some ways, this is perhaps the most important question to answer.

In this chapter, four former White candidates, all of whom demonstrated a deep commitment to social justice and equity upon completing the program, share aspects of their journey as they work to enact these dispositions in practice. The chapter introduces each candidate individually, in their own words, wherein the reader has the opportunity to learn a bit about their unique experiences and perspectives. Candidates' stories are arranged by teaching experience, beginning with those closest to their time in the program and ending with those who have been in the field the longest. We then move to discuss common themes and offer some recommendations to teacher educators in preparing future candidates to successfully do this work. These four candidates are highlighted specifically because of their strong social justice commitment as well as three other significant reasons: (1) they all identify as White, (2) they are currently teaching in districts serving students from marginalized backgrounds in terms of race and social class, and (3) they were among the most pedagogically talented candidates in their respective cohorts.

That all the candidates were White was of critical importance. While in an all-encompassing and supportive space like SCC where it is expected that all candidates commit to equity and justice, it isn't always clear how deep this commitment runs. As White people, these candidates can "turn it off" when they leave the program; their privileged status in our society allows them to choose whether or not they engage in fighting for social justice and the extent of this engagement. It is thus imperative to better understand how their commitment is enacted over time. This is not to suggest that Black, Indigenous, and People of Color (BIPOC) candidates, because of their racial identity, automatically express a commitment to social justice. As Jackson and Knight-Manuel (2019) argue, "Color does not equal consciousness" (p. 65); however, in a racialized society like the United States and in a predominantly White teacher preparation program like ours, BIPOC candidates are always aware of the racial politics and cannot simply "turn it off." Further, the four candidates featured in this chapter also experienced significant growth in their commitment. They arrived in the program with little prior knowledge of social justice, and some even expressed that they were initially "turned off" by the term *social justice* itself. Learning whether their commitment persisted over time and through experience in the field would be telling.

It is also critically consequential that these candidates demonstrated pedagogical skill, as culturally responsive and sustaining teaching requires academic rigor (Ladson-Billings, 1995; TFAEvents, 2016). If we, as teacher educators, are to understand how to prepare all educators to carry out this important work, we must look to the exemplars. Of all our White candidates, these four showed the greatest potential when it came to possessing both the *will* and *skill* to be social justice educators.

KAYLIE'S JOURNEY: "A VERY LONELY WAY OF TEACHING"

> Prior to SCC and EDEL 244 [another course on campus], I was not at all familiar with the term *social justice*. I had grown up [White] in a rural, small, predominantly White community where there was never any discussion of social justice. Even after I became familiar with the term, I still did not place much action behind what it truly meant to teach for social justice. It wasn't until during and after my SCC experience that I fully understood what social justice was and what it meant to teach for social justice. Before SCC, I didn't understand how a teacher could teach for social justice in the classroom. I remember thinking that it felt too political to bring topics like race, gender, SES, sexual orientation, etc., into the classroom. Now, I understand that education in and of itself is inherently political and it's not about teaching for or against a certain political party, it's about exposing students to the realities of our society and developing empathetic, culturally competent, and critically conscious citizens of our world.

Typical of most candidates we work with, Kaylie had little prior connection to social justice prior to her participating in the program but now strongly identifies as a *"community-engaged, equity-focused educator."* Moving into additional practicum placements and now in student teaching, Kaylie has been anxious to enact this orientation in practice, but doing so has been anything but easy. She says:

Upon leaving the program, I felt a sense of empowerment to operationalize my social justice disposition and support my students to become empowered and effective individuals. After all, this is an essential disposition for effective citizenship in our democratic society. However, I was aware that this style of teaching—teaching students in a way that empowers them to analyze aspects of history and common core curriculum through a critically conscious lens— was not a popular style of teaching in most schools. Once I was in my practicum and student teaching placements, I felt the pressure to conform to traditional aspects and forms of teaching that did not allow room for students to question, critique, or speak up about "hard topics." Students were expected to receive the whitewashed versions of history without question and were not encouraged to open up discussions about these topics as it is deemed "not appropriate" for school.

For example, during her current student-teaching placement, Kaylie suggested that as part of a study of women's history, the students learn about an updated and diverse group of women. When suggesting they add Malala Yousafzai to the women they discussed, Kaylie shares what happened:

I said "Let's consider Malala . . . well, I'm not actually sure yet how to pronounce her last name but—" when I was interrupted by my mentor teacher, who retorted, "Well we don't even know how to say her name, so I don't think we should teach about her," and instead offered up a list of "appropriate" women that she wanted covered.

Kaylie, opting to "choose her battles," decided to drop this push for the moment, determined to teach differently when she had control of planning instruction.

While students like Kaylie expect to receive some resistance from classroom teachers, they do not always anticipate the resistance from their peers. As Kaylie shares:

I also personally experienced pushback from fellow preservice teachers who I collaborated with to create lesson plans for my practicum experiences who had not had the teacher preparation I had. Whenever I suggested to add more elements of cultural connections that our students could relate to and that would foster deeper critical discussions, my group members were fearful to bring up those types of conversations in schools because they felt "unprepared and unqualified to hold those types of discussions in the classroom."

Her peers also shared that it was not worth the "extra" work to make lessons culturally responsive. For example, Kaylie further shares:

> While planning a lesson for a 2nd-grade class, I suggested to the other preservice teachers in my group that we should include social justice standards into our lesson plan to make the learning more meaningful and authentic for our students [. . .] I suggested to my group members that we try and incorporate some aspect of our students' community in order to make meaningful connections. My idea was to go out into the community and take pictures of the local fire station, police station, and their own school, and incorporate these into the lesson. My fellow preservice teachers were not keen on the idea, as they said that it would require too much work to go out and get that kind of information. I had explained to my group members that if we divided the work between all of us, it wouldn't be as much of a task and the students would benefit greatly from it. However, they were still not willing. I had explained to my group members that this type of connection would only enhance their learning experience and more than likely help students better retain the material. This was a lot of work for me to complete on my own with the timeline, but I did take as many photos as I could of certain aspects of the community and found as many photos as I could online.

The constant and continuous resistance that candidates receive upon leaving the program—be it from peers, mentor teachers, or, as other candidates have shared, faculty—is taxing, and has the potential to dim candidates' sense of agency to effect change. As Kaylie explains:

> I still possess a strong commitment to social justice and teaching for social justice in particular. However, this passion at times has diminished or become discouraged because it is hard to find educators who also stand for the same pedagogical teaching practices in their classrooms. Educating for social justice can be a very lonely way of teaching. Many educators in school systems today conform to the traditional styles and forms of teaching that seek to perpetuate racial, religious, sexist, ablest, etc., discrimination. This can cause a sense of discouragement in a teacher like myself who has the complete opposite view of teaching and building relationships with students.

When asked what helps her stay committed, Kaylie mentions the "potential of helping create accepting, critically conscious, culturally competent, empowered, and effective individuals who will participate in our democratic society" and:

> Having contact and communication with the preservice educators and faculty who are passionate about this work. It allows us to have a space where we can share our struggles, successes, and a place to share new information with one another about current events and findings that pertain to social justice education. Keeping this contact and communication open upon leaving the program allows preservice educators to stay connected with a network of teachers who are also dedicated to this type of work and makes the work that we are doing feel much less lonely and daunting.

HAILEY'S JOURNEY:
"IT JUST FEELS RIGHT IN MY HEART TO TEACH FOR SOCIAL JUSTICE."

Hailey's journey in becoming an educator committed to justice and equity was anything but preordained. As she explains:

> Before SCC I had never really thought much about social justice and always had more "conservative views" when it came to schools. I thought that everything came back on the parents, that children needed to be saved from their "bad homes" and "unsafe neighborhoods." I even had the thought that police in schools were necessary to keep everyone safe and that force was something that was hardly ever used and, if it was, it was because of the student. I had no idea how prejudiced I was toward people of color and that I looked down on them without even realizing it. SCC and 244 [another class on campus] led me to believe and understand that, above all else, students are human, and for such a long time, I realize now, that I didn't look at them as if they were. I expected that students should just comply to my directions and, if not, something was wrong with them, not me. I am very thankful for SCC because it helped me understand the power a teacher has and what can happen if that power is used negatively and how it should be used to empower students, families, and communities. I always thought I loved children and families, but I learned quickly that what I was doing wasn't loving and teaching—it was controlling, judging, and harming. I knew which teacher I wanted to be, and I have strived to be that ever since then. I know I have so much more to learn and so much more work to do on myself, but I don't want to be that teacher.

In this excerpt, Hailey reflects on her prior assumptions and how her experiences in SCC helped to transform her understanding of teaching and herself. As a result of these new insights, Hailey states that building strong relationships with children and providing humanizing learning experiences have been essential to her ability to enact her social justice orientation in the classroom. "When planning for activities in my own classroom and even during student teaching, I try to always consider my students, who they are and where they come from," she says. Discussing her student-teaching experience, she further explains:

> I had a lot of freedom, so I was able to create learning experiences
> that provided my students with mirrors and windows and then hold
> incredible conversations about race, gender, sexual orientation,
> current events, and unfair historical events. I was able to build
> relationships during my student-teaching experience that my
> supervising teacher was not able to or willing to build. Now that
> I have finished my student teaching and I have transitioned into a
> teaching position in the same building, I have been able to be a part
> of some really close relationships with my students. Most days I have
> extra students in my classroom who come in to take breaks with me,
> talk about some rough moments, to vent, or just to hang out.

It is these very relationships that have been at the crux of the challenges Hailey has experienced since moving into the field:

> Because I am always working at building strong relationships with
> students and families, I have received a lot of pushback. Not from
> administration in my building, but from other adults in the building.
> I've had other people say, "Well they like YOU." "They act right for
> HER." "I don't know what goes on in that room, but it has to be a
> wild party because they like her too much." "She encourages them
> to speak up to adults."
>   I intentionally eat my lunch in the staff lounge because
> when I hear someone say something negative about students, I
> like to combat that and say something positive or tell a positive
> story about a child that I've experienced, or maybe even give an
> explanation or defend a child. I find myself sometimes biting my
> tongue and telling myself to watch it and to make sure that what
> I'm saying won't come back to negatively reflect on me. One
> experience that comes to mind is overhearing a teacher talk about
> how "bad all of these kids are. It's not a school, it's a jungle. I can't
> even teach. I have to parent." I responded, full of heat, "Your kids

are my kids too! Watch what you're saying and keep your rude comments to yourself."

This [has] caused me to question myself. I have had an extremely hard time feeling a lot of the negativity that other adults in our building speak about the children we share space with. I don't want it to affect me and how I view the students, and I know that it can. Speaking up like this helps me stay focused on what matters.

It is in the challenges that Hailey has found much success, too. Hailey, who does not describe herself as an outspoken person, has found that when it comes to her students and their families, she is extremely vocal. Explaining this, she says, *"I never was somebody to speak up and rock the boat. But no matter what they [colleagues] say, I'll continue to do what I believe is right for me to do with my students and their families.* It's simply the right thing to do."

The belief that "it's the right thing to do" prompted her, as a student teacher, to intervene in a situation wherein a school resource officer (SRO) forcibly attempted to remove a kindergarten student from a classroom. As this was happening, Hailey pulled up a chair next to the SRO, and the following ensued:

Child (to SRO): Don't take me away!
SRO (to child): I'll let you go if you stop crying.
Hailey (to child): You have the option to sit with me.

As Hailey recounts, the SRO looked at her, bewildered, and continued to go back and forth with the child. Finally, seeing that Hailey was not going to leave, the SRO let go of the child, who promptly fell to the floor and crawled to Hailey, hiding from the SRO behind her chair.

Hailey (to child): Are you okay?
Child: Don't take me away!
Hailey: Were you scared? Had you seen that before?
Child: Yes.
Hailey: He [SRO] won't do that. It's not his job to take you away. His job is to keep us safe from threats.

After deescalating the situation, Hailey reported the incident to the principal. She also spoke with the kindergarten teacher to understand what prompted the call to the SRO. The teacher told Hailey that the child had taken a pair of headphones home and the parents, upon realizing this, notified the teacher, returning the headphones with the child the next day.

Despite how things had played out, the teacher told Hailey that "this was stealing" and that the child "needed to talk to the police."

Hailey: What was the point of calling the SRO?
Teacher: To teach her a lesson. That when you steal, you go to jail.
Hailey: Kindergarteners go to jail for stealing?
Teacher: Well . . . I don't know . . .

When asked why she intervened, Hailey said: "I knew it was the right thing to do. The SRO could break the child's relationship with the school, and I had an obligation to reassure her and jump in to make sure she was safe." Hailey also mentioned that intentional preparation during her SCC experience where "we had conversations about police in schools and how to push back against negative comments" helped her act in these moments.

During student teaching, Hailey's principal was so impressed with her that, in an email to Kristin, he expressed that he saw her as someone who could shift the culture of the school; she was subsequently offered a full-time job at the school. Now in her first teaching position, Hailey is just as committed to social justice and equity in her teaching:

It just looks different from what I had imagined. I believe that my commitment is stronger than it was before, due to working with students and being able to see the injustice and struggles that my students face on a daily basis and how it impacts every move they make inside and outside of our building. SCC picked me up and showed me what the teaching profession is really all about. The love for my students, families, and communities that is necessary [to teach effectively]. The determination that is essential to keep going and to continue doing the hard work on myself. The injustice that our students, families, and communities face that is strong enough to bring you to your knees and leave you with your head on your desk wondering why our society is the way that it is. And then the constant reminder of all of these things are why this work is hard, but necessary. It just feels right in my heart to teach for social justice. It's a personal commitment for myself, but more importantly, for my students. It's what they deserve. Our goal as teachers is to help our students grow and learn so that one day, they will be active members in a democratic society. If that is what we are trying to do then we should teach students to think critically and question the world around them, to stand up and speak out. And we need to do that too. I'm committed to teaching for social justice because it's necessary for a better and more just society.

KYLIE'S JOURNEY:
"NOT ONLY SOMETHING I COULD DO BUT NEEDED TO DO..."

I am a middle-class White woman teaching in a low-income and highly diverse elementary school, with the desire to generate change. The stereotypical and culturally incompetent savior teacher that most likely came to your mind after reading my last statement is not who I am. The unfortunate truth that typically feeds that stereotype compels me to justify myself through self-reflection and honesty.

As a 5th-grade teacher in her 1st year at a school on the south side of Indianapolis, Kylie's path to this place has been anything but straight. Prior to participating in SCC, social justice was not on her "radar." By the end of the program, however, not only had she developed a strong commitment to social justice, she sought to put it into practice in her daily life. Upon completion of the program, she and a small group of students sought to revive a student group for education majors—which they named Educators for Equity and Justice—in order to influence their peers and continue to develop their own capacity for social justice teaching. Despite this commitment, she doubted whether she wanted to teach. In fact, she says:

> I decided I did not want to teach, and I stuck with that decision all the way up through student teaching. I fully believed that I could not enact my social justice orientation in the classroom.

Kylie's classroom and field experiences post-SCC profoundly affected her and helped her to see that teaching, and teaching in ways that prioritize equity and social justice, was *"not only something I could do but needed to do."* She explains:

> I found myself completely immersed back into the traditional education system, where none of the ideologies I just fell in love with are taking place. I was back in the role of being seen as only a student, not an equal. However, this caused me to have a huge revelation. If I was feeling unseen, disrespected, and mistreated as an adult woman in college, how are our elementary students surviving? It helped me gain a greater perspective of how some of our younger students feel daily.

Despite these insights, Kylie still thought she could not enact her social justice orientation in the classroom. She says, *"I felt as though I would have an easier time doing so in a different field related to children and their families."* She elaborates:

> When leaving the program, having a commitment to social justice felt like a huge amount of pressure. I hadn't witnessed a teacher take the practices we had learned and successfully implement them in their elementary classroom, and I started to believe that it might not be possible. I thought the pushback would be too strong, and I wouldn't have the necessary support.

For Kylie, her student-teaching experience was pivotal:

> I was placed in another former SCC teacher's classroom for my student-teaching placement, and my world changed. Finally, I saw someone implementing everything we learned. Through watching her, I realized that this was something *I could not only do, but something I needed to do.* I had the tools. I had the mindset. I had the support. To not make use of all of that by having my own classroom would be doing a disservice to so many students.

Seeing the types of pedagogies that aligned with her philosophy in practice, Kylie was able to move from thought to action, and finally envision how she could enact her values in the classroom. Now in her 1st year, Kylie explains how she does this:

> Once I began my 1st year of teaching, I realized that being culturally responsive isn't something you can "do enough" of. It's honestly not something you can measure. It is a different way of thinking; it's your perspective on life. Of course, you can say, "Oh, yes! This lesson is totally focused on social justice and will be culturally relevant to my students!" However, throughout my 1st year I have learned that being a culturally responsive, socially just teacher has less to do with manipulating content and standards to your benefit, and more to do with your perspective. When you have that social justice switch turned on in your brain, it's forever turned on. You can't turn it off. When that happens, your commitment to social justice becomes interwoven into your being. You pause, acknowledge, and think with a different intention than others. Yes, it is important to still intentionally input socially just content into your students, but to me what is more powerful is the small moments. The moments where your students are communicating their needs to you. Those small moments are when I am most thankful for my

social awareness. The moments where I truly see my students, when I hear them, when I can acknowledge who they are . . .

While Kylie has found a way to enact her values in the classroom, it hasn't been easy. She explains:

The biggest challenge I have faced is with staff. When you are surrounded by staff who are not culturally responsive, it can become daunting. There is already a stigma that comes with being a 1st-year teacher, so when you come in with culturally responsive ideas the judgment begins to grow. My classroom is filled with flexible seating, intrinsic motivation, and student-created rules and boundaries. That looks vastly different from most classrooms, and when you pair that with being a 1st-year teacher, you find yourself with a lot of the staff questioning if you have any idea what you are doing. I respectfully ignore those judgments and seek out others who have similar mindsets, which I am very fortunate to have found a select few at my school. Although it is important to try to educate those around you who lack social justice knowledge, it is equally as important to look out for your own mental health and well-being. You can't be a hero, not all people will be receptive to your ideas and values, and that is something you have to accept.

Finding likeminded people to sustain her has been critical for Kylie. Similarly, staying focused on her reasons for teaching have helped her to persist in the face of the challenges. Kylie discusses a story that has been a landmark for her as she navigates her 1st year:

The essence of the story is that someone keeps throwing babies into a river, and a group of people rush into the river and save the babies. One man leaves, and when the group of people question him, he states he is going upstream to stop whoever keeps throwing the babies into the river. This acted as a metaphor to systematic oppression, and how we could begin dismantling the system. I posed questions to [my professor] about this story. Parts of the metaphor didn't sit right with me. I didn't like the idea of "saving" the babies, as we know savior teaching is toxic. However, what are we to do with those drowning babies who keep on coming down the river? Dr. Eva had the most brilliant revelation, that instead of pursuing the impossible task of saving all the babies, *we teach them how to swim.* This was everything to me, and it still is. Our students have and will continue to have many struggles in life. They are in a world where they have less opportunity and face more oppression than others.

While we work on dismantling the system, we can't forget about those babies in the river, and we need to realize they do not need saving. We need to teach our children how to swim, how to survive and thrive in a world that at times can be completely against them. We need to teach them the skills and give them the tools in order to be successful citizens. What keeps me going is seeing those babies in the river, eager to survive, and knowing that all they need is someone to teach them how to swim.

JACOB'S JOURNEY: "I WAS NOT READY FOR THE TRUTH"

Before SCC, I was oblivious to the term *social justice*. I always knew that people grew up in different circumstances, but I never figured that the deck would be stacked against certain groups of people. I knew I was fortunate enough to have both of my parents who loved me and supported me, but I didn't realize the amount of privilege I had until SCC. The reason I got into teaching was the same old lofty goal of changing the world for the better. Social justice wasn't even on my radar at the time. SCC reinvigorated my purpose and passion for teaching. Upon completing the course, I was astonished at the lack of cultural knowledge I had received as a child. My instructors had not purposely deceived me, but I still felt a frustration that I did not want any other child to experience. The commitment to teach for social justice began at that moment. A commitment that soon became a lifestyle. It became a part of me that I couldn't shut off. SCC transformed my perspective on teaching, as I now use it as a tool to help heal the deep wound of social injustice in this country.

For Jacob, a young White male from a small rural town in Indiana, teaching for social justice was not the obvious or automatic choice. Emblematic of one of the program's touchstones—when we know better, we do better—Jacob explains that his purpose for teaching was transformed and a fire was lit within him, deeply influencing his decisions as an educator. For example, as a result of this new orientation, Jacob made the decision to student-teach in Texas, where he actively attempted to put his community-engaged, social justice philosophy to work. As an outsider to the community, Jacob was committed to building authentic relationships with students and families. Teachers in the building warned him to avoid the neighborhood; instead, Jacob approached a paraprofessional whom he knew lived in the community and asked to attend community events with her as a way to learn more about the lives of his students. Now in his 2nd year of teaching in a public school just outside of New Orleans, in a racially and socioeconomically marginalized community, he continues to put his principles into practice. Explaining this commitment, Jacob says:

> Everywhere I would go, every video I see, I immediately begin to think of ways I could get my students to question and think critically about all parties involved. Each of my lessons are now framed within this scope. It would be a disservice to my students if I continue sharing only one perspective of the complex story we call life. Every year I will continue to empower the youth at a young age. I will continue to discuss injustices faced by cultural groups. I will continue to ask thought-provoking questions. I will continue to teach them how to analyze sources and think critically. I will continue to give my students a space to make connections about what has happened in the past and how it influences our lives today. I will continue to develop tomorrow's leaders. Powerful young men and women who will soon help bridge the divide and bring our great country together.

Jacob speaks at length about how he enacts his social justice orientation, and the successes and challenges that have resulted from his attempts to practice what he teaches (Picower, 2012):

> My successes are due to my teaching position. I am responsible for teaching U.S. history and science to a group of 90 4th-graders. How much luckier can I get? Both subjects are the perfect combination to reflect upon the injustices cultural groups have faced and how we can use science and engineering to help save the planet and build for a better future. The state social studies curriculum literally gives me the opportunity to discuss the Transatlantic Slave Trade, Native American desecration, the Civil Rights Movement, and immigrant experiences, just to name a few. For a teacher enacting social justice, a more perfect scenario does not exist. The state science curriculum follows the new NGSS standards, which in 4th grade emphasize the use of energy in our society and its effects on the environment. My students investigate how our use of nonrenewable energy is leading to the dangers of climate change—a reality that they will be responsible for solving when they grow up, like it or not. I count my blessings every day knowing that I am truly teaching my students the knowledge and skills they will need to fix the problems of this world.
> [I have found] the best way to implement social justice is allowing the students to experience the content. They need to have a personal stake and feel invested in the topics being discussed. I use

a three-step approach. I begin by having my students pair up and critically examine sources. These can be an image, painting, object, video, or other source. They are responsible for pointing out what they "see" and what they "think" it means. This "I See, I Think, I Wonder" activity captures their curiosity and allows them to respond to one another's ideas. A vested interest has been captured as they want to find out if their predictions were right throughout the lesson. The second step is to provide a role-playing experience of the day's lesson. My students have played the parts of Thomas Jefferson, Sacagawea, the Freedom Riders, immigrants during the Industrial Revolution, and so on. They've predicted, and now they have experienced, the content. Throughout the role-playing activity I sprinkle in the higher-order thinking questions and have my students evaluate and critique the decisions people made throughout history. Both step 1 and step 2 take no longer than 20 minutes. I provide them with whatever the Tier 1 curriculum is for step 3 in order to strengthen their understanding of the investigated topic. Afterward, I have them complete an exit ticket or work on part of a project that measures the standard being tracked.

Luckily, I have never been challenged on the content I teach. What I have been challenged on is my use of time. I have had administrators recommend that I shorten these periods [experiential learning outlined above] down to provide for more "instructional" time. In response, I took a week and taught using both styles. Half the week I provided an experience before my students started annotating their text, and the other half of the week we went straight into our reading/questions. Guess which lessons they were able to master the standards on? The ones I provided an experience with. I brought the results to my administrators, and they gave me the green light to keep doing what I was doing as long as it didn't take up my whole class. Yet, the hidden enemy lurks in the back of the room at all times, serving as a constant reminder that the activities I'm providing must come to an end. Time has stifled my commitment to social justice more times than I can count. I'm emailing parents, grading tests, consoling students, adapting my instruction—the list just goes on and on. The time I thought I would have for creating curriculum that would target social justice is being taken, minute by minute. When I left SCC, I anticipated I would be able to create these amazing lessons that would impact my students and blow their minds. Walking into my room, you would hear, "What! That's not fair!" "Are you serious! How could they let this happen?" "Is this still going on?" "What can we do to help stop this?" I honestly felt that I would receive autonomy over my lesson planning and

could create meaningful learning experiences that highlighted the
injustices of the past. Of course, I would adhere to the standards, but
ultimately, I would get the final say in how much time I could take.
Boy, was I wrong. Naïve would be an understatement. I was not
ready for the truth about teaching and the realities of being a public
educator.

When I go home and finally take a breath, I realize that my
commitment to social justice is not as strong as it was upon leaving
SCC, but it still will always be there. No matter how hard or long
the days are, I will stay committed to teaching for social justice.
What keeps me going is the anticipation my students have for a
learning experience. The way they talk about my lessons when they
get home. How they come in talking about what they saw on the
news and how it relates to our teaching. The rapid pace of questions
they ask me and each other when they realize an injustice throughout
history. A student standing up and deciding to cast her "vote" in a
lesson on Jim Crow voting laws and explaining she would rather live
freely than be afraid of the repercussions of Whites in the South. The
class standing up and giving her a standing ovation for her bravery.
When my students are thinking critically, displaying kindness and
empathy for others, these are the moments I live for. These are the
moments that keep me committed.

DISCUSSION

As the quotation from Greg Michie at the onset of this chapter states,
having beliefs and guiding principles is one thing, but putting those into
practice is an entirely different matter. The candidate perspectives shared
in this chapter are a testament to this. Kaylie, Hailey, Kylie, and Jacob
have all struggled to enact their values in practice despite possessing a
deep commitment to equity and social justice. Yet, in the face of the many
obstacles in their paths, they have persisted, finding ways to "creatively
maladjust" (Kohl, 1994) to both explicitly and covertly challenge schooling as usual. While each is on their own specific and idiosyncratic journey,
their stories reveal numerous parallels from which we, as teacher educators, can learn.

First and foremost, it is abundantly evident that a strong commitment
to equity and social justice matters. As Kylie states, "When you have that
social justice switch turned on in your brain, it's forever turned on. You
can't turn it off. When that happens, your commitment to social justice
becomes interwoven into your being. You pause, acknowledge, and think
with a different intention than others." Jacob, too, talks about how social

justice became a "lifestyle," something that was with him "everywhere [he] would go" and could not be turned off. While none of the candidates entered the program with this orientation, the schematic shift that they made was lasting and served as the foundation and motivation for their teaching. Without this switch, the rest would not be possible. To those of us engaged in preparing future teachers, this should be encouraging news: We can help candidates develop the necessary dispositions for teaching (Diez & Murrell, 2010).

Additionally, all four candidates possess a robust understanding of systemic inequality and are deeply committed to mitigating it through education—knowledge that scholars consider essential to effective teaching (Cochran-Smith et al., 2009; Picower, 2012; Sleeter, 2012). In fact, each candidate discussed the way in which social justice became a "mission" in and of itself, and not in some stereotypically savior way wherein they believe it is their job to fix children. Rather, they believe in the power of teaching to empower children to think critically about the world around them. As Kaylie shares, "it was my personal mission to ensure that the students who entered my future classroom would not only be cognizant of these issues but become empowered to stand up for social justice in their own life." Understanding oppression, power, and privilege, as well as their own positionality, was an essential component of their development.

As part of this mission, candidates saw it as their role to speak up and challenge institutional structures and schooling as usual. We see this most explicitly in the stories from Hailey and Jacob. Hailey makes it a point to combat the negative talk of colleagues and intervene in situations that are harmful to children. Jacob uses the curriculum to challenge the single stories (Adiche, 2009) often peddled in our history books and, using student learning as evidence, pushed back on administrators who sought to curb his teaching. Kaylie and Kylie both share examples of this, too. Kaylie found herself curtailed by both her peers and mentor teachers; Kylie talks of colleagues in her building who disagree with her approaches. Both have pushed forward despite these criticisms, albeit less forcefully.

While the candidates knew that this work would be hard and anticipated resistance, they all admit that they did not realize just how hard it would be. Given few opportunities to see socially just, culturally responsive and sustaining pedagogies in practice was discouraging. Kaylie talks of a diminished commitment; Jacob of frustration to find his footing; Kylie of almost not teaching. Most explicit in her critique, Kylie laments the impacts of traditional teaching on campus and in practicum placements, sharing that she felt "unseen, disrespected, and mistreated as an adult woman in college." While a negative experience for her personally, she shares that this also led to a significant insight for her regarding the daily experience of children in schools and motivates her to do better by her students. This, in particular, should give us pause. If our strongest candidates sometimes struggle in their conviction to do this work, what of our less strong candidates? How will they persist?

Finding success has often meant a recalibration in what candidates envisioned enacting their social justice orientation to look like. Jacob discusses the many constraints of the school day and the lack of autonomy many teachers today experience, prompting him to make small changes to work within the system. Kylie speaks to the power of the small moments and that while it's important to infuse social justice content into the curriculum, it is one's perspective and how they interpret students' actions and communication that makes a difference. Hailey, on the other hand, while acknowledging that the work is messier than she anticipated and she sometimes "bites her tongue," is probably the most vocal in expressing her values. She credits having models of what it looks like to speak up and practicing doing just that as helping her find her courage to persist.

Lastly, the candidates discussed the importance of finding others who are likeminded to sustain their passion and commitment. Hailey says: "Another landmark I have is my cohort and professors from SCC 2018. We all still communicate and have created a positive community where we can share our experiences, thoughts, successes, and our failures." While they acknowledge that they knew this would be "lonely work," it is apparent that it is easy to get caught in the undertow when swimming in unsupportive waters. As Kaylie explained earlier in this chapter, having a network made the work "less lonely and daunting" and aided in her continuous education. In Kylie's case, she was lucky enough to locate a small network in her school. When this isn't possible, having an outside, established network becomes a lifeline for candidates.

In summary, what we learn from the candidates is that while knowledge of and a desire to address inequality and oppression are required, they are simply not enough to sustain them in their journey to becoming culturally responsive and sustaining, equity-focused, socially just educators. In light of what candidates share, there appear to be several concrete actions teacher educators can take to help support candidates to enact this identity in the field.

IMPLICATIONS AND RECOMMENDATIONS: A WORD TO TEACHER EDUCATORS

Just as we want our candidates to work to make change both inside and outside of the classroom, teacher educators have the same responsibility. As we listen to the candidates' voices, it is clear that a great deal of work remains to be done in order to change the system of teacher preparation. While all four candidates retained their commitment to social justice, the lack of understanding and the resistance to this orientation, which they sometimes found on campus and in the field, hindered their ability to enact social justice pedagogy. We, as teacher educators, have an obligation to work for change in our departments, in our colleges, and in our school partnerships. As the saying goes, *You can't be what you can't see*, and without more opportunities to observe and practice teaching for social justice, we may find more candidates reverting to traditional ways of teaching. Based on the experiences of these four candidates, in addition to the many anecdotes we have heard from other candidates, we offer some suggestions for what teacher preparation might do differently.

First and foremost, candidates need examples—several examples—of culturally responsive and sustaining, socially just, equity-focused practice. Kylie's story, in particular, highlights just how important this is. Had she not been placed with a former SCC candidate, where she was able to see a philosophy similar to hers put into practice daily, we might have one fewer educator in the field today. While many programs prioritize getting candidates into the field earlier and more frequently, it is imperative that we consider the *quality* of these placements over the *quantity*. Hailey makes this point clearly:

> This work is incredibly hard, and it is so easy to fall off track and say or do things that you don't believe in. It's easy to shame students, it's easy to hear negative words being spoken and instead of speaking up, you agree and keep your comments to yourself [. . .] It would have been amazing to be placed with a supervising teacher during student teaching that would help and encourage a commitment to social justice.

Placing candidates in classrooms that model traditional approaches rather than engage in culturally responsive and sustaining pedagogy, engage the community, and prioritize equity and social justice offers our candidates, at best, little more than the opportunity to see what *not* to do and, at worst, undermines their agency while socializing them into "school as usual" (Daniels, 2016).

Of course, candidates need these experiences on campus as well, a point Hailey makes: "You should know that the thing that has helped me along this journey the most is having professors to look up to who are doing this work not only in their own spaces, but they are working alongside previous and current students to do this work as well." Faculty members' actions on campus were profoundly powerful for candidates. Here again, recall Kylie's words as she describes her experience back on campus: "unseen, disrespected, and mistreated." While the other candidates did not speak in such stark terms, Hailey shares, "If there was anything at all that would have made this transition easier it would have been being able to return to campus and continue doing this work without the incredible amount of pushback from other teacher educators." In addition to direct resistance, Hailey explains that, through omission, some faculty made clear that social justice, equity, and being community and culturally responsive were not always valued. This omission, while not labeled as such, is also evident in Kaylie's remarks when she talks about her peers feeling "unprepared and unqualified" to have conversations about issues like race.

This is not surprising, as the scholarship shows, far too frequently, that courses "addressing diversity" are relegated to standalone courses (Daniels, 2016; Sleeter, 2001) and terms like "social justice" are seen as outside the purview of teacher preparation (Landorf & Nevin, 2007), thus giving the impression that diversity and social justice have little to do with the practicalities of teaching. Instead, social justice and equity must be organizing principles around which all teacher preparation programs are based. To do otherwise is to leave intact the traditional paradigm— one that serves to reinforce and reify dominant norms, marginalizes students and families from nondominant* backgrounds, and exacerbates the opportunity gap (Carter & Welner, 2013). Teacher education has a responsibility to demystify how power and privilege work and assist candidates in having the "difficult conversations" in the classroom. This will require change on the part of teacher education, which often perpetuates, maintains, and legitimizes oppression (e.g., see Allen et al., 2017) for discussions of teacher education, Whiteness and racism), as well as teacher educators, the majority of whom are White (American Association of Colleges for Teacher Education, 2018) and have a vested interest in protecting Whiteness.

Second, it is important that programs of teacher preparation help build candidates' social network. All four of the candidates discuss encountering some level of resistance, be it from teacher educators, mentor teachers and other adults in the school, and/or their peers. There is no guarantee that one will find likeminded people in one's school, as happened for Kylie. Helping candidates build a network of likeminded

---

*We use "dominant" and "nondominant" to describe a broad range of individuals, groups, and institutions relative to their positioning within the larger field of power. Importantly, the term "nondominant" includes terms used to define populations by race and class (e.g., low-income, marginalized, minoritized, underrepresented). Similarly, "dominant" also encompasses a broad range of terms (e.g., privileged, elite, affluent, White). These terms align with our use of "dominant" and "nondominant" cultural capital (Carter 2003, quoted in Cipollone & Stich, 2017).

educators helps them know they are not alone, and gives them a space to share ideas, triumphs, struggles, and questions. It also serves as an educational space where candidates can continue building their knowledge and skill. As Kaylie shares, candidates need this space while still in the preservice stage as well as when they are in the field. In fact, all four candidates were part of a group, Educators for Equity and Justice, and regularly reach out to peers from that group today. Thus, building a network for candidates before they enter the field who can move with them is essential to sustaining both their commitment to social justice and their agency to enact it.

Third, it is imperative that we help candidates learn how to, as Herbert Kohl (1994) calls it, "creatively maladjust." Many of our candidates find themselves in schools in which their autonomy is curtailed. While they are not provided with a scripted curriculum, what they are expected to teach is highly proscribed and, especially as new teachers, they may feel little ability to deviate. To address this challenge, Jacob suggests that we

> advise preservice teachers to take what their district has given them to teach and make minor adjustments to it the 1st year. Once they feel more comfortable the 2nd year, they can begin to teach more critically from a social justice lens. I would tell them that it isn't giving up or giving in. It's more so finding your footing before you start the race.

If we are to effectively prepare candidates, we must help them learn how to adapt curriculum so that they can make it culturally responsive and sustaining. Often, practicum assignments require candidates to develop lessons from scratch or develop units of their choosing—a somewhat unrealistic exercise given the current realities of the classroom. If we were to help students practice adapting and, perhaps more accurately, subverting the curriculum, they may feel more efficacious in the field. Jacob's example of using data to speak back to an administrator is also instructive. Creating opportunities wherein candidates can practice speaking up and back could go a long way in helping develop the confidence to do just that in the field.

Lastly, as teacher educators, we have an obligation to help candidates identify their "landmarks." Michie (2010), using the metaphor of the (mythical) undertow to discuss teaching, explains:

> The undertow was an invisible current beneath the ocean's surface that, if you weren't careful, could pull you down the coastline or out to sea before you knew what was happening. It tugged you along almost imperceptibly, she said,

so you had to consciously keep your bearings: Pick a recognizable landmark and don't lose sight of it. (p. 705)

The pull of schooling as usual is powerful. There are real obstacles that could (and often do) prevent candidates from realizing their vision for teaching. As we heard in the candidates' stories, having a passion for social justice is not enough to ensure that students enact teaching that is socially just. Having knowledge about the gross injustices that exist in our society, which are frequently perpetuated in and through schooling, is not enough. They will need to be resilient in the face of such challenges, so having a recognizable landmark, something that meaningfully motivates them to persist, is imperative. We must be honest about the challenges of this work and engage our candidates in frequent and continuous discussions that prompt them to reflect on their personal motivations for teaching for equity and social justice.

CONCLUSION

The candidates' stories demonstrate just how difficult it can be to translate belief into action. How does one put into practice a social justice orientation in environments that are not supportive, at best, and, at worst, actively obstructionist? In her role as teacher educator, Kristin expends a significant amount of effort in helping students develop dispositions toward social justice, equity, inclusion, and democracy. While she strives to model these dispositions in her everyday practice, without authentic opportunities to practice and greater support for their beliefs, she worries that our teacher candidates may get caught in the undertow of school as usual (Michie, 2010). While the stories of Kaylie, Hailey, Kylie, and Jacob provide hope that candidates can indeed live their social justice values in their practica, in their student teaching, and in their own classrooms, they also demonstrate just how daunting the task is. As some of our strongest candidates, these four possess the *will* and the *skill*, and are resilient and resourceful, able to adapt and creatively maladjust. While these four have thus far been able to persist in the face of institutional challenges, would candidates with less confidence and self-assuredness be able to do so? Will these four educators burn out? As we work to make institutional and programmatic changes, let's use the candidates' words as our landmarks.

REFERENCES

Adiche, C. (2009). *The dangers of a single story*. TED. https://www.ted.com/talks/chimamanda_ngozi_adichie_the_danger_of_a_single_story?language=en

Aldridge Sanford, A. (2020). *From thought to action: Developing a social justice orientation*. Cognella Academic Publishing.

Allen, A., Hancock, S. D., Starker-Glass, T., & Lewis, C. W. (2017). Mapping culturally relevant pedagogy into teacher education programs: A critical framework. *Teachers College Record*, *119*(1), 1–26.

American Association of Colleges for Teacher Education. (2018). *Colleges of education: A national portrait* (Executive Summary). https://secure.aacte.org/apps/rl/res_get.php?fid=4178&ref=rl

Anyon, J. (1980). Social class and the hidden curriculum of work. *Journal of Education*, *162*(1), 67–92.

Anyon, Y., Jenson, J. M., Altschul, I., Farrar, J., McQeen, J., Greer, E., Downing, B., & Simmons, J. (2014). The persistent effect of race and the promise of alternatives to suspension in school discipline outcomes. *Children and Youth Services Review*, *44*, 379–386.

Apple, M. W. (2004). *Ideology and curriculum* (3rd ed.). Routledge.

Apple, M. W. (1992). The text and cultural politics. *Educational Researcher*, *21*(7), 4–19.

Bowles, S., & Gintis, H. (1976). *Schooling in capitalist America*. Basic Books.

Carter, P. L. (2003). "Black" cultural capital, status positioning, and schooling conflicts for low-income African American youth. *Social Problems*, *50*(1), 136–155.

Carter, P., & Welner, K. G. (2013). *Closing the opportunity gap: What America must do to give every child an even chance*. Oxford University Press.

Cipollone, K., & Stich, A. (2017). In the shadows: "Democratizing" college preparatory education in two urban schools. *Sociology of Education*, *90*(4), 333–354.

Cipollone, K., Stich, A., & Weis, L. (2020). STEM for all: Student identities and the paradox of STEM democratization. *Teachers College Record*, *122*(2), 1–67.

Cochran-Smith, M., Shakman, K., Jong, C., Terrell, D., Barnatt, J., & McQuillan, P. (2009). Good and just teaching: The case for social justice in teacher education. *American Journal of Education*, *115*(3), 347–377.

Daniels, S. M. (2016). Grappling with culturally responsive pedagogy: A study of elementary-level teacher candidates' learning across practicum and diversity coursework experiences. *Urban Review*, *48*(4), 579–600.

Diez, M., & Murrell, P. (2010). Dispositions for teacher education: Starting points for consideration. In P. Murrell, M. Diez, S. Feiman-Nemser, & D. Schussler (Eds.), *Teaching as a moral practice: Defining, developing, and assessing professional dispositions in teacher education* (pp. 7–26). Harvard Education Press.

Haberman, M. (1991). Can cultural awareness be taught in teacher education programs? *Teaching Education, 4*(1), 25–31.

Jackson, I., & Knight-Manuel, M. (2019). "Color does not equal consciousness": Educators of Color learning to enact sociopolitical consciousness. *Journal of Teacher Education, 70*(1), 65–78.

Kohl, H. (1994). Creative maladjustment. *Education Week, 5*(7), 26–31.

Labaree, D. 2010. *Someone has to fail.* Harvard University Press.

Ladson-Billings, G. (1995). Toward a theory of culturally relevant pedagogy. *American Educational Research Journal, 32*(3), 465–491.

Landorf, H., & Nevin, A. (2007). Social justice as a disposition for teacher education programs: Why is it such a problem? In S. M. Nielsen & M. S. Plakhotnik (Eds.), *Proceedings of the Sixth Annual College of Education Research Conference: Urban and International Education Section* (pp. 49–53). Florida International University Press.

Love, B. L. (2019). *We want to do more than survive: Abolitionist teaching and the pursuit of educational freedom.* Beacon.

Michie, G. (2010). Teaching in the undertow: Resisting the pull of schooling-as-usual. In T. Burant, L. Christiensen, K. Dawson Salas, & S. Walters (Eds.), *The new teacher book* (2nd ed., pp. 705–710). Rethinking Schools.

Moll, L. C., Amanti, C., Neff, D., & González, N. (1992). Funds of knowledge for teaching: Using a qualitative approach to connect homes and classrooms. *Theory into Practice, 31*(2), 132–141.

Oakes, J. (1985). *Keeping track: How schools structure inequality.* Yale University Press.

Orfield, G., & Lee, C. (2005). Segregation 50 years after Brown: A metropolitan change. In L. Weis & M. Fine (Eds.), *Beyond silenced voices: Class, race and gender in United States schools* (pp. 3–20). State University of New York Press.

Paris, D., & Alim, H. S. (Eds.) (2017). *Culturally sustaining pedagogies: Teaching and learning for justice in a changing world.* Teachers College Press.

Picower, B. (2012). *Practice what you teach: Social justice education in the classroom and the streets.* Routledge.

Sciuchetti, M. B. (2017). Addressing inequity in special education: An integrated framework for culturally responsive social emotional practice. *Psychology in Schools, 54*(10), 1245–1251.

Skiba, R. J., Chung, C.-G., Trachok, M., Baker, T. L., Sheya, A., & Hughes, R. L. (2014). Parsing disciplinary disproportionality: Contributions of infraction, student, and school characteristics to out-of-school suspension and expulsion. *American Educational Research Journal, 51*(4), 640–670.

Sleeter, C. (2001). Preparing teachers for culturally diverse schools: Research and the overwhelming presence of whiteness. *Journal of Teacher Education, 52*(2), 94–106.

Sleeter, C. (2012). Confronting the marginalization of culturally responsive pedagogy. *Urban Education*, *47*(3), 562–584.

Spring, J. (2004). *American Education* (11th ed.). McGraw-Hill.

TFAEvents. (2016, February 11). *All together now: Academic rigor and culturally responsive pedagogy* [Video]. YouTube. https://www.youtube.com/watch?v=OzNl4unAe20

U.S. Department of Education Office for Civil Rights. (2014). *Civil rights data collection data snapshot: School discipline* (Issue Brief No. 1.)

Weis, L., Eisenhart, M., Cipollone, K., Stich, A., Nikischer, A., Hanson, J., Ohle, S., & Dominguez, R. (2015). In the guise of STEM education reform: Opportunity structures and outcomes in inclusive STEM-focused high schools. *American Educational Research Journal*, *52*(6), 1024–1059.

Yosso, T. (2005). Whose culture has capital? A critical race theory discussion of community cultural wealth. *Race Ethnicity and Education*, *8*(1), 69–91.

Zygmunt, E., Cipollone, K., Tancock, S., Clausen, J., Clark, P., & Mucherah, W. (2018). Loving out loud: Community mentors, teacher candidates, and transformational learning through a pedagogy of care and connection. *Journal of Teacher Education*, *69*(2), 127–139.

Zygmunt, E., & Clark, P. (2016). *Transforming teacher education for social justice*. Teachers College Press.

Part III Reflection

In 2017, the population of Black and Brown students in United States classrooms tipped the 50% mark, with a now-documented 52% of students representing minoritized populations—a trend predicted to grow exponentially over the next decade (National Center for Education Statistics [NCES], 2020). While the student population has shifted dramatically in the last 2 decades, those who teach remain disproportionately White—equipped and often emboldened with power and privilege that inform who they are and how they move through the world. According to Greene and colleagues (2017), a typical White person in the United States lives in a neighborhood that is 75% White, diminishing opportunities for interracial interaction and cross-cultural connection. The danger of this divide is articulated by Tyrone Howard, who explains:

> I think what happens is we tend to live in our own world, and we tend to think that our way of being, that our own cultural orientation is pretty much "normal." And when we do that, what happens is that we then determine, or we then designate other kinds of behavior that isn't in line with ours as being abnormal or somehow problematic. And I think that when we step outside our own cultural comfort zone and begin to recognize that just because something is different doesn't make it deficient, that is when our competency can begin to enhance and expand. (Clark et al., 2016, p. 270).

And so, according to Howard's counsel, community-engaged teacher preparation, as described in these chapters, provides the opportunity for preservice teachers to experience, reflect upon, and integrate into their consciousness the experiences of the "other" as not decidedly deficient, but, in the words of Davis (2008), "as a unique manifestation of the human spirit." In tandem, community-engaged teacher preparation offers the opportunity to examine the systemic structures that perpetuate inequity, and to dedicate oneself to the elimination of such: developing both the *skill* and, more importantly, the *will* to work toward equity and social justice in schooling—a historically elusive and contemporarily stubborn target, even amongst those with a patent pursuit of such.

It is daunting to consider that recent research (Stark et al., 2020) comparing teachers to nonteachers in a national data set found that teachers from all demographic groups evidenced as much pro-White/anti-Black bias as members of the general population—bias that proves challenging to mitigate without concerted opportunities to critically reflect upon one's values in practice (Cook et al., 2018). Although the first chapter in this section underscored the disparate realities of preservice teachers of color and their White peers and how their lived experience impacts their predispositions toward equity and social justice, research suggests that teachers of color experience internalized racism (Kohli, 2014) and are not immune from negative bias toward students of color in general, and Black boys in particular (Gilliam et al., 2016). This research further supports a program of preparation during which contextualized, critical reflection is embedded in practice. Community-engaged teacher preparation addresses the pressing needs of deconstructing prior schema and rebuilding a new lens through which to reconsider what equity and justice look like in education, and to begin to develop the efficacy to be agents of change.

Absent justice in education, much is lost for students *and* their teachers, including, according to Howard (2019), "any semblance of hope." According to Howard, "hope is a source of strength, an asset of possibility, and a tangible way of grasping for a reality that is not seen but is believed to be within reach" (p. 143). And yet hope devoid of informed action becomes blind faith, which, according to Wilson (1998), "no matter how passionately expressed, will not suffice" (p. 260). Possessing both the efficacy and agency to address injustice positions the students and teachers in these chapters with the capacity to not only dream of a different reality in schools, but to "creatively maladjust" (Kohl, 1994, p. 26) to begin to make it so.

Shedd (1928/2006) wrote, "ships are safe in harbor, but that's not what ships are built for." The two chapters in this section portray their characters venturing into untested waters—dissatisfied with past praxes and committed to the precepts of equity and justice in education. This work, engaged in alongside school and community partners in authentic collaboration, endeavors to prepare "community teachers" (Murrell, 2001) who not only privilege students' cultures and experience in their formal education, but who additionally understand the systemic and institutional forces that perpetuate systems of disadvantage. These teachers commit to work collaboratively with children, families, and the community in order to reshape the deeply rooted systems and practices that undermine equity. Recalling Shedd's sage counsel, the community teacher does not cling to the safety of the shore, but instead practices patience, persistence, bravery, and boldness, as they navigate their emerging passion and embrace their purpose in ensuring the equitable access and opportunity that are the founding principles of public education in our country.

A testament to finding the courage to take a stance against the current of injustice is offered by poet Audre Lorde (2006), who writes, "When I dare to be powerful, to use my strength in the service of my vision, then it becomes less and less important whether I am afraid" (p. 13). These chapters allude to the discovery of personal power, and to the audacity required to exercise an ardent energy in pursuit of educational justice for *all* students. They offer that a concerted and creative effort to reimagine teacher education is well worth the investment of reaching across borders and building bridges—structures that, if carefully nurtured, will ensure our collective advent in the schools we dare to dream are possible.

REFERENCES

Clark, P., Zygmunt, E., & Howard, T. (2016). Why race and culture matter in schools and why we need to get this right: A conversation with Dr. Tyrone Howard. *The Teacher Educator, 51*, 268–276.

Cook, C., Duong, M., McIntosh, K., Fiat, A., Larson, M., Pullman, M., & McGinnis, J. (2018). Addressing discipline disparities for Black male students: Linking malleable root causes to feasible and effective practices. *School Psychology Review, 47*(2) 135–152.

Davis, W. (2008). *The worldwide web of belief and ritual.* TED. http://www.ted.com/talks/wade_davis_on_the_worldwide_web_of_belief_and_ritual

Gilliam, W., Maupin, A., Reyes, C., Accavitti, M., & Shic, F. (2016). *Do early educators' implicit biases regarding sex and race relate to behavior expectations and recommendations of preschool expulsions and suspensions?* Yale Child Study Center.

Greene, S., Turner, M., & Gourevitch, R. (2017). *Racial residential segregation and neighborhood disparities.* U.S. Partnership on Mobility from Poverty.

Howard, T. C. (2019). *Why race and culture matter in schools: Closing the achievement gap in America's classrooms.* Teachers College Press.

Kohl, H. (1994). Creative maladjustment. *Education Week, 5*(7), 26–31.

Kohli, R. (2014). Unpacking internalized racism: Teachers of color striving for racially just classrooms. *Race Ethnicity and Education, 17*(3), 367–387.

Lorde, A. (2006). *The cancer journals: Special edition.* Aunt Lute Books.

Murrell, P. C., Jr. (2001). *The community teacher: A new framework for effective urban teaching.* Teachers College Press.

National Center for Educational Statistics (NCES). (2020). *The condition of education 2020*. Washington, DC: Author. https://nces.ed.gov/programs/coe/pdf/coe_cge.pdf

Shedd, J. (2006). *Salt from my attic*. Cited in F. Shapiro (Ed.), *The Yale book of quotations* (p. 705). Yale University Press. (Original work published 1928)

Stark, J., Riddle, T., Sinclair, S., & Warikoo, N. (2020). Teachers are people too: Examining the racial bias of teachers compared to other American adults. *Educational Researcher*, 49(4), 273–284.

Wilson, E. O. (1998). *Consilience: The unity of knowledge*. Vintage Books.

Thoughts on Hope and Healing

Eva Zygmunt

Growing up, I had a great-aunt who would now be 109. She was an elementary school teacher, and a storyteller. She had no children of her own but would spend hours recounting the exploits of the students with whom she worked, some sidesplitting, others serious, and always a few "peculiar," which seemed to fascinate her. She never spoke poorly of the children and their families in her rural Indiana school system, but on more than one occasion, she divulged how it was standard practice on "state test day" for the bus driver to be given a list of children to "not pick up." In my 35 years as an educator, this story has resonated in my memory. I have wondered who these children were, why they were marginalized, and when and how the system lost hope in them. I have wondered how, and if, schools and teachers worked to learn about the context of their lives, to develop relationships with their families, and to invest the effort required to make school relevant and engaging. I think about how these children didn't "fit" school, and how school, therefore, saw fit to leave them behind.

Reflecting on this memory and considering much of my and my colleagues' experience in and out of schools over the course of our careers, we lament that we may be more similar in current practice than we are to the contrary. While schools are significantly more diverse racially, ethnically, linguistically, and socioeconomically than they were nearly a century ago, our ethic of who "fits" school, and who is pushed to the margins is determined by the historical underpinnings of public education, the contemporary political systems that inform the standards children must accomplish in order to be classified as "educated," and the governing bodies that determine who is sanctioned, and how one becomes "qualified," to teach. Our global history of colonization and resulting systems of power and privilege continue to dictate whose stories are told, whose wisdom is honored, and whose voices, indeed, whose *lives* matter—phenomena that play out in classrooms every day to the advantage of some, and to the detriment of so many others.

Traditional teacher preparation has neither aimed to contest, nor has sufficiently disrupted, a system that has been propagative of inequity. In fact, we may be further away from this ethic than we were several decades ago, when the rhetoric of social justice was in vogue, and at least a sector of society was on board with the idea that everyone should have access and opportunity that would lead to the realization of their individual promise and potential. We argue that a market-driven, context-neutral standardization of content, pedagogy, and assessment in the current environment of teacher preparation well-serves *some,* but belies the intention of liberty and justice for *all.*

Suggesting that the constructs of liberty and justice in school are elusive requires a more nuanced elaboration of how forces of oppression and inequity often subjugate students, ill-positioning them as the critical and free-thinking citizens we aim to establish in a dynamic and democratic society. As we consider such inequity, we reflect on our experience in schools where we have seen advantage bestowed upon children because of the privileged position of their families, contrasted with the violence, both figurative and physical, perpetuated upon students whose teachers did not—and perhaps due to their experience and preparation, *would not* and therefore *could not*—imagine their greatness. We have experienced children's inequitable access to facilities and materials; inequitable access to high-quality teachers; inequitable access to a climate of high expectations; and inequitable access to an education that is culturally relevant, affirming, responsive, and sustaining. We have observed disciplinary referrals and escorts by "resource officers" reinforcing for Black boys, as young as kindergarten-aged, the perception of danger that their small figures already embody.

Angela Davis (1998) waged a battle against the "prison industrial complex," and similarly, Michelle Alexander (2010) has discussed mass incarceration as "the New Jim Crow" (further elaborated in Ava Duvernay's haunting 2016 documentary *13th*). As mentioned in the introduction to this book, Bettina Love (2019) draws on Davis's language in articulating an "educational survival complex" wherein "students are left learning to merely survive, learning how schools mimic the world they live in, thus making schools a training site for a life of exhaustion" (p. 27).

Within the confluence of these constructs, it seems important to consider what constitutes incarceration, and the psychology of how this plays out in school. As Black and Brown children are effectively denied access to their histories; as their families are restricted in terms of their "visitation"; as the program of their day is often dictated, if not scripted, uninformed by the pedagogies and community wealth of their lived experience; as their language and communication traditions are denied the respect they deserve; and as forced isolation is the consequence for understandable rebellion, one can easily see the parallels. The psychology of days and months and years of experience with such systems of oppression categorically contradicts the constructs of culturally responsive and sustaining pedagogies that give students voice and position them as co-creators of change. It is critical to consider, then, that carceral conditions in schools have emerged as a *newer* Jim Crow, literally and figuratively detaining students from the freedom that access and opportunity afford.

Research over the last decade has addressed the need for "trauma-informed" practices and pedagogies in school (Souers, 2016)—often presented as strategies through which to mediate adverse childhood experiences (ACEs) that students *bring* to school and that present obstacles to their successful adaptation in educational spheres. Much less attention is directed to the individual and institutional trauma inflicted on children *in* school, and the healing practices and pedagogies required in order to create a climate of restoration. While we do not deny that the trauma children can and do experience in families and communities is real and relevant, we argue that substantial energy and significant resources are devoted to social and emotional learning programs aimed at building students' "resilience," "grit," and "mindfulness"—strategies we believe are often more required of students in negotiating substantial trauma sanctioned within school buildings.

We know that schools alone are not the problem. Broader cultural and contextual forces, such as racism and classism, indirectly and directly influence children's, families', and communities' lived experience. Access to fair housing, living-wage employment, an adequate supply of healthy food and clean water, and preventive health care—basic human needs—are disproportionately impacted by race and income. According to Chatmon and Watson (2018), "To improve the entire ecosystem, specific institutional targets need to expose, address, and uplift those who are least served. Strategic inputs then create improvements that cascade out, affecting the policies and practices of the larger collective" (p. 8). In this book, we argue that a new paradigm of teacher education can be such an uplifting and cascading lever.

The antithesis of oppression is liberation. Juxtaposed against school-sanctioned captivity and control, the construct of educational liberation focuses on consciousness raising, and the empowerment of student voice in the work of creating a more a civil and just society. According to Freire (1996), absent liberatory practices in education, students fail to develop the critical consciousness that "would result from their intervention in the world as transformers of the world" (p. 54). An alternative is emphasized by Shalaby (2017), who asserts that we need schools

fueled by the imperative to imagine and to create a world in which there are no throwaway lives. Any of us invested in the rights of persons to be free have cause to care about the lives of children at school and to resurrect our imagination for schooling as deeply human, wildly revolutionary sites of possibility. (p. xviii)

In this volume, we argue that traditional teacher education positions future teachers as cogs in a machine that reproduces schools and classrooms as they *are* instead of the healing spaces they can *become*. We assert a resurrection of imagination in teacher education as requisite to fulfilling Shalaby's plea for a deeply human and wildly revolutionary renaissance.

As we consider the potential contribution of community-engaged teacher education as a means through which to reimagine the field of educator preparation, it is important to consider the words of Freire (1993):

The future is something that is constantly taking place, and this constant "taking place" means that the future only exists to the extent that we change the present. It is by changing the present that we build the future, therefore history is possibility, not determinism. (p. 84)

Our aim in this volume is to provide evidence that we *can*, and, indeed, currently *are* changing the present, by building a new future in teacher preparation: one that honors traditionally unrecognized sources of wisdom and expertise, informed by an ethic of "radical healing" (Ginwright, 2015). Such healing requires the concerted cultivation of community, informed by the meaningful relationships of individuals and institutions committed to the work of changing the systems that create, support, and reinforce inequity. According to Wallace (2012), "healing justice" is an emerging movement that seeks individual and collective healing, as well as works to transform the institutions and relationships that are causing the harm in the first place.

Restorative justice in schools (Hopkins, 2002, 2004) has received a lot of notice of late as an alternative to traditional practices of operant conditioning and exclusionary practices of suspension and expulsion. Originally coined by Eglash (1958) as "creative restitution," this approach focuses on how an offender, with appropriate scaffolding, makes amends to those he has hurt by his offense. As we consider the future of educator preparation and our collective obligations to the children, families, and communities we serve, we believe it is imperative to not only raise, but to effectively embrace, with grace, the sobering realization that traditional teacher education has been the offender, and we now find ourselves in the enviable position to make amends and to turn the tide of tradition to one of restoration and hope.

George Washington Carver said, "where there is no vision, there is no hope" (Boyd, 2015, p. 83). The communities in which we have been privileged to work, and those elevated in these chapters, provide great hope for the future. These are communities whose fierce love for their children, their culture, and their communities inform their collective resolve to have voice, and to co-create a vision for what schools can and should be. We assert that, as programs of educator preparation, we must position ourselves to be grateful recipients of the knowledge and expertise of communities, humbling ourselves to the admission that our work, even though it shamefully was granted license to be, ought never to have been possible absent this partnership.

The eight illustrations of community-engaged teacher preparation in this volume speak to the impetus for innovation, but also accentuate the complex task of interrupting, disrupting, reimagining, and rebuilding firmly established schema, structures, and systems. Contradicting the simple relocation of a course or a clinical experience into a community space, this work is political and requires creative strategy, authentic collaboration, concerted commitment, and "radical hope" (Gannon, 2020; Lear, 2006). This hope requires an essential critical consciousness involving a resolute reflection on self, other, and the mechanisms through which inequity is routinely reproduced, as we work together toward positive change.

The current racial, political, economic, cultural, and religious divides in our country and world are rampant and raging—the flames of which, at the time of this writing, are being fanned by leadership exhibiting negligence and brazen bravado. If we are to rewrite divisive narratives, we must together forge a different path—a path mobilized by our collective power. Native spiritualists Jamie Sams and David Carson (1988) wrote, "Compassion, caring, teaching, loving, and sharing your gifts, talents, and abilities are the gateways to power." The chapters in this book clearly mirror this ethic as members of communities, school systems, and university programs of educator preparation have joined hands to develop a powerful new approach to teaching future teachers. This effort, ignited by the injury of far too many children, fuels an energy to reimagine what could replace systems that damage, with practices that restore. Such power is indeed promising as we push forward.

In February of 1968, Dr. Martin Luther King Jr. spoke the words, "We must accept finite disappointment, but never lose infinite hope" (Harding, 2008). So perhaps hope lies at the nexus of despair and prospect; perhaps our discontent fuels our endeavors to rectify and resolve, and it is this that propels us forward. A local pastor with whom our program has a long-standing and close connection recently preached from Romans 12:12, in which Paul guides us to "be joyful in hope." Love (2019) describes this as joy that originates in "resistance, agitation, purpose, justice, and love" (p. 15). We argue that education can be one of the principal arbiters of a society grounded in the ethic of social justice. Perhaps this directive to be joyful in our hope will energize us in our united appeal to the field of teacher preparation to redefine spaces and places where education can actually bring about the social change that we so desperately need.

In 2016, Tyrone Howard called community-engaged teacher preparation a "paradigm of possibility" (Clark et al., 2016). As evidence of such, the chapters in this book are offered as a collective energy determined to continue the successful launch of a movement. With Freire's reminder that we write our history in the present, we embrace these efforts, the principal aims of which are to prepare teachers to persist in decolonizing the knowledge, pedagogy, and practices that continue to privilege some and disenfranchise many, so they might equip their students with the efficacy and agency to continue the struggle. While Langston Hughes reminds us that this is a "land that never has been yet" (2004), we choose to ground our hope in the promise and possibility of our power and the will with which we exercise our collective commitment.

We close with a quote from Rebecca Solnit (2015), who forecasts the future of our force in rewriting a new narrative in the preparation of teachers:

His name was privilege, but hers was possibility. His was the same old story, but hers was a new one about the possibility of changing a story that remains unfinished, that includes **all of us**, that matters **so much**, that we will watch, but also **make** and **tell** in the weeks, months, years, and decades to come. (p. 53)

To this end, we invite you to radically hope, with joy, and to commit to the work ahead.

REFERENCES

Alexander, M. (2010). *The new Jim Crow: Mass incarceration in the age of color-blindness.* New Press.

Boyd, B. (2015). Six leadership lessons from photography. *Journal of Applied Christian Leadership, 9*(2), 80–90.

Chatmon, C., & Watson, V. (2018). Decolonizing school systems: Racial justice, radical healing, and educational equity inside Oakland Unified School District. *Vue, 48,* 7–12.

Clark, P., Zygmunt, E., & Howard, T. (2016). Why race and culture matter in schools, and why we need to *get this right*: A conversation with Dr. Tyrone Howard. *The Teacher Educator, 51,* 268–276.

Davis, A. (1998, September 10). Masked racism: Reflections on the prison industrial complex. *ColorLines.* https://www.colorlines.com/articles/masked-racism-reflections-prison-industrial-complex

DuVernay, A. (Director). (2016). *13th* [Film]. Kandoo Films.

Eglash, A. (1958). Creative restitution: Some suggestions for prison rehabilitation programs. *American Journal of Correction, 20*, 20–34.

Freire, P. (1993). *Pedagogy of the city*. Continuum.

Freire, P. (1996). *Pedagogy of the oppressed*. Penguin Books.

Gannon, K. (2020). *Radical hope: A teaching manifesto*. West Virginia University Press.

Ginwright, S. (2015). *Hope and healing in urban education: How urban activists and teachers are reclaiming matters of the heart*. Routledge.

Harding, V. (2008). *Martin Luther King: The inconvenient hero*. Orbis Books.

Hopkins, B. (2002). Restorative justice in schools. *Support for Learning, 17*, 144–149.

Hopkins, B. (2004). *Just schools: A whole-school approach to restorative justice*. Jessica Kingsley Publishers.

Hughes, L. (2004). *Let America be America again and other poems*. Vintage Books.

Lear, J. (2006). *Radical hope: Ethics in the face of cultural devastation*. Harvard University Press.

Love, B. L. (2019). *We want to do more than survive: Abolitionist teaching and the pursuit of educational freedom*. Beacon.

Sams, J., & Carson, D. (1988). *Medicine cards*. Bear and Company.

Shalaby, C. (2017). *Troublemakers: Lessons in freedom from young children at school*. The New Press.

Solnit, R. (2015). *Things men explain to me*. Haymarket Books.

Souers, K. (2016). *Fostering resilient learners: Strategies for creating a trauma-sensitive classroom*. Association for Supervision and Curriculum Development (ASCD).

Wallace, R. (2012). Healing justice workshop. http://www.crossroadsfund.org/blog/healingjustice

About the Contributors

Editors

Patricia Clark is professor of early childhood education in the Department of Early Childhood, Youth, and Family Studies at Ball State University. She is a co-founder of Schools Within the Context of Community, a community-engaged program of teacher preparation at Ball State University. Along with colleagues, Dr. Clark has obtained over $3 million in funding to support the priorities of the community for the education of children. Dr. Clark has presented extensively at national conferences and has published numerous articles on early childhood education and diversity. She is co-author, with Eva Zygmunt, of *Transforming Teacher Education for Social Justice* (2016). Dr. Clark is committed to preparing future teachers who engage with the communities they serve in order to provide education that is socially just and equitable for all children.

Eva Zygmunt is the Helen Gant Elmore Distinguished Professor of Elementary Education at Ball State University and a co-founder of the Schools Within the Context of Community immersive learning semester—a nationally recognized model of community-engaged teacher preparation. Eva is also the co-founder of the Alliance for Community-Engaged Teacher Preparation—an international network of teacher educators committed to authentically embedding their programs of educator preparation in the communities in which their institutions of higher education are situated. Eva has dedicated her career toward furthering community-engaged teacher preparation and its emphasis on culturally responsive, equity-focused, and socially just pedagogies as a compelling and justifiable direction for the field.

Susan Tancock is associate dean for undergraduate and graduate studies at Ball State University Teachers College and a professor in the Department of Elementary Education. Susan earned her PhD at The Ohio State University and served as a Reading Recovery and Title 1 teacher early in her teaching career. She was a member of the faculty team in the Schools

Within the Context of Community program for 8 years, where she worked with teacher candidates to facilitate culturally responsive literacy experiences for children and families in school, after school, and in community spaces. Susan is committed to finding ways to better prepare teacher candidates to serve racially, culturally, and linguistically diverse students and to address issues of equity in today's schools. She believes that community engagement is imperative to fully prepare teacher candidates to engage in culturally responsive, sustaining instruction and to teach for social justice.

Kristin Cipollone is associate professor of curriculum and instruction in the Department of Elementary Education at Ball State University. She is director of the Schools Within the Context of Community program and advisor to the student group Educators for Equity and Justice. Her research interests include the development of equity-focused educators, preservice teacher dispositions, and the ways in which inequality is (re)produced in and through schooling. She is committed to pedagogies of community engagement, anti-racism, and social justice, and is passionate about working with preservice teachers to cultivate the political awareness, dispositions, and pedagogical skill necessary to make education a force for justice.

Chapter 1

Wilisha Scaife is a passionate educator who describes herself as a believer, dreamer, and lifelong learner. She is employed at Ball State University in the Department of Early Childhood, Youth, and Family Studies, where she consults and collaborates with faculty on matters of family and community engagement, provides frequent guest lectures, and serves as the Family Engagement Coordinator for the MuncieP3 academic enrichment program. Along with her service as a child, family, and community advocate, Wilisha is a licensed minister at Union Missionary Baptist Church in Muncie, where her husband, Robert, is the senior pastor. She is a champion for children and families and has presented at numerous conferences and professional forums nationwide.

Chapter 2

Candance Doerr-Stevens is assistant professor of reading at the University of Wisconsin-Milwaukee, where she teaches courses on digital and disciplinary literacies. She received a PhD in critical literacy and English education from the University of Minnesota, Twin Cities. Her research focuses on the emergent literacy practices and identity work involved in multimodal composition. Her work has been published in *Pedagogies*, *English Journal*, and *English Teaching Practice and Critique*.

Joëlle Worm is director of ArtsECO and systems director of ACCESS—two grant programs at the University of Wisconsin-Milwaukee that work with teacher candidates and in-service teachers in the Milwaukee area. She holds degrees in dance from the University of Minnesota–Twin Cities (summa cum laude) and a master's in public administration from Baruch College–City University of New York. Her professional background is in the facilitation and management of arts and education programs in K–12 schools and outreach settings in New York and Milwaukee.

Kelly R. Allen is an urban education doctoral candidate at the University of Wisconsin-Milwaukee. She earned her BA in urban social studies education with an emphasis in history, political science, and sociology, as well as her MS in urban education, from the University of Wisconsin-Milwaukee. Informed by her experience as a high school social studies teacher, her current research interests focus on issues of equity and race/ism in social studies education.

Chapter 3

April Mustian is associate professor of special education at Winthrop University and Director of its BS in Special Education program. A former K–12 urban special educator, she provides in-depth instruction to preservice teachers and graduate students on culturally responsive behavioral and academic practices. Prior to joining the Winthrop University community, Dr. Mustian served at Illinois State University (ISU) for a decade. During that time, she was the coordinator of the National Center for Urban Education's (NCUE) specialized urban course sequence called Innovative Network of Future Urban Special Educators (INFUSE). Additionally, she served as the director of faculty development for NCUE, where she, along with other NCUE staff, supported new NCUE urban faculty each summer through an immersive professional development course redesign experience. Her research interests include culturally responsive academic and behavioral interventions for students with high-incidence disabilities, community-engaged special education teacher preparation, teacher bias and its impacts on school outcomes for marginalized student populations, restorative practices, and decreasing disproportionality (challenging the school-to-prison pipeline) of Black and Latinx students in disciplinary action.

Jennifer O'Malley serves as director of the Chicago Teacher Education Pipeline (CTEP) within the National Center for Urban Education (NCUE). A former middle and high school public school teacher and current public school parent, she has worked at CTEP since its founding, collaborating with school and community partners to design the comprehensive programming that now encompasses the NCUE model of community, school, and university integration. NCUE programming spans from K–12 students and families through preservice teachers, including supporting program graduates in their teaching careers in urban districts. Jennifer earned a master's degree in writing and a master's degree in education from DePaul University in Chicago.

Gynger Garcia is a public school graduate and former public school teacher. She has worked at Breakthrough Urban Ministries for the last 12 years, most recently as a community liaison for the Chicago Teacher Education Pipeline. Breakthrough is a nonprofit community organization located on Chicago's West Side, partnering with the community to build connections, develop skills, and open doors of opportunity. Gynger earned a bachelor of science degree in elementary education from DePaul University in Chicago. She lives in Chicago with her husband and two daughters, who are also public school students.

Carlos Millan is a coordinator for educational partnerships at The Resurrection Project, where he sustains and builds partnerships to strengthen the resources of elementary schools in the Pilsen neighborhood in Chicago, Illinois. Carlos is a community liaison for the Chicago Teacher Education Pipeline for Illinois State University, increasing preservice teachers' level of readiness for urban school settings. Previously he worked for Providence St. Mel's admission team in the East Garfield Park community. Carlos earned his master's degree from Marquette University in Spanish literature and culture with a concentration in second language acquisition.

Maria Luisa Zamudio-Mainou serves as the executive director of the National Center for Urban Education (NCUE). For the last 19 years, Dr. Zamudio-Mainou has worked at Illinois State University (ISU) in various capacities, including teaching multicultural education and coordinating the Bilingual–Bicultural Program, where she was directly responsible for all grant management activities and recruitment of teachers interested in becoming certified in bilingual education and ESL. She also has led study-abroad programs in Mexico and Spain. Dr. Zamudio-Mainou has secured and led multimillion-dollar federal grant projects that have empowered bilingual paraprofessionals to become classroom teachers. She earned her undergraduate degree from Instituto de Estudios Superiores de Tamaulipas (IEST) in business administration; her master's degree in Latin American literature and culture at ISU; and her doctorate degree in higher education administration at ISU. Her area of research expertise includes culturally responsive practices for Latinx students and families.

Chapter 4

Nadine McHenry has been at Widener University since 2002 and in higher education since 1993. She is currently a professor in the Center for Education and coordinator of Widener University's Community Engaged Teacher Education program, where teacher candidates learn the importance of cultural proficiency, culturally responsive pedagogy, and equity literacy when working in diverse communities. Dr. McHenry is also the director of Widener's Science Teaching Center, where she facilitates community outreach and a variety of local and global service-learning programs. She has worked over the past 11 years conducting professional development and sustainability projects with teachers and other environmental educators in Trinidad and Tobago, where she is co-founder of the Protect and Nurture Trinidad and Tobago initiative. Dr. McHenry has received the Lindback Foundation Award for Excellence in Teaching, Neumann University's Excellence in Teaching Award and Excellence in Research Award, and Widener University's Faculty Award for Civic Engagement.

Janet Baldwin recently retired as an elementary school principal after 46 years in education. When it came time to leave, she shared with the children that the school did not belong to her, the new principal, or the teachers, but *to them*. The children would determine its future. If we can live by this principle and instill in our children that they have the power to carve out their destiny, then we will leave something that will carry forward a future of hope and possibilities. Her wish is that the words that we share in this book will inspire readers to do just that. Janet is now enjoying time with her husband, four grown children, and six grandchildren while teaching a Community Teacher course and pursuing projects that will fulfill her desire to make a difference in the lives of others.

Rev. Hilda M. Campbell received a dual degree in applied science and construction technology from Delaware Technical Community College. She also holds a degree in science and professional studies from Widener University. She is a retired member of the United Brotherhood of Carpenter's LU#626 and the International Brotherhood of Electrical Workers #1238. She is a United Methodist pastor as well as a thespian/theatrical performer. Ms. Campbell volunteers with EMIR's Healing Center (Every Murder Is Real) using "The Arts" as therapy to provide an outlet for trauma experienced after acts of violence and/or death. She works mainly with youth and teens, providing arts-and-crafts activities (making dolls and jewelry), painting, quiltmaking, journaling, writing poetry, playing games, and participating in conversations discussing the impact and loss of their loved ones.

Essence Allen-Presley is an assistant professor of teaching and the program coordinator for special education at Widener University. She is a consultant and adjunct with several companies, including Community College of Philadelphia and the University of Pennsylvania. Dr. Allen-Presley collaborates with and trains child care programs and various organizations throughout the region on multiple ways to enhance their services to children with special needs and behavior challenges in early learning programs. Dr. Allen-Presley has presented at conferences, lectures, and seminars throughout the country. She understands the need for *quality* child care programs and their impact on school readiness in the K–12 system. Dr. Allen-Presley earned her doctoral degree in education leadership from Saint Joseph University. She holds two master's degrees, in urban and regional planning and in special education. She also holds a Special Education, K–12 Leadership, Special Education and Curriculum & Instruction Supervisory Certificate in the state of Pennsylvania.

Bretton T. Alvaré is associate professor and chair of the Department of Anthropology at Widener University. Dr. Alvaré is an urban ethnographer who conducts participatory action research with grassroots nongovernmental organizations in the United States and Trinidad and Tobago, many of which focus on improving access to education. His research has been published in *Ethnography and Education, Political and Legal Anthropology Review, The International Journal of Environment and Science Education,* and *The Journal of Latin American and Caribbean Anthropology.* Dr. Alvaré is a Periclean Faculty Leader, Borislow Community-Engaged Research Fellow, and the recipient of a Fitz Dixon Innovation in Teaching Award and a Widener Faculty Award for Civic Engagement. He is also a co-founder of Protect and Nurture Trinidad and Tobago and the former vice president of Trinidad and Tobago Rastafari United.

Taylor Borgstrom was born and raised in Columbus, New Jersey, with her twin brother and her dogs. She attended Widener University as an Early Childhood Education and Special Education major and was selected to be in the Honors College program. During her time at Widener, she was in the National Honors Fraternity Phi Sigma Pi, Phi Sigma Sigma, and Kappa Delta Pi. She combined her love for travel and learning when she studied human development in Barcelona, Spain, for a summer. During her spring breaks, she participated in the Alternative Spring Break Program, where students would travel to different locations around the United States and volunteer with Habitat for Humanity. Taylor graduated in 2019 with cum laude honors. Since then, she has been an educator in the Chester Upland School District, where she participated in the Community Engaged Teacher Education Program and completed student teaching prior to her employment there.

Chapter 5

Jo Lampert is a professor in the School of Education at La Trobe University in Australia and director of the NEXUS alternative pathway into teaching. Her research includes Aboriginal and Torres Strait Islander education, teacher education for high-poverty schools, and community engagement in teacher education.

Eric Dommers has taught in secondary schools in Melbourne, Australia, and was principal research fellow at the Brotherhood of St. Laurence. He is currently co-director of the Northern Centre of Excellence for School Engagement at Banksia Gardens Community Services in Melbourne, Australia. Eric's research interests are in the impacts of poverty and disadvantage on educational opportunity.

Jaime de Loma-Osario Ricón is deputy chief executive officer at Banksia Gardens Community Services. Jaime is responsible for the establishment of many of the organization's current programs and played a pivotal role in the redevelopment of the organization's headquarters. Jaime's interests include social and environmental issues, science, and languages.

Stevie Browne is a doctoral student at La Trobe University in Melbourne, Australia. Stevie has been a teacher in low-socioeconomic secondary schools in Brisbane and Southwest Sydney. Her research is presently focused on the experiences of teachers who come from backgrounds of adversity.

Chapter 6

Heather K. Olson Beal is a professor of education studies and the co-creator and co-director of the CREATE program at Stephen F. Austin State University. She teaches courses in educational foundations, family and community engagement, educational policy and advocacy, and literacy. Her scholarship examines the issues of school choice, second language education, and the experiences of women and mothers in academia. She has three feisty and big-hearted children who guide and shape her scholarship and teaching.

Lauren E. Burrow is an associate professor of elementary education and the co-founder and co-director of the CREATE program track at Stephen F. Austin State University. She is a MotherScholar of three inspirational, intelligent, and kind-hearted children and wife to a husband who helps her accomplish so much. She is an engaged scholar committed to service-learning as pedagogy in order to improve preservice teachers' awareness of social in/justices. Additionally, her research agenda includes best practices for teachers in early literacy and instructional technology.

Linda Autrey has served students in Texas public schools for 25 years as a teacher and administrator. She is married to another passionate educator and the proud mother of three children, two of whom are still in school. In addition to advocating for students and teachers at the local and state levels, she loves to read, travel, and watch films.

Crystal Hicks is a reformed academic who taught literature and film studies at Texas Tech before leaving the field to pursue a career in librarianship. She is the assistant director of the Nacogdoches Public Library and heads up programming and outreach, which is driven by the notion of radical collaboration with the community.

Amber Teal is a mom of two children, Xavior and Iyana. She has a passion for giving back to her community and for educational advocacy. She is a licensed community health worker and a licensed speech language pathologist assistant.

Chapter 7

Tasha Austin is a lecturer in language education and urban education at the Rutgers Graduate School of Education. She is also an educational consultant with expertise in supporting schools' and districts' shifts toward problem-based learning and the development of cultural competence. In her current doctoral studies, she uses critical race theory and Black feminist epistemologies to qualitatively examine language, identity, and power, and the ways in which anti-Blackness emerges in language education and language teacher preparation. Tasha is the author of a bilingual children's book entitled *El Barrio Mío / My Neighborhood*, available on amazon.com and authorhouse.com. She is also the NJTESOL/ NJBE Teacher Education SIG Representative.

Kisha Porcher, PhD, is an assistant professor of English education in the Department of English at the University of Delaware. An emerging scholar-practitioner, her research focuses on antiracist, community-engaged teacher education. Her research draws on a framework she is developing that engages in the interrogation of self; exploration of the assets, genius, and conditions of students of color and their communities; antiracist instructional strategies, and critical service-learning.

Mary Elizabeth Curran is a professor of practice in language education and director of local-global partnerships at the Graduate School of Education at Rutgers, the State University of New Jersey, where she coordinates the language education program. She frequently collaborates with a broad range of stakeholders at local community organizations, K–12 school districts, the New Jersey Department of Education, and national and international centers and universities. Her scholarship focuses on language and community-engaged teacher education for social justice, and has appeared in *The Journal of Teacher Education*, *TESOL Quarterly*, *Foreign Language Annals*, *Theory into Practice*, *The Language Educator*, and *Learning Languages*. She is an academic co-director for the Collaborative Center for Community-Based Research and Service at Rutgers. She holds a doctorate in curriculum and instruction and a master's degree in English applied linguistics from the University of Wisconsin–Madison.

Jaime DePaola is a 1st-year ESL teacher at Franklin High School in Somerset, New Jersey. She received both her bachelor's degree in linguistics and her master's degree in ESL education from Rutgers University. She has also completed certifications in elementary education and special education. She continues to build connections and strengthen her practice by working as the Franklin High School Warriors Unite club advisor, a Special Olympics–sponsored after-school program facilitating the socialization and inclusion of students in the severe LLD, autism, and general education programs. She is also an active member of the high school's equity team, a team of teachers who supervise professional developments addressing educational equity influenced by race, gender, and socioeconomic status.

Jessica Pelaez-Merino is an elementary school teacher at New Brunswick Public Schools. She holds a BA in English and an MA in elementary education from Rutgers University.

Lauren Raffaelli is a dance educator based out of New Jersey. She most recently taught at Teaneck High School, where she taught dance levels I–IV and directed the Dance Ensemble, the school's performance-based dance group. In addition to K–12 education, she teaches at numerous dance studios throughout New Jersey. She is also a 200-hour registered yoga teacher with Yoga Alliance and started a community yoga program at Midland Park Memorial Library. In addition to her teaching career, she dances professionally with Nikki Manx Dance Project, a modern dance company focused on social justice–based art. Raffaelli received her master's degree in dance education from the Graduate School of Education at Rutgers University and her bachelors of fine arts in dance from the Mason Gross School of the Arts at Rutgers University.

Chapter 8

Kaylie Johnston currently teaches 3rd grade at Noble Crossing Elementary School in Noblesville, Indiana. Her teaching pedagogy focuses on creating culturally responsive and equitable educational opportunities for all students in order that they may become productive global citizens. Kaylie is a 2018 graduate of the SCC program.

Hailey Maupin currently teaches 4th grade at South View Elementary School in Muncie, Indiana. She was a 2018 graduate of the SCC program. Hailey takes pride in the knowledge she gained during her time in SCC and believes that because of this program she is able to truly reach her students, families, and community. Hailey's time in SCC has inspired her to set meaningful goals, and she plans to return to college to further her education by attending graduate school in urban administration.

Kylie Kaminski currently teaches 5th grade at Chapelwood Elementary School in Indianapolis, Indiana. Her classroom is student-centered, focusing on cultivating genuine relationships and creating culturally relevant learning opportunities. She was a 2017 graduate of the SCC program, the pedagogy of which continues to inspire her both personally and professionally.

Jacob Layton currently teaches 4th grade at Converse Elementary School in Converse, Texas. His goal is to create community-engaged citizens through culturally relevant, project-based instruction. He is a 2015 graduate of the SCC program.

Index

The letter *f*, *n*, or *t* after a page number refers to a figure, note, or table, respectively.